THOUGHT-IMAGES

Cultural Memory
in
the
Present

Mieke Bal and Hent de Vries, Editors

THOUGHT-IMAGES

Frankfurt School Writers' Reflections from Damaged Life

Gerhard Richter

STANFORD UNIVERSITY PRESS

STANFORD, CALIFORNIA

2007

Stanford University Press
Stanford, California

© 2007 by the Board of Trustees of the Leland Stanford Junior University.
All rights reserved.

No part of this book may be reproduced or transmitted in any form or by any means, electronic or mechanical, including photocopying and recording, or in any information storage or retrieval system without the prior written permission of Stanford University Press.

Printed in the United States of America on acid-free, archival-quality paper

Library of Congress Cataloging-in-Publication Data

Richter, Gerhard, 1967–
  Thought-images : Frankfurt School writers' reflections from damaged life / Gerhard Richter.
    p. cm.—(Cultural memory in the present)
  ISBN 978-0-8047-5616-7 (cloth : alk. paper)
  ISBN 978-0-8047-5617-4 (pbk. : alk. paper)
    1. German literature—20th century—History and criticism.   2. Adorno, Theodor W., 1903–1969—Criticism and interpretation.   3. Benjamin, Walter, 1892–1940—Criticism and interpretation.   4. Kracauer, Siegfried, 1889–1966—Criticism and interpretation.   5. Bloch, Ernst, 1885–1977—Criticism and interpretation.   6. Frankfurt school of sociology.   7. Literature and society. I. Title.
PT405.R479   2007
830.9'355—dc22   2007001246

Typeset by BookMatters in 11/13.5 Garamond

Für Lexi—für später

"*Optimists write badly.*" (Valéry.) But pessimists do not write.
—Maurice Blanchot, *The Writing of the Disaster*

The concept of *Verstehen*, interpretive understanding, cannot be applied without further ado to a hermetic text. Essential to such a text is the shock with which it forcibly interrupts communication. The harsh light of unintelligibility that such a work turns toward the reader renders the usual intelligibility suspect as being shallow, habitual, reified—in short, pre-artistic.
—Theodor W. Adorno, "Presuppositions" (*Notes to Literature*)

Thought-images (*Denkbilder*) are not images like the Platonic myths of the cave or the chariot. Rather, they are scribbled picture-puzzles, parabolic evocations of something that cannot be said in words (*des in Worten Unsagbaren*). They do not want to stop conceptual thought so much as to shock through their enigmatic form and thereby get thought moving, because thought in its traditional conceptual form seems rigid, conventional, and outmoded. What cannot be proved in the customary style and yet is compelling—that is to spur on the spontaneity and energy of thought and, without being taken literally, to strike sparks through a kind of intellectual short-circuiting that casts a sudden light on the familiar and perhaps sets it on fire.
—Theodor W. Adorno, "Benjamin's *One-Way Street*" (*Notes to Literature*)

Contents

	Acknowledgments	*xiii*
	Paleonomies of the Thought-Image: An Introduction	*1*
1.	A Matter of Distance: Benjamin's *One-Way Street* through the *Arcades*	*43*
2.	Bloch's Dream, Music's Traces	*72*
3.	Homeless Images: Kracauer's Extraterritoriality, Derrida's Monolingualism of the Other	*107*
4.	Nazism and Negative Dialectics: Adorno's Hitler in *Minima Moralia*	*147*
	Coda	*191*
	Notes	*193*
	Index	*229*

Acknowledgments

I would like to record my gratitude to those friends and colleagues who kindly responded to individual chapters of my study: Klaus L. Berghahn, Fritz Breithaupt, Stanley Corngold, Alex Düttmann, Peter Fenves, Michael Jennings, Dirk Oschmann, and Liliane Weissberg. I also thank Peter Uwe Hohendahl and the attendees at the Cornell colloquium where I presented an early version of the material on Adorno. I am particularly grateful to Rodolphe Gasché, Jost Hermand, and Martin Jay, who read the entire manuscript and shared their valuable thoughts.

Scholarly audiences in Amsterdam (Netherlands), Athens, Atlanta, Berkeley, Bonn (Germany), Buffalo, Davis, Hartford, Irvine, Ithaca, Los Angeles, Madison, Minneapolis, New Orleans, New York, Philadelphia, San Diego, San Juan (Puerto Rico), State College, Stony Brook, and Washington, D.C., listened patiently to my arguments about the Frankfurt School over the past few years. I thank my hosts and interlocutors on these occasions and can only hope that their hospitality, intellectual generosity, and exactitude of spirit have left traces on my pages.

The research and writing of this book were supported by a generous grant from the Dean's Office of the Division of Humanities, Arts, and Cultural Studies in the College of Letters and Science at the University of California, Davis, as well as by an H. I. Romnes Faculty Research Award from the Wisconsin Alumni Research Foundation, a Vilas Associate Research Award from the Trustees of the William F. Vilas Estate, and multiple faculty summer research grants awarded by the Research Committee of the Graduate School at the University of Wisconsin, Madison. A research sabbatical spent at the Universität zu Köln allowed me to devote myself exclusively to this project for one semester during the spring of 2004, while a grant from the Andrew W. Mellon Foundation (2004–5) enabled me to co-direct a yearlong multidisciplinary seminar on Theodor W. Adorno for students and faculty through the University of Wisconsin's Center for the Humanities. The Mellon seminar provided an invigorating forum in which to test ideas presented in this book.

I appreciate the generosity of the Schiller-Nationalmuseum and Deutsches Literaturarchiv in Marbach am Neckar for making available to me a print of the surviving shards from the original glass plate of the 1930 photograph of Siegfried Kracauer that appears on the cover of this book and again in chapter 3. Christoph König of the Deutsches Literaturarchiv, now a professor at the Universität Osnabrück, extended warm hospitality during my visit to Marbach in 2004, furnishing access to rare documents—some unpublished—by Adorno, Benjamin, and Kracauer.

I wish to thank Norris Pope of Stanford University Press for his enthusiastic support of my project, as well as Carolyn Brown, Emily-Jane Cohen, and Barbara Norton for their efforts in seeing the publication process through to completion.

Finally, I wish to extend my thanks to the following publishers for granting me permission to use portions or versions of texts of mine that have appeared previously: "Bloch's Dream, Music's Traces," *Sound Figures of Modernity: German Music and Philosophy*, ed. Jost Hermand and Gerhard Richter (Madison: University of Wisconsin Press, 2006), and "Nationalsozialismus und Negative Dialektik in Adornos *Minima Moralia*," in Gerhard Richter, *Ästhetik des Ereignisses: Spache—Geschichte—Medium* (Munich: Fink, 2005). An English version of the latter first appeared in *Unmasking Hitler: Cultural Representations of Hitler from the Weimar Republic to the Present*, ed. Klaus L. Berghahn and Jost Hermand (Oxford: Lang, 2005), and "A Matter of Distance: Benjamin's *One-Way Street* through the *Arcades*" was also included in *Walter Benjamin and the Arcades Project*, ed. Beatrice Hanssen (London: Continuum, 2006).

SAN FRANCISCO EAST BAY
APRIL 2006

THOUGHT-IMAGES

Paleonomies of the Thought-Image

AN INTRODUCTION

The Frankfurt School and the Thought-Image

A paleonomy, as Jacques Derrida explains, is the "maintenance of an *old name* in order to launch a new concept."[1] Extending Derrida's observation, we could say that all serious engagement with philosophical and aesthetic concepts and their political and historical traditions may require a form of paleonomic work. In modern writing, key examples include Kant's *critique*; Friedrich Schlegel's *irony*; Hegel's *system*; Marx's *ideology*; Nietzsche's *genealogy*; Freud's *unconscious*; Kafka's *law*; Heidegger's *Being*; Brecht's *gesture*; Lacan's *real*; Foucault's *author*; Levinas's *Other*; Derrida's *writing*; de Man's *allegory*; and Debord's *spectacle*. In every case, the paleonomic gesture requires us to stand inside and outside a tradition at the same time, perpetuating the tradition while breaking with it, and breaking with the tradition while perpetuating it.

This book wishes to reread the often neglected literary genre of the *Denkbild*—"thinking image," "image of reflection," or simply "thought-image"—as a paleonomy by examining the philosophical and literary texts of a constellation of friends and colleagues associated with what came to be known as the Frankfurt School of Critical Theory (Frankfurter Schule): Theodor W. Adorno, Walter Benjamin, Siegfried Kracauer, and, more indirectly, Ernst Bloch. Deeply connected by complex personal and intellectual relations to each other and to the project of critical theory, these major German Jewish writers strategically chose the minor genre of the Denkbild because it belongs to those apparently marginal speculative and aesthetic phenomena that, upon closer inspection, emerge as the secret avenues of critical insight. Denkbilder are neither programmatic treatises nor objective manifestations of a historical spirit, neither fanciful fiction nor mere reflections of reality. Rather, the philosophical miniatures of the Denkbild can be understood as conceptual engagements with the aesthetic and as aesthetic engagements with the conceptual, hovering between philosophical critique and aesthetic production. The Denkbild encodes a poetic form of condensed, epigrammatic writing in textual snapshots, flashing up as poignant meditations that typically fasten upon a seemingly peripheral detail or marginal topic, usually without a developed plot or a prescribed narrative agenda, yet charged with theoretical insight.

The Denkbild was of such concern to these writers because it reconfigures the relationship between conceptual and aesthetic categories, between philosophy and art, not only thematizing but also enacting the difficulty that Adorno diagnoses in his *Aesthetic Theory* and that organizes both his own Denkbilder and those of his friends around a common core, namely that "art stands in need of philosophy that interprets it in order to say that which it cannot say, whereas art is only able to say what it says by not saying it."[2] The practice of the Denkbild constitutes an abiding and obsessive response to the rigorous demands of this axiom.

Engaging the material inscription of logic and poetics through the figure of the Denkbild, I wish to read Adorno, Benjamin, Bloch, and Kracauer not merely as philosophers and cultural critics, but as *writers*. My guiding assumption is that much of what is most valuable in these writers, and what connects them as a group of thinkers who pay close attention to the status of writing itself, is the view that *what* they say cannot be thought in isolation from *how* they say it, that any philosophical truth-content their writing may contain invariably is tied to, and mediated by, its specific and potentially unstable figures of presentation. In their writerly production, each of them responds, implicitly or explicitly, to Nietzsche's famous metaphor of a metaphor: "What, then, is truth? A mobile army of metaphors, metonyms, and anthropomorphisms—in short, a sum of human relations which have been enhanced, transposed, and embellished poetically and rhetorically, and which after long use seem firm, canonical, and obligatory to a people: truths are illusions about which one has forgotten that this is what they are."[3] As is the case with Nietzsche's moveable army of tropes, the tropes of the Denkbild insist that any truth, even the truth of the existence of untruth, can be arrived at only by attending to the metaphor of the metaphor, the figure of the figure. In this way, the Denkbild shows itself responsible to the idea that only a writing that takes account of its own irreducibly figurative qualities can allow the historical nature of an utterance, the historicity of language, to begin to speak.

To insist on the figurative qualities of these writers' philosophical and poetic production and to read them primarily as writers is also to problematize the very notion of a homogenous, self-contained Frankfurt School. This name today refers loosely to the members of the Institute for Social Research, founded by Felix Weil as a progressive interdisciplinary research center in Frankfurt in 1924, and the name was not normally used by the members themselves. The Frankfurt School's foremost historians, Martin Jay and Rolf Wiggershaus, have excavated the complex circumstances under which the label "Frankfurt School" was retroactively applied, beginning in the 1950s, to this group of thinkers and writers, all of whom were affiliated with the project of a fundamental ideologico-philosophical cultural critique that took the political, epistemological, and psychoanalytic insights of Marx, Nietzsche, and Freud as seriously as the aesthetic, moral, and historical ones of Kant and Hegel.[4]

But can a "school" ultimately be "read"? Is it a homogenous entity that can be arrested long enough for us to make generalizations about it? Or is it not rather a richly textured network of heterogeneous traces and singularities? And if the designation "Frankfurt School" privileges the geographic location of a German city, do the proper names New York, Los Angeles, Berlin, and even Paris not play just as important a role in the group's complex history of displacement, exile, and extraterritoriality? Should the Frankfurt School be content to consider itself a school at all, or does it, in the very moment of this designation, cease to be a school dedicated to transformative thinking and to a critical thought that is permanently in flux? Perhaps the Frankfurt School can remain faithful to its transformative aims as a school only when it no longer is a school, when it is the particular school that can be no school, the school without school. From the perspective of such a reflection, we should set aside any preconceived notions or political appropriations and allow the term Frankfurt School to rearticulate itself along the lines of a careful and probing reading of the singular and specific texts that were produced in its orbit. I wish to propose, then, that the Denkbild offers one fruitful opportunity for such a reconsideration. My use of the term "Frankfurt School" therefore also deserves to be read as a paleonomy, the retention of an old name for a new concept.

One dimension of this paleonomic mobilization of the term "Frankfurt School" involves my choice of writers for inclusion in this study. In focusing on a specific engagement with the poetic Denkbild, my study does not address the work of those important writers associated, more or less intimately, with the first generation of the Frankfurt School, members of what then was called the Institute for Social Research, such as its director, Max Horkheimer, or Erich Fromm, Otto Kirchheimer, Leo Löwenthal, Herbert Marcuse, Franz Neumann, Friedrich Pollack, Karl August Wittfogel, and many others.[5] Even among the writers whom I have selected, individual relationships to the Institute are anything but homogenous. Although Adorno, especially through his close ties to Horkheimer, clearly belonged to the inner circle of that group—indeed, their coauthored book, *Dialectic of Enlightenment* (1947), became the one text most canonically associated with the Frankfurt School—other writers such as Kracauer belonged to this group only in a more peripheral and indirect sense, despite the vital importance of their work to the group's theoretical formulations. Moreover, Bloch, who never belonged to the Institute or the Frankfurt School in any official sense, maintained deeply involved relationships with many of its members. He was an important early mentor to Adorno, Benjamin, Kracauer, and others in the Frankfurt School, and his work unfolded in constant dialogue with that produced by its members.

There are important correspondences between Bloch and several members of this group, and it is no accident that both Adorno and Benjamin considered his *Spirit of Utopia* (1918) a formative work in their own intellectual development. Bloch, for his part, produced his book of Denkbilder, *Spuren* (1930), in the context of frequent discussions with Benjamin during the time when the latter was composing his own Denkbilder book, *One-Way Street* (1928), a publication that Bloch also reviewed for a journal. Further links between Bloch and these other writers were forged by his contribution of book reviews to the Institute for Social Research's journal, "Zeitschrift für Sozialforschung," and the invitation he received in the late 1930s from Horkheimer, Adorno, and other members of the Institute to contribute to a planned collective volume on questions and theories of materialism.[6] By including Bloch in this constellation, I am less interested in performing an act of revisionist intellectual history than I am in allowing Bloch's *Denkbilder* to illuminate, and be illuminated by, the intellectual projects of those writers who comprised such an important part of his writerly orbit. In so doing, I am in agreement with a growing group of critics, including, among others, the intellectual historian Wiggershaus, the philosopher Eduardo Mendieta, and the Germanist Jack Zipes, who advocate the broad inclusion in the orbit of the Frankfurt School of writers such as Bloch and Kracauer who were close personal and intellectual allies with members of the Institute without ever officially belonging to it. For instance, Wiggershaus's sentiment in his history of the Frankfurt School is that the works of these colleagues, especially those of Bloch, Benjamin, Kracauer, and Adorno, are inextricably interlaced in their shared gesture of micrological thinking:

> This history, which external circumstances rendered highly uneven, suggests that one should not understand the term "Frankfurt School" too narrowly. Two further considerations confirm this: first, the fact that the "charismatic figure," Horkheimer, gradually assumed an ever less decisive position that therefore was not suitable to the formation of a school: second, there is the following circumstance related to the first. If one looks at the four decades of the older Frankfurt School in its totality, one sees that neither a unified paradigm developed nor a paradigm shift that could accommodate everything that is evoked when one speaks of the Frankfurt School. The two main figures, Horkheimer and Adorno, worked from different positions on shared themes. . . . Adorno represented a micrological-messianic thinking that connected him closely with Walter Benjamin, who, through his efforts, became a contributor to the *Zeitschrift für Sozialforschung* and eventually a member of the Institute for Social Research, as well as with Siegfried Kracauer and with Ernst Bloch.[7]

As Wiggershaus elaborates this imbrication in another text:

> As little as Kracauer can be said to have belonged to the so-called Frankfurt School, he nevertheless belongs, along with its most important representatives, to a common constellation. It consists of Ernst Bloch, Siegfried Kracauer, Walter Benjamin, Theodor W. Adorno, and Max Horkheimer. What makes all of them elements in the same constellation is that they can be understood as critical materialists whose critical materialism was either sharpened by theological motifs or harbored theological motifs within itself . . . The combination of article, essay, and book; the combination of notes, aphorisms, and occasional works with montage-like or encyclopedic form; the inclusion of literary forms in the spectrum of means

of presentation and the use of literary means appropriate to the objective in philosophico-theoretical contexts: all of this was an expression of the attempt to combine a sensory spectrum broadly opening up to contemporary experience with a philosophical and theoretical thinking that resisted ossification.[8]

Likewise, as Zipes reminds us, while "Bloch has never received the critical attention that the Frankfurt School has received," it is important to note that "he shared many things in common with them, especially with Walter Benjamin."[9] And, most recently, Mendieta justifiably includes Bloch's texts in an anthology that collects the Frankfurt School's major statements on the relation between religion and critique, reminding us that Bloch's "work was determinant for the development of the Frankfurt School's thinking about religion, theology, and Judaism," especially in light of the messianic elements that Bloch's work constantly interjected into Adorno's uncompromising negativity.[10] As a case in point, we may recall that Benjamin writes to Ernst Schoen as early as 1919 that, for all the reservations he has with regard to Bloch's work, *Spirit of Utopia* "is the only book . . . against which I can measure myself."[11] This view is shared by Adorno many years later when he writes of Bloch's *Spirit of Utopia*: "The book, Bloch's first, bearing all his later work within it, seemed to me to be one prolonged rebellion against the renunciation within thought that extends even into its purely formal character. Prior to any philosophical content, I took this motif so much as my own that I do not believe I have ever written anything without commemorating it, either implicitly or explicitly."[12] As early as the 1930s, the time in which most of the Denkbilder that are the focus of this study were being composed, Adorno for his part directly confirms his desire to involve Bloch with the Frankfurt School Institute. He writes to Bloch on 2 October 1937, "as you are aware, I am now a member in good standing of the International Institute for Social Research, to which I have always been closely connected through my friendship with Max Horkheimer. . . . It goes without saying that the personal reestablishment of our contact [that is, between Adorno and Bloch] at the same time signifies its material and factual [*sachlich*] one. And it is no less self-evident that I would like to extend our contact to the Institute as well." Adorno closes his letter by asking Bloch, to whom he refers as his "red brother," for copies of his latest manuscripts and by assuring Bloch that he is "burningly interested" in his most recent work and that "Horkheimer, with whom I briefly corresponded about it, also feels a great affinity for it."[13] Finally, a remarkable 1964 radio conversation between Bloch and Adorno on the internal contradictions in utopian longing highlights the many shared concerns and fundamental agreements that form the relays between Bloch and the Frankfurt School.[14] With his poetic and philosophical concerns, especially in the context of the Denkbild, Bloch belongs without belonging, belonging only in his non-belonging, as a ghostly yet abiding presence in the thinking of his Frankfurt School friends.

These friends' engagement with their sense of constitutive loss and trauma proceeded by their refunctionalizing and redefining of the literary and philosophical tradition of the Denkbild during their time in Germany in the late 1920s and 1930s and continued (except for Benjamin, who committed suicide before he could escape from the Nazis in 1940) while they were in American exile during the Hitler regime. Deepening and elaborating the micrological turn in critical thought that Georg Simmel had helped to effect through his philosophical and sociological writings since the late nineteenth century—indeed, Benjamin, Bloch, and Kracauer all were students of Simmel and were deeply influenced by his philosophy during their years as university students and beyond—the friends worked on the level of speculative thought to interrogate the imbrication of cultural analysis and aesthetic form that was at the core of Simmel's unorthodox microphenomenology of the object world.[15] Even though they objected to the nationalist spirit and patriotic attitude that at times characterized Simmel's largely bourgeois perspective (Bloch eventually even went so far as to disown his teacher on these grounds), the phenomenological and theoretical rigor that Simmel brought to the micrological analysis of the culture of objects, whether in his analyses of everyday human encounters with the face or in his subtle readings of the cultural logic of money, as in his *Philosophie des Geldes* (1900), remained a key touchstone for the friends. After all, their project, too, was to read certain surface phenomena of modernity as ciphers of deeper cultural and political processes.

The Denkbild, as this group of friends conceived of it, is a brief, aphoristic prose text typically ranging in length between a few sentences and a couple of pages that both illuminates and explodes the conventional distinctions among literature, philosophy, journalistic intervention, and cultural critique. As creative appropriations of the tradition of the baroque emblem and of subsequent eighteenth-century versions of the genre in Herder and others, modernist Denkbilder, which were a preferred medium not only for authors of the Frankfurt School but also for such contemporary writers as Karl Kraus, Robert Musil, and Bertolt Brecht, tend to focus on the specificity of a quotidian object or a seemingly negligible phenomenon: a dream, a gas station, an advertisement, a film, a shadow, a hotel lobby, a sports event, affective states such as boredom, even the telephone—in order to place these objects and phenomena into a new, unexpected constellation that enables them to be read and evaluated as signs of a larger cultural semiotics. The Denkbild can be understood, borrowing a phrase from Adorno, as an innovative "philosophical form . . . in which spirit, image, and language are linked." The fragmentary, explosive, and decentering force of the Denkbild also served Adorno and his friends in their concrete and conceptual struggle against the reactionary modes of cultural and political coordination that constituted the so-called conservative revolution in Germany in the 1920s and 1930s, a set of right-leaning nationalistic tendencies associated with such names as Oswald Spengler, Ernst Jünger, Arthur Möller van den Bruck, and Ernst von Salomon.

Figuring the Thought-Image

Two examples may provide us with a better sense of some of the formal trajectories encrypted in the Denkbild. The first is one of the most famous Denkbilder to have emerged from the corpus of this group of writers, the angel of history that Benjamin evokes in his theses on the concept of history. The second one, also by Benjamin, is less well-known but vigorously bespeaks the formal thrust of this mode of writing.

Benjamin's famous image of the angel constitutes the axis around which the entire constellation of his theses on history pivots, namely, in the ninth of eighteen theses. In this Denkbild, he writes:

There is an image by Klee named "Angelus Novus." It presents an angel looking as though it were about to distance itself from something at which it is gazing. Its eyes are staring, its mouth is open, and its wings are spread. This is what the angel of history must look like [*Der Engel der Geschichte muß so aussehen*]. Its face is turned toward the past. Where we perceive a chain of events, it sees a single catastrophe which keeps piling wreckage upon wreckage and hurls it in front of its feet. The angel would like to tarry, awaken the dead, and reassemble what has been shattered. But a storm is blowing from paradise; it has got caught in its wings with such violence that the angel can no longer close them. This storm inexorably propels it into the future to which its back is turned, while the pile of debris before it grows skyward. This storm is what we call progress.[16]

Benjamin here records his general wish to reconceptualize history, which involves a rejection of historicist linearity, a strategic exploding of the teleology of progress, and a rupture of temporality that results in a revolutionarily charred moment of "now-time," in the image of Paul Klee's angel. Depending on one's reading of the phrase "must look like," this angel is an Angelus Novus—a *new* angel—either because it is the image of what already has taken place, or because it prefigures something that has yet to take place, something that only can be imagined in the future figure of this angel. Whether read as an affirmation or as a predictive promise, in Benjamin's text Klee's angel becomes invested with the figurative force that alone could underwrite the "*weak* messianic power" and open "the small gate [*kleine Pforte*] through which the Messiah might enter."[17] Benjamin appropriates the image of Klee's angel for a rearticulation of the historical that understands messianism neither as a concrete historical movement nor as a religious doctrine but rather as a more general commitment that refuses to foreclose hope for what is still to come. In order to keep the promise of the narrow gate alive, the angel of history admonishes us to "articulate the past historically," rather than fetishize the ultimately elusive image of "the way it really was." To articulate the past historically means to activate the historicity of our objects of study in a way that places them on the far side of the teleology of progress and the grand claims of conventional historicism. As in his frequent evocation of photography, which memorializes the image of an event while at the same time removing it from the stream of history, Benjamin's "true image of the past flits by," "flash[ing] up in the moment of its recognizability never to be seen again."[18] The angel of history presents itself as just such an image. For Benjamin, this historical elusiveness, its vacillation between an affirmation and a negation, embodies a political hope. On a certain level all Denkbilder share this aesthetico-political movement, even as the individual tropes and images within an author's corpus remain in every case irreducibly singular.

The second example is a Denkbild entitled "The Sock," which Benjamin included in the 1938 version of his *Berlin Childhood around 1900*. It reads:

The first cabinet that would yield whenever I wanted was the wardrobe. I had only to pull on the knob, and the door would click open and spring toward me. Among the nightshirts, aprons, and undershirts which were kept there in the back was the thing that turned the wardrobe into an adventure for me. I had to clear a way for myself to its farthest corner. There I would come upon my socks, which lay piled in traditional fashion—that is to say, rolled up and turned inside out. Every pair had the appearance of a little pocket. For me, nothing surpassed the pleasure of thrusting my hand as deeply as possible into its interior. I did not do this for the sake of the pocket's warmth. It was "the little present" rolled up inside that I always held in my hand and that drew me into the depths. When I had closed my fist around it and, so far as I was able, made certain that I possessed the stretchable woolen mass, there began the second phase of the game, which brought with it the unveiling. For now I proceeded to unwrap "the present," to tease it out of its woolen pocket. I drew it ever nearer to me, until something rather disconcerting would happen: I had brought out "the present," but "the pocket" in which it had lain was no longer there. I could not repeat the experiment on this phenomenon often enough. It taught me that form and content, veil and what is veiled, are the same. It led me to draw truth from works of literature as warily as the child's hand retrieved the sock from "the pocket."[19]

The *Mitgebrachte*, that which has been brought along as a gift in a covering sheath, not only cannot be separated from its carrier, it also *is* this carrier. To unroll the sock for its inner core of meaning is to make it disappear, even as it ceaselessly demands to be unrolled. Our attempt to extract the gift of a Denkbild from the language that carries it to us always leads us to the discovery that the language is the gift. There is no semantic, extratextual truth-content that could be excavated from the material fibers of a Denkbild's rhetoric. To learn from the literary form of the Denkbild is thus to learn from a potentially open-ended series of significations that signify not only *that* but also *how* they signify, becoming allegories of the ways in which they mean and fail to mean. In this sense, every Denkbild is a sock.

While proximate to such short forms of modernity as aphorism, fragment, parable, and maxim, the poetico-philosophical Denkbild is traceable along a distinct genealogical development. In the 1920s, Benjamin was the first among his Frankfurt School colleagues to employ the term Denkbild for his writing, even as others were writing in this mode at the same time. In this condensed textual formation, form itself becomes content, and one's perception of a seemingly trivial object becomes, through sustained reflection, an exemplary theoretical reflection. Benjamin was aware, through the study of German baroque drama that gave rise to his early theory of modernity in the *Trauerspiel* book, that the notion of the Denkbild descends from the baroque emblem.[20] Based on Benjamin's meticulously kept record of the books he read and his sources for the *Trauerspiel* study, we know that he drew heavily on the baroque emblem books of such writers as Giovanni Piero Valeriano Bolzani, Diego de Saavedra Fajardo, and Julius Wilhelm Zincgref, and that he engaged the theories of the emblem by such writers as Franz von Baader, Jacob Boehme, Karl Giehlow, and Georg Phillip Harsdörfer.[21] The baroque emblem consisted of a tripartite structure: motto or *inscriptio* (the title), icon or *pictura* (the image of the described object), and epigram or *subscriptio* (the interpretive commentary). Here, the singular and concrete signification of *pictura* is the ground for an interpretive strategy that recognizes in the singular a more universal and abstract meaning.[22] (The short, epigrammatic titles that head the Denkbilder of Benjamin's *One-Way Street*, such as "Construction Site," "For Men," and "Optician"; or of Adorno's *Minima Moralia*—such as "Cat out of the Bag," "Baby with the Bathwater," and "Table and Bed"—reenact this function of the baroque emblem's *inscriptio*.) In Dutch baroque art, one also finds the term *denkbeeld*, which refers to a broadly conceived figural presentation or instantiation of a non-empirical idea.[23] In the eighteenth century, writers such as Lessing, Goethe, Hamann, and Winkelmann used the term Denkbild in various philosophical contexts, where the usage encompassed a range of meanings, from the sensuous cognition of form to the Idea of the Platonic *eidos*. Winkelmann, for instance, employs the term when lamenting the whimsical superficiality of rococo porcelain design in favor of reviving the more "dignified" and didactically suffused forms of classical antiquity that, in his estimation, constitute the only Denkbild of worthy proportions and qualities. Herder, too, employs the term Denkbild—though he uses it at times interchangeably with the more Kantian-inflected *Sinnbild*, a sensuous image or allegorized idea—in his discussion of symbolic figuration in the context of an emerging German classicism and in the context of an insistence on the sensually mediated relation between intuition (*Anschauung*) and reflection.

In the nineteenth century, important touchstones for the development of the Denkbild as it later would coalesce in Adorno, Benjamin, Bloch, and Kracauer were the aphoristic philosophical prose of Nietzsche and, concerning the trope of urbanity and the obsessive analysis of modern city phenomena, the literary work of Baudelaire and his "reading" of Paris in terms of what Benjamin came to call the capital of the nineteenth century. When German and Austrian writers of the early twentieth century and of the Weimar Republic, such as George, Kraus, Musil, Brecht, and, first and foremost, the writers of the emerging Frankfurt School, employed the Denkbild as a privileged literary form, they inscribed themselves into a subterranean poetic tradition while at the same time refunctionalizing that tradition for their own aesthetic and philosophical purposes. It is from the perspective of this refunctionalization that Adorno writes apropos of the Denkbilder in Benjamin's *One-Way Street*:

> In the poem from the *Siebente Ring* in which George expresses his gratitude to France, Mallarmé is praised as "*für sein Denkbild blutend,*" bleeding for his "thought-image." The word *Denkbild*, from the Dutch, replaces the word *Idee*, idea, which has been spoiled by usage; a conception of Plato which is opposed to Neokantianism comes into play here, a conception in terms of which the idea is not a mere mental notion but rather something existing in itself, something that can then be contemplated, if only intellectually. The expression *Denkbild* was attacked sharply in Borchardt's review of George and has made little headway in the German language. But like books, the words of which books are made have their destinies. While the Germanization of the idea did not prevail against linguistic tradition, the impulse that inspired the new word has remained active. Walter Benjamin's *One-Way Street*, first published in 1928, is not, as one might at first think, a book of aphorisms but rather a collection of Denkbilder: a later series of short prose pieces by Benjamin, related in their substance to *One-Way Street*, does in fact bear that name. The meaning of the word has of course shifted. The only thing Benjamin's meaning has in common with George's is that precisely the experiences that a trivial view considers merely subjective and contingent are granted objectivity—that in fact the subjective as such is conceived as the manifestation of something objective. Benjamin's Denkbilder are Platonic, in other words, only in the sense in which people have spoken of the Platonism of Marcel Proust—someone with whose work Benjamin converges, and not merely as Proust's translator. The pieces in *One-Way Street*, however, are not images like the Platonic myths of the cave or the chariot. Rather, they are scribbled picture-puzzles, parabolic evocations of something that cannot be said in words [*des in Worten Unsagbaren*]. They do not want to stop conceptual thought so much as to shock through their enigmatic form and thereby get thought moving, because thought in its traditional conceptual form seems rigid, conventional, and outmoded. What cannot be proved in the customary style and yet is compelling—that is to spur on the spontaneity and energy of thought and, without being taken lit-

erally, to strike sparks through a kind of intellectual short-circuiting that casts a sudden light on the familiar and perhaps sets it on fire.[24]

For Adorno, a Denkbild, which works to say in words what cannot be said in words, launches an impossibility, indeed, wishes to take that very impossibility as its principle. While Wittgenstein famously insists that one must remain silent about that of which one cannot speak, the Denkbild seeks to speak only of that about which one cannot speak. The Denkbild therefore works to create an image (*Bild*) in words of the ways in which it says what cannot be said. It is a snapshot of the impossibility of its own rhetorical gestures. What it gives us to think (*denken*) is precisely the ways in which it delivers an image (*Bild*) not only of this or that particular content, but always also of its own folding back upon itself, its most successful failure.

Adorno locates in Benjamin's Denkbilder an enigmatic impulse that flows through his own Denkbilder and through those of their common friends Bloch and Kracauer as well. The poetic prose of the Denkbild works both with and against conceptual thought, remaining faithful to the concept by betraying it, illuminating remnants of experience in the service of an unknown futurity that those remnants still may harbor. The Denkbild wishes to comment on its own contingency, even as it strives to assert propositions of truth that also wish to remain unfettered by the contingency that they themselves diagnose.

The sentences that the Denkbild gives us to read arrest thought in an image composed of words. Each sentence, ghostly in its apodictic illumination, thematizes its non-transparent relationship to the sentences that both follow and precede it. The individual sentence of the Denkbild calls attention to itself as a sentence in order to thematize, by involving the reader in a serious play and a vexing dance of meaning, not simply its denotative meaning but also its participation in the larger process of hermeneutic decoding that it at the same time resists. Woven from the material fibers of language, the image that the Denkbild gives us is a picture of this resistance.[25]

Pre-Histories of the Thought-Image

In this self-conscious mode of writing and thinking, the Denkbild hopes to preserve something of the poetic consciousness that conceptual prose has repressed in the service of reason alone. As the Germanist Heinz Schlaffer puts it, "the remainder of lyric poetry that still adheres in 'Critical Theory' achieves its unfolding in the Denkbild."[26] It is precisely this valorization of poetry—understood in the extensive sense of *Poesie*, the larger aesthetic practice in which, since German Romantics such as Novalis, Tieck, Schlegel, and Wackenroder and the Idealist philosophy of Schelling and Hegel, the term points beyond mere writing—that the writers of the Denkbild wish to retain for their own project. It comes as no surprise, then, that Adorno, in the dedication introducing his Denkbilder collected in *Minima Moralia*, explicitly positions his textual production with and against Hegel. "Hegel," Adorno reminds us there, "whose method schooled that of *Minima Moralia*, argued against the mere being-for-itself of subjectivity on all its levels." Within this frame of reference, Adorno's Denkbilder "take upon themselves the duty to 'consider the evanescent itself as essential,'" and they "insist, in opposition to Hegel's practice and yet in accordance with his thought, on negativity."[27]

The Denkbild thus operates both with and against Hegel, in a way that remains faithful to Hegel by departing from him always one more time. In the Denkbild's perpetual and uncontainable movement of negativity—a negativity that in its relentlessness also activates a sense of the futurity of the positive, even if only as a mirror image of loss and trauma—the idea of redemption and the hope that attaches to it never can be declared fully dead, even as there can be no naive or triumphalist initialization of any program that would seek the restoration of damaged life to a condition of wholeness and presence. The damaged life cannot be restored because it was always already damaged; it cannot be made present because it was always already absent; but the lack and the traumatic void can be made the poetic and philosophical occasions for a vigilant stance that will neither simply revel in resignation nor fully relinquish the madness and enigmatic stimulus of non-deluded hope. Here, the Denkbild refuses to give up on the Hegelian "labor of the concept," even when its aestheticized form and rhetorical flourishes seem to privilege *Spiel* over *Arbeit*, just as the melancholic dramatic tensions of a *Trauerspiel* can never fully be explained away or arrested by any achieved result of *Trauerarbeit*.

The writerly praxis of the Denkbild that Adorno, Benjamin, Bloch, and Kracauer pursue cannot be thought in isolation from Hegel's insistence, so significant to these writers, that the absolute spirit can know and be known in different ways, and that the self-knowing of absolute spirit can occur in more ways than one. The Absolute, which derives from the Latin *absolvere* (to detach or release), is that which gives itself its own laws and which situates its conditions of possibility only in itself, rather than in any other. For the early German Romantics, the Absolute is the category of the unsayable as such. Hegel's system, however, attempts to specify the conditions under which the Absolute is thought and aesthetically performed. One privileged way in which the absolute spirit in Hegel's aesthetics can come into its own, that is, come to know itself as a form of absolute spirit, resides precisely in art. In art such as poetry and music—what Hegel calls *das sinnliche Erscheinen der Idee*, or the sensuous appearance of the idea— the Absolute grasps itself as such. For instance, as Hegel writes in the section entitled "The Position of Art in Relation to Finite Reality and to Religion and Philosophy" in his *Lectures on Aesthetics*, "artistic beauty [*das Kunstschöne*] is neither the logical Idea, absolute thought as it develops in the pure element of thinking, nor is it the natural Idea, but it belongs to the *spiritual or intellectual* realm [*dem* geistigen *Gebiete*], without, however, stopping at the cognitions and actions of *finite* spirit." Rather, Hegel continues, "the realm of beautiful art is the realm of absolute spirit."[28] Art stages, in Hegel's aesthetics, the overcoming of the finite in the Absolute, that is, in speculative truth. The Absolute appears as aesthetic presence in the singularity and finitude of individual works of art. Rather than working against the appearance of the Absolute, the unverifiable singularity and relentless finitude of the artwork individuates and specifies the Absolute in non-programmatic, unforeseeable ways. The singular and finite artwork, then, encrypts philosophy as the speculative truth of the Absolute in the variegated appearance of an aesthetic form. In this way, a speculative thinking of the Absolute in Hegel's aesthetics requires a manifest form beyond the realm of abstraction, such as the work of art, to concretize it and to make it sensually experienceable.

It is possible to understand Hegel's view of the aesthetic form as a response to, and elaboration of, one of the basic distinctions introduced to European philosophy by Kant: the fundamental difference between theoretical and practical philosophy. In Kant's view, one never acts according to the precepts of theoretical principles alone. Rather, elements inevitably are present in one's actions and being that correspond to movements of thought that cannot be contained in advance by this or that theoretical system, whether in the realm of ethics or in the realm of one's public use of reason. By the same token, Hegel's Absolute could not realize itself merely as a theoretical law, or as a mode of systematic abstraction, without recourse to an aesthetic, figurative, and, by extension, non-theoretical and non-systematic experience such as the work of art supplies. Only in the work of art, then, can truth emerge as an estimation of the appropriateness of any link forged between reality and concept.[29]

Schelling extends Hegel's insistence on the artwork's special claim to the speculative truth of the Absolute and argues—following the romantic Friedrich Schlegel, whose work exerted such a powerful influence on the early Benjamin's intellectual concerns—that the infinite qualities of the Absolute may become graspable and experienceable in the concrete aesthetic manifestations offered by the work of art. In Schelling's system of transcendental Idealism, art is the site where that which philosophy seeks but always fails to grasp takes place. As Schelling argues, for instance, in his 1802–3 *Philosophie der Kunst*, "art corresponds precisely to philosophy" and "art itself is an outflow of the Absolute [*ein Ausfluß des Absoluten*]."[30] What exceeds philosophy in its conceptual system manifests itself in the work of art, representing that which refuses itself to the mere concept. In Schelling's view, and as mediated by Hegel, art, rather than logic, is the *organon*, or tool, of philosophical speculation. Whereas mere logic fails as the systematic medium in which the truth of speculative thought might manifest itself, art contains and reveals what philosophy cannot, forming, in its unification of absolute differences, a bridge between thought and concept. As such, art acts as the sensuous appearance of speculative truth, that is, the only truth that matters, one that unfolds beyond mere empirical observation and logico-formal deduction.

Although the writers of the Frankfurt School often were critical of certain elements of the so-called German Idealism with which Schelling and Hegel are identified, they nevertheless subscribed in mediated ways to the Idealist notion that the work of art participates in crucial ways in sublating the negative presence of the infinite within the finite. Thus, to mediate their theoretical views in the sphere of the artwork meant to produce a form of writing that would allow the theoretical content of their work to be performed—rather than merely described by the logical and formal categories of philosophy one more time. The form they chose, the Denkbild, was meant to embody this appearance of the infinite in the finitude of the aesthetic text, the *Scheinen* (appearance or shining through) of one determinant in the form of another. The literary Denkbild, then, is the sensuously graspable form that does not just mimetically reflect the content of a theoretical system but performs it precisely by exceeding itself, pointing beyond itself and, by extension, beyond any pre-programmed systematic content. The Denkbild, as an artwork that differs from and with itself, enacts speculative truth as a sensuously concrete manifestation of the spiritual truth that, as in Hegel, thinks the ways in which it differs with and from itself. The Denkbild constitutes itself as an aesthetic and speculative form precisely by returning again and again to the demands of thinking this self-differentiation. From such a perspective, the Denkbild can be thought as embodying the negative presence of the infinite in the formal aesthetic features of its very finitude. In this one regard, then, the artistic practices of Adorno, Benjamin, Bloch, and Kracauer convene with those of Hegel, Schelling, and their poet friend and Tübingen classmate Friedrich Hölderlin—as especially Adorno and Benjamin, who devoted lengthy studies to the latter's writing, well knew.

Tracing the Law of Genre

To mediate and complicate these aesthetico-philosophical concerns by the concrete production of Denkbilder is a task that, for all their individual differences, will not leave this group of Frankfurt School writers. In fact, it is their shared hope that these ethico-political and epistemo-aesthetic concerns can be made sensuous in the Denkbild. Bloch elucidates this hope with regard to Benjamin's writings:

A sense for the peripheral: Benjamin had what Lukács so drastically lacked: a unique gaze for the significant detail . . . things which do not fit in with the usual lot and therefore deserve particular, incisive attention. Benjamin had an incomparable micrological-philological sense. . . . He was not only up to his ears in books, but up to his ears in the experience of a *world* that had to be read with the greatest care . . . that made external appearances and precisely the strikingly unnoticed (or rather that which is striking and yet goes unnoticed) in this perception and the structures of appearance appear to him as written signs. This happened in a slightly uncanny [*unheimlichen*] manner, as if the world were a text, as if the course of things . . . were writing an unknown book out of mere emblems . . . [and] making ciphers that had to be read, read in a micrological-philological way. . . . Precisely the "text" structure emerges here . . . as Benjamin thought, because the objective hieroglyphics of the thing become visible to us in this way.[31]

In what simultaneously is a comment on his own Denkbilder and on those of his and Benjamin's mutual collaborators, Bloch emphasizes the intuition in Benjamin's texts that the world in which Denkbilder unfold deserves to be read according to a textual model of history and of experience. This is not to say that, for any of the Frankfurt School's writers, the world *is* a text, but only that the understanding of the world upon which the practice of the Denkbild is predicated approaches the world *as if it were* a text, that is, as a signifying structure full of figures and tropes to be carefully deciphered and confronted in their potential withdrawal from transparent meaning.[32] These "hieroglyphics" demand to be read—indeed, they can *only* be read— yet at the same time, one cannot take their readability for granted. One can only engage the Denkbilder that one is given to read one more time.

Yet the primary aim of this study is neither to establish a philological history of a genre nor to revel in the securities offered by the taxonomic administration of that phenomenon. Rather, my mobilization of the Denkbild is meant to contribute to the activity of theoretical thought as conceptual creation, and to allow the figure of the Denkbild to open up ever more speculative perspectives across the texts that it traverses. Here, I wish to think of the Denkbild less in terms of a narrow philological category than, even as it is also mediated by philological issues, in terms of what Gilles Deleuze and Félix Guattari call a concept's perpetual creation. For them, "philosophy is not a simple art of forming, inventing, or fabricating concepts, because concepts are not necessarily forms, discoveries, or products. More rigorously, philosophy is the discipline that involves *creating* concepts." Because concepts "are not waiting for us ready-made, like heavenly bodies," we might say that "the task of philosophy is to create concepts that are always new."[33] The Denkbild, then, should be understood not simply as a prefabricated concept and fixed genre, ready for us to initialize, but as the formal site for singular and unpredictable—but not arbitrary or facile—acts of conceptual creation. The Denkbild is thus inseparable from the aesthetic dimension of conceptual thought.

Moreover, in specifying the generic history and formal features of the Denkbild—that is, by making it a genre and thereby generalizable—one runs the risk of eliding the resistance that the Denkbild itself mounts against such taxonomic and classificatory impulses. After all, what connects various Denkbilder across time and across thematic concerns is their very disconnection from one another and from any truth-content that could be detached from the specificity of each singular occurrence. A Denkbild therefore cannot be paraphrased. Rather, the Denkbild will not remain unaffected by what Adorno, in *Negative Dialectics*, underscores with regard to philosophical thought itself. Here, "the presentation of philosophy is not an external matter of indifference to it but immanent to its idea."[34] Therefore, Adorno emphasizes that

> philosophy would need first, not to turn itself into a series of categories but rather, in a certain sense, to compose itself. It must, in the course of its progression, relentlessly renew itself, as much from its own strength as from the friction with that against which it measures itself; it is what happens in philosophy that is decisive, not a thesis or a position; its texture, not the deductive or inductive single-tracked train of thought. Therefore philosophy is in essence not summarizable. Otherwise it would be superfluous; that most of it allows itself to be summarized speaks against it.[35]

Likewise, what prevents a Denkbild from being superfluous, even when it addresses philosophical issues, is its resistance to being fully translatable into philosophical truth-claims or formal propositions. Indeed, its very resistance to such translation and paraphrase is part and parcel of what it signifies and of what it gives us to think philosophically.

The resistance of the Denkbild to paraphrase and translation, and thus also implicitly to its own generic classification, situates it as a liminal case in which it thematizes the very idea that an act of signification could be designated by a genre. In "The Law of Genre," Derrida argues that whenever what is at stake is the issue of genre and its attendant issues of gender, genus, classification, taxonomy, and category, the membership of a certain phenomenon or event in a particular genre is signified by a certain marker or mark. This mark, which signals the belonging of something to a genre with respect to certain self-identical principles, codifiable traits, and verifiable characteristics, can itself not belong to the very genre it names. It is thus in the position of naming belonging without itself belonging; it belongs to the idea of belonging in that it signals belonging, yet at the same time it does not fully belong. The mark of genre, then, can be said to be inside and outside at the same time, not unlike Benjamin's figure of the flaneur who, taking a stroll through the glass-covered Parisian Arcades, can have the sensation of being inside and outside at the same time. Acknowledging that it is possible to have more than one genre at once—say, a novel that also is an autobiography—an intermingling of various genres and even the genre of "genre" itself, Derrida emphasizes that the remark of a generic designation need not explicitly mention the genre, as often is the case in the title of literary works, such as a novel or drama. He continues:

A text would not *belong* to any genre. Every text *participates* in one or several genres, there is no genreless text . . . yet such participation never amounts to belonging. And not because of an abundant overflowing or a free, anarchic and unclassifiable productivity, but because of the *trait* of participation itself, because of the effect of the code and of the generic mark. In marking itself, the text unmarks itself [*se démarque*]. If remarks of belonging belong without belonging, participate without belonging, then *genre-designations cannot be simply part of the corpus*. . . . This inclusion and the exclusion do not remain exterior to one another; they do not exclude each other. But neither are they immanent or identical to each other. They are neither one nor two. They form what I shall call the *genre-clause*, a clause stating at once the juridical utterance, the designation that makes precedent and law-text, but also the closure, the closing that excludes itself from what it includes. . . . At the very moment that a genre or a literature is broached, at that very moment, degenerescence has begun, the end begins.[36]

In the context of the Denkbild, then, this generic form, whenever it is remarked as a generic or formal designation in this study, also is incapable of fully belonging to what it designates. The generic designation "Denkbild" cannot itself be a Denkbild. If writers such as Benjamin bestow the generic title Denkbild and Denkbilder on their texts, these markers only can stand in for that to which they cannot belong but for whose belonging they are indispensable. The Denkbild proclaims membership while remaining both inside and outside, perched on the fence of multiple generic commitments and determinations, closing its genre without closure, being interior and exterior at the same time. As a liminal form of discourse, a minor form of writing and a marginal textual practice, the Denkbild, perhaps unlike more dominant literary forms such as the novel, the poem, or the drama, not only participates in this play of non-closure and excess, it also comments on it, staging it not as an embarrassment to be overcome but inviting it as part of the constellation of aesthetic forms and philosophical points that it gives us to think in so many singular events. We could even say that the Denkbild is the genre-without-a-genre par excellence, that is, the genre that both lacks a genre and that relies on what is "genreless" for its affirmation as a genre—similar to Benjamin's preference for thinking the moment of expression in terms of the "expressionless" (*das Ausdruckslose*). The double coding of generic belonging and non-belonging will remain operative throughout my readings of individual Denkbilder in this study: they give us to think, among other things, the ways in which they never fully can belong.

This emphasis on the simultaneity of belonging and not belonging, and on the ways in which this simultaneity is mediated by the material inscriptions of the Denkbild, may help us to resituate certain aspects of humanistic inquiry today. After all, my study of the Denkbild also is motivated by the sense that today's humanistic inquiry often is characterized by a tacit return to certain models of mimetic correspondence between the aesthetic and the political, between the material artifact and an allegedly non-aesthetic world. In short, there is a tendency to regress to systems of reading that ascribe, often with understandable political motivations, a status of transparent and fully referential functionality to aesthetic modes of production and reception. This attempt at formalizing in a political agenda the often uncontrollable significations of aesthetic form has been called "aesthetic ideology." My claim is that the genre of the Denkbild deserves to be reconsidered in this context. The Denkbild belongs, I argue, to those aesthetically self-conscious critiques of aesthetic ideology that work to uncover and to interrogate the problematic unspoken assumptions that allegedly connect the sphere of the aesthetic directly and *without further mediation* to the realm of concrete social praxis. The Denkbild is politically charged in that it offers a mode of thinking, reading, and writing that allows us to inquire into the history and logic of aesthetic ideologies. It affords insight into the often subterranean ways in which seemingly disinterested claims of taste or artistically mediated forms of sensate cognition reinforce an uncritical view of social norms and a tendentious imposition of constructed and contingent worldviews as the expression of an alleged political necessity. Because the Denkbild remains suspended in a charged tension between the figural and the literal as it stages its overdetermined relation to the sphere of non-aesthetic discursive practices, it offers us bold new strategies for the future of critical inquiry. Even while it shares Marx's oppositional spirit, the new form of materialism that the Denkbild stages cannot be reduced to the materialist critique that Marx marshaled against aspects of the Idealist systems of Kant and Hegel. Rather, as a radicalized form of *textual* materialism—concerned with the materiality of language—it ceaselessly engages the moment of critical *inscription* rather than mere *description*.[37]

Thought-Images and the Scenes of the Political

For our writers, each in his own way, the kind of aesthetics named by the Denkbild is invested with a promise, the promise of literature, which, for them, cannot be thought in isolation from a rethinking of the political.[38] This implies not only that there is a connection between the literary text and politics but also that this connection can be thought, and even thought again, in terms of a promise, the promise of literary writing. But today, in our digitized global era, who or what can still assume the responsibility of this promise? Who or what promises what to whom? And what would it mean to keep this promise? Or to break it? Does a promise not need to be repeated, affirmed again and again, in order to remain what it is? What the Denkbild shows is that the promise of literature, if there can be such a thing, lies not in what it teaches about the political—how it reproduces political issues that seem to be prevalent in the empirical or historical time in which a text is embedded—but rather in its invitation to reconsider, again and again, the non-identical forms of political thinking that are enacted in artistic presentation. "This is not the time," Adorno writes, "for political works of art; rather, politics has migrated into the autonomous work of art, and it has penetrated most deeply into works that present themselves as politically dead."[39]

Far from subscribing to any straightforwardly realist ideology, the self-conscious writings of Adorno, Benjamin, Bloch, and Kracauer remind us of the ways in which the poetic text enacts the inseparability of language and presentation from issues of politics. But perhaps poetic forms such as the Denkbild do not afford the luxurious but misleading comfort of mimesis—much less a mimesis of what is political. The Denkbild neither simply affirms nor negates what is, nor does it give us a new political agenda that we might implement in lockstep fashion, a utopia that already has been decided. Rather, the promise of the Denkbild may reside in the invitation that it extends to us to open up the complexity of the concept of the political to its perpetual non-self-identity and thus to its unpredictable future. This opening up can occur even—or especially—when the language of a Denkbild seems, on the surface, to have little or nothing to do with questions of politics or history. Like the non-synchronicity of Bloch's utopia, the promise of the Denkbild always resides in an unnamable elsewhere.

Why do such aesthetic questions continue to be relevant today? Undoubtedly, these are difficult times for theoretically inflected literary and cultural criticism. As modes of inquiry that are hard to describe, and even harder to quantify, these forms of critique are badly suited to the demands of a globalized system that is rooted in the principles of consumption and the maximization of profit. Literary writing especially denies itself to the ideals of instrumentality and the economy of exchange value that so thoroughly have gripped our academic institutions. In fact, the dangers inherent in an ideology of institutional knowledge that espouses corporate models of globalized production have been made vivid for us by such critics as Bill Readings, J. Hillis Miller, and Christopher Fynsk, among many others. Readings subtly uncovers the ways in which the new "university of excellence" prepares its human products for conformist and affirmative roles in the transnational network of conglomerates. The "excellence" that is attained in such an education need not—indeed must not—be excellence *in* anything in particular, much less be based on a critical stance. Just excellence; perhaps even, in corporate speak, "McExcellence." This generalized excellence then easily can be instrumentalized for this or that corporate purpose.[40] Appropriate programs already have been implemented. For instance, as Miller points out, when the current president of a large public university system in the United States assumed office a few years ago, he immediately hired consultants from the business world in order to determine how the application of corporate models of thinking to teaching and research could make the university more "productive."[41] In the face of these institutional pressures, Fynsk reminds us, it is incumbent upon us to reclaim the significance of fundamental research in the humanities so that it preserves its material and linguistic specificity as a politics of engagement.[42]

Hand in hand with corporate transformations of the university has come a backlash against literature, aesthetics, literary theory, and theoretical speculation more generally. As Fredric Jameson, one of the most astute American interpreters of the Frankfurt School's political heritage, recently wrote, "Ours is an antitheoretical time, which is to say an anti-intellectual time; and the reasons for this are not far to seek. The system has always understood that ideas and analysis, along with the intellectuals who practice them, are its enemies and has evolved various ways of dealing with the situation, most notably—in the academic world—by railing against what it likes to call grand theory . . . at the same time that it fosters more comfortable and local positivisms and empiricisms in the various disciplines." For instance, Jameson continues, "If you attack the concept of totality . . . you are less likely to confront embarrassing models and analyses of that totality called late capitalism or capitalist globalization; if you promote the local and the empirical, you are less likely to have to deal with the abstractions . . . without which the system cannot be understood."[43] It is not necessary to share Jameson's sustained commitment to such concepts as totality to follow the cultural and therefore political logic that his assessment sketches out. The antitheoretical bias, often coupled with an attack on the continued study of literature, its culture, and its concepts, pushes humanistic studies into a position in which they often work to reinforce, rather than place out of joint, the logic of the economy of systemic mediations that produced them. The humanities are confronted with a corporate situation ruled by a model of immediate transparency in which, to use Adorno's formulation, people are taught to valorize instant clarity, with the unfortunate result that only that which "they do not need first to understand, they consider understandable; only the word coined by commerce, and really alienated, touches them as familiar."[44] Whenever writing and thinking fail to conform to this demand of immediate transparency they are met with intolerance and even hostility.[45] But then again, as Paul de Man has taught us, "Nothing can overcome the resistance to theory since theory *is* itself this resistance."[46] What will this have meant? What are the implications for us, today? And what is the place of literature and the aesthetic in this self-referential resistance, Adorno's *Widerstand*?

As in the Denkbild, speculative thought and literary aesthetics are, in the understanding of our Frankfurt School writers, intertwined. The universal of theory assumes the form of the particular in literature. This is not to say that literature functions merely as an illustration of theoretical points elaborated outside of it. On the contrary, the uncontainably performative nature of literature hardly will allow it to function as a mere repository of examples for this or that theoretical discourse. Rather, we may say that literature, even when it implicitly is concerned with general theoretical questions, can approach these questions only in local and circumscribed instances that may or may not correspond to the claims to generality that a theoretical account of a phenomenon strives to offer. Kafka's texts, for example, are concerned not merely with this or that law, but with the idea of the Law as such; but they can approach this generality only through specific, local, ungeneralizable, and unverifiable narrative situations: a man from the country standing before the gates of the law; a land surveyor visiting a mysterious castle; or Joseph K. suddenly being arrested one fine morning under dubious circumstances. Similarly, if Proust is concerned with a general philosophy of time and memory, *In Search of Lost Time* can "only" offer us a series of specific moments, singularities that show Marcel in his cork-insulated room, reflecting on his grandmother's death or on devouring a madeleine. And if Flaubert's wish was to write the great nineteenth-century novel about "nothing," the characters in *A Sentimental Education* always are involved in *something*, beginning with Frédéric Moreau's return to Nogent-sur-Seine. This is to say neither that literature somehow is deficient in its representative powers, nor that it, at its best, simply illustrates an a priori general concept. After all, even the kind of theoretical discourse that strives most vigorously to avoid specific and explicit examples to sustain its philosophical points cannot always escape the potentially disruptive particularity of figurative speech. The uneasy status of the "example," often tacitly bending in its illustrative strength under the weight of all the metanarratives it is meant to support, in the aesthetics of Kant and Hegel is a good case in point.

But this is not the crux of the matter. Rather, the relation between the literary and the theoretical shows how the reality of a concept always and of necessity is based in a singular linguistic moment, a trope whose materiality of signification it never fully can shuck. Because there can be no theoretical concept that is free from the (unreliable) singularity of the particular shape that it necessarily assumes upon entering language, literature, such as the Denkbild, self-consciously exposes the inescapable contamination of the theoretical by the figurative—rather than glossing over this tension in an effort to create the false semblance of disembodied meaning. We thus could say that literature not only contains a network of metaphors and metonymies, but also is itself a metonymy of the linguistic specificity of any theoretical act. Because this double signature of literature does not happen in a vacuum, and because the interpretive reading of this signature is a matter of contention rather than of self-evidence, its analysis is an eminently political act with properly political stakes—even when a literary text at first seems to have little or no political content.

By extension, the Denkbild always operates as a double performative. As a special mode of literary writing, it enacts the relationship between the universal and the singular: each Denkbild thematizes a singular content—in other words, it is "about" something, and its "aboutness" opens onto larger questions of writing to the extent that each Denkbild is itself the singular instantiation, regardless of its specific theme, of a larger, universal idea of literature. It is the wager of the Frankfurt School writers who work in this mode that this double performative of the Denkbild renders it politically and philosophically charged.

The Denkbild helps us to ask if there can be such political potential in the literary, that is, if there can be a promise in literature that goes beyond the pleasure principle and, if so, what it would mean for such a promise to unfold on the far side of mimesis and realist criticism. The question to ask is thus not simply when serious and even "hermetic" literature, literature that thematizes its own literariness, putatively ceased being political, but rather, what it means that it breaks, within the realm of the aesthetic, with the referential links that often are adduced as the guarantors of its social commitments. (One thinks of the German systems theorist Niklas Luhmann, who, implicitly deepening an observation previously made by La Rochefoucauld, traces the invention of modern love back to readers of eighteenth-century novels, who believed that they too must feel this emotion called "love," in the same way as the characters about whom they were reading.)[47] In this scenario, our Frankfurt School writers become the undead of aesthetic theory who, like the revenants evoked by Bloch in his reading of the German Romantic Ludwig Tieck's literary fairy tale "Blond Eckbert," return to haunt.

Such concerns place us squarely within the network of questions regarding the relation between formal structure and social resonance, between essentially aesthetic issues and urgently political ones. After all, for Adorno as for his Frankfurt School colleagues, there can be no immanent meditation on the aesthetic that is not simultaneously either an enactment or a determined negation of the social and political structures in which its particular manifestation, the rigors of its form, are embedded. Yet what determines the political content of an encounter with the aesthetic is neither its transmission of this or that content, nor its revelation of a communicable message. Rather, the aesthetic remains to be understood in terms of the specific and formal ways in which it *resists* appropriation and instrumentalization. We thus encounter the aesthetic, particularly in the domain of writing, in a series of hieroglyphs that demand to be read but that also refuse to yield their full meaning. Pointing to the ways in which "the concept of *écriture* has become relevant," Adorno argues in the section "Enigmaticness, Truth Content, Metaphysics" of *Aesthetic Theory* that "all artworks are writing, not just those that are obviously such; they are hieroglyphs for which the code has been lost, a loss that plays into their content. Artworks are language only as writing." Although these hieroglyphs cannot be reduced to a singular truth statement or stable meaning without being canceled, they also cannot *not* be read. Rather, what is at stake in reading—in the emphatic sense—the hieroglyphs of the aesthetic is the determination of the specific ways in which they resist determination. As Adorno tells us, the "aim of the artwork is the determination of the indeterminate" (*AT* 189; 124). Because the hieroglyphs of the aesthetic reveal themselves in the form of enigmas, that is, as "script [*Schrift*]" in which "as in linguistic signs, its processual element is enciphered [*verschlüsselt*] in its objectivation" (*AT* 264; 177), the artwork only can be understood as a system whose internal laws are out of joint: "Each artwork is a system of irreconcilability [*ein System von Unvereinbarkeit*]" (*AT* 274; 184).

Once this system of *Unvereinbarkeit* becomes visible in a literary text such as a Denkbild—and just when such a point has been reached remains an open matter of discussion—what reveals itself to the reader is that in "artworks nothing is literal, least of all their words" (*AT* 135; 87). This means that to read artworks such as the Denkbild and the realm of the aesthetic to which they belong entails a decisive turn away from the realist or mimetic effect that they may simulate on the surface. In an act of dissimulation, they become thinkable only in and as something irreducibly figurative. One might call this their material moment of inscription. Artworks become material and readable in what Adorno calls "their own figuration," that is, the allegorical enactment of "the solution" to problems "which they are unable to provide on their own without intervention." The specific intervention that the artwork can perform thus unfolds not in the sphere of immediacy or street violence, but precisely in the aesthetic and incommensurate event marked—but not containable—by its inscription. This suggests, according to Adorno, that "every important work of art leaves traces behind in its material and technique, and following them defines the modern as what needs to be done, which is contrary to having a nose for what is in the air. Critique makes this definition concrete." He continues: "The traces to be found in the material and the technical procedures, from which every qualitatively new work of art takes its lead, are scars: They are the loci at which the preceding works misfired." For Adorno, the material inscription of the aesthetic event as a political act presents itself in the figure of the scar. A scar, as a trace of corporeal writing, marks the place of a previous incision or injury. A sign of what no longer is, it also is a deeply historical marker. The scar always occurs as a double gesture: it represents itself as the concrete and present image of a disfiguration, excessive in its reference to something that no longer exists, a signifier with a signified but without a referent. The scar bespeaks that utopian moment of coming to terms with and recovering from a traumatic injury, even as it continues to render the forgetting of that trauma impossible. After all, a scar is a sign both of healing and of danger: it always threatens to be reopened. Seen from this perspective, the scar occupies a ghostly locus between the various axes of time and of cognition. We even could say that the figure of the scar, like Adorno's sentences themselves, not only signifies the historical and theoretical complexity of material inscription, but also embodies it. Following Adorno's lead, the history of Western art and aesthetics deserves to be rewritten not in terms of teleological succession, but as an archive or constellation of scars. The scar, and "not the historical continuity of [the works'] dependencies, binds artworks to one another" (*AT* 59; 35).

The insistence on the materiality of this scarred inscription, articulated by Adorno and shared by his Frankfurt School colleagues, often has been overlooked, even by readers sensitive to the desire to articulate political commitments in and with the aesthetic. Among the many suggestive dimensions of Adorno's work, this insistence is especially relevant today in the face of a widespread return to models of mimetic correspondence between the aesthetic and the political, between the material artifact and its relation to a non-aesthetic world. Rather than heed Roland Barthes's warning against the seductions of the "reality effect"—that is, the confusion of a complex rhetorical construction or semblance of reality within an artwork with reality itself, as in the case of Flaubert's inexplicable barometer[48]—there is a regression to models of reading that ascribe, often with fully understandable political motivations, a status of transparent and fully referential functionality to aesthetic modes of production.

The Denkbild, in its excessiveness and resistance, should be read alongside trenchant critiques of this kind of "aesthetic ideology," critiques that work to uncover the problematic unspoken assumptions that underlie any attempt to connect the sphere of the aesthetic directly and without further mediation to the non-aesthetic realm of concrete or political praxis. Aesthetic ideology thus becomes visible as the name for a movement that strives to deduce a social or political model from an aesthetic one. In the case of Schiller's aesthetics, for instance, one often can discern the utopian impulse to construct a new state in accordance with an "aesthetic education" that adheres to certain principles of reflective contemplation. It can be argued, however, that the confusion of aesthetic and non-aesthetic reality itself is the birth of ideology, and the work of critics as different as, for example, de Man and Terry Eagleton has done much to question this ideology.[49]

However, this is not to say that, in a flash of recognition, the tradition of modern aesthetic speculation from Baumgarten onward suddenly has become suspect, exposed in all its irrecuperable corruptness.[50] Neither would it be useful to construct "The Aesthetic" as a transhistorical, self-identical category of theoretical reflection without first considering the extent to which this category has been reworked and rethought across historical and philosophical specificities in ways too heterogeneous and too contradictory to be reducible to any monolithic entity of meaning. By the same token, not all aesthetic discourse must be equated a priori with bad faith and delusions; it certainly is possible and desirable to imagine an aesthetic discourse that liberates itself from and subverts the ideology of the aesthetic from within while retaining its status *as* aesthetic discourse. Aesthetic ideology, then, can be understood as the name for a *particular movement* of thought within an aesthetic discourse, a slippage from the formal to the political. A sustained examination of the logic and history of aesthetic ideologies thus may reveal the often subterranean ways in which seemingly disinterested claims of taste or artistically mediated sensate cognition work to create and reinforce an uncritical, organicist view of social norm and a tendentiously violent imposition of highly constructed and contingent worldviews as the expression of an alleged political necessity. That is to say, critiques of aesthetic ideology are most persuasive when they focus on the nodal points in that ideology's historical and systematic formation that require the conflation of cognitive and sensate encounters with an absolute state of empirical reality or even with the unforgiving demands of narrowly conceived Reason. Viewed in this light, it becomes incumbent upon any critique of aesthetic ideology to ask what it is in the rhetorical presentations of an aesthetic discourse that enables and, just as important, does not preclude its proponents from seeking to buttress empirical power by strategically imbricating the sphere of the real with claims of taste and judgment.

An abiding assumption in this kind of aesthetic ideology is the idea that works of art communicate something other than themselves, a content that exceeds their material form. But a reconsideration of the Denkbild in this context makes clear that, rather than relying on a model of transparent communication and the secure ground of referentiality, this mode of writing conceives of the aesthetic as a realm in which signs first and foremost exhibit how writing communicates nothing but its own non-communicability. As Adorno tells us with regard to Paul Celan's poetry, "Art is integral only when it refuses to play along with communication" (*AT* 476; 321). Seen from this perspective, the sphere of the non-aesthetic becomes thinkable as an irreducible alterity not only to the aesthetic, but also to what the aesthetic communicates, that is, what Adorno calls its non-communicability. This communication of non-communicability is the scar of the Denkbild—in both the genitive and the ablative case.

The orientation of these reflections, however, does not lend credence to more literalist readings that are tempted to see, albeit for understandable reasons, in Adorno's self-reflexive model of the aesthetic and in the Denkbild more generally the threat of negating the artwork's political relevance, thereby reducing it to a purely parasitic and domesticated entity. On the contrary, for Adorno, as for his fellow writers of the Denkbild, the political function of the aesthetic paradoxically is located in the very space in which it is inaccessible to instrumentalist reasoning and unmediated political intervention. Here, "art becomes social by its opposition to society." Adorno argues that "by crystallizing in itself as something unique to itself, rather than complying with existing social norms and qualifying as 'socially useful,' it criticizes society by merely existing, for which puritans of all stripes condemn it" (*AT* 335; 225–26). Because even art that is socially and politically engaged can become affirmative of the status quo by fulfilling the function of critique that the status quo already has assigned to it—that is, by offering a critique that is co-opted by the system that spawned it—Adorno prefers to think of the aberrant event of art in terms of a "determinate negation of a determinate society." Therefore, art "keeps itself alive through its social force of resistance," without which it becomes, even in its critical forms, "a commodity." Because "nothing social in art is immediately social, not even when this is its aim," what art can contribute to society "is not communication with it but rather something extremely mediated: It is resistance" (*AT* 335–36; 226). For Adorno and his friends, there can be no resistance lodged in artworks and literary texts that is not perpetually retreating from what it signifies and from the determinate nature of the relays between it and the context that mediates it. What interests Adorno, specifically in the literary aesthetics to which *Aesthetic Theory* takes frequent recourse, cannot be reduced, as so often has been attempted, to the concept of artistic autonomy. Rather, what Adorno ceaselessly seeks in literature, and what he and his fellow writers of the Denkbild engage, is the determinate indeterminacy of what in its own tropes spells the name "resistance" in ever new ways and in the ever new and unforeseeable movements of its textual signature.

Adorno's philosophical model of aesthetics is most political—and, therefore, given the Frankfurt School's commitments, most itself—when it moves toward something else, that is, when, in its refusal to remain itself, it resists any unmediated form of political intervention. The Denkbild exploits the gestures by which the aesthetic imbues its own negativity not with a utopian model for practical action, but with an excessive alterity that cannot fully be accounted for. The aesthetic thus stages its conflictual relationship to the sphere of non-aesthetic discourse in that charged tension between the beautiful and the true. When seen against this background, we can appreciate Adorno's assertion that all "artworks, even the affirmative, are a priori polemical. The idea of a conservative artwork inherently is absurd. By emphatically separating themselves from the empirical world, their other, they bear witness to the idea that the world itself should be other than it is; they are the unconscious schemata of that world's transformation" (*AT* 264; 177).[51]

Adorno, along with his friends, thus conceives of the aesthetic neither as a mere abstraction divorced from any actuality nor simply as the conglomerate of canonical artistic practices such as writing, painting, sculpture, and music. Rather, he endows the aesthetic with a conceptual specificity that allows it to encompass and simultaneously to exceed all of its individual components. This is the double movement that Adorno often calls lyric poetry or simply, as in his *Notes to Literature*, "literature." Next to the musical composition—which, for Adorno as for Bloch, is the most exalted model of non-communicable materiality and stands, through such figures as Beethoven and Schönberg, at the core of their philosophico-political aesthetics—literary writing such as that of the Denkbild becomes a privileged stage upon which to engage with the aesthetic. For Adorno there can be no rigorous thinking of the aesthetic that does not proceed in terms of the alterity and non-communicable materiality of the literary text. This is so in part because literary writing, in its refusal to remain *buchstäblich*, or literal, demonstrates what is always the case in aesthetic experience: there can be no direct or realist reading of an aesthetic creation capable of doing justice to art's irreducibly figurative nature. For Adorno, literary works, not unlike the twelve-tone music that he so championed in Schönberg and the Second Viennese School but unfolding in a different materiality, are figurative or allegorical, possessing "a wordless syntax even in linguistic works. What these works say is not what their words say," so that meaning cannot be synonymous with authorial intention. What Adorno calls the allegorical *Wahrheitsgehalt*, or truth-content, of a text becomes perceptible when it divorces itself from its author's intended meaning: what speaks in a work of art is not the author's voice but the artwork's own formal echoes: "The dynamic of artworks speaks in them" (*AT* 275; 184). If the Greek root of allegory, *allegorein*, signifies the process of speaking differently or of saying something else, then literature works to retain and, indeed, to intensify this otherness.

Yet although the Denkbilder of our Frankfurt School writers are theoretical through and through, they do not lay out a unified aesthetic theory of literature (or of anything else, for that matter). They enact a principle of reading and thinking in which theory always already *is* praxis. That is to say, they prefer instead to approach the construction of theory with an openness to the shifting requirements of the *singularity* and *specificity* of the object, reinventing their theoretical procedure with the new form and figurative shape of each object of analysis. For instance, Bloch's commitment to an unorthodox form of utopian thought, one that does not content itself with merely predictive or programmatic forms of the future, also plays a role in his Denkbilder. In the same way that Bloch's utopian gesture points not to a foreclosed future but to something that is unpredictable, excessive, and always yet to come, his image of the self never is quite present to itself. The self always is the location of an elsewhere, gesturing beyond itself in a constellation of analyses, dreams, and imaginative acts. What is required for Bloch's Denkbilder, as for those of his friends, is a thinking of the ways in which the self transgresses itself and of the movements by which it becomes the object and telos of transgression.

What names the otherness of the literary Denkbild as a form of material inscription is language itself. To read closely, slowly, and with an eye to the materiality of a text's figures is the challenge that the Denkbild offers to us. As Bloch writes in "On a Metaphor in Keller": "He who has learned to write does not necessarily know how to read. This is especially obvious when someone reads quickly and indiscriminately." But "sentences in good books can be so beautiful that one hardly wishes to read any further," as is the case with Keller, where figurative language poses special and "relentless" challenges.[52] Here, individual figures and metaphors work to attract and to distance the reader at the same time. In Keller's rhetorical metamorphoses, spiders "do not sit in their webs but 'hover' in them," a "dog eats by 'conversing' with its plate," a beard is depicted as a "thicket," and misery itself "comes calling like a 'taciturn messenger of the judiciary.'"[53] For Bloch, Keller's metaphors do not simply serve to convey this or that plot: as epistemological instances, they show us the reality of a thinking that both refers to something at hand and reminds us of the strategies that it itself—*as* figurative language—employs to prevent us from accessing the kind of truth that pretends to be self-evident and unchangeable, that is, not governed by the hope lodged in the unpredictable contingency of tropes. "For," Bloch writes, "especially when the contours of things are glimmering with such intensity, the totality of what comes to pass in a given time is precisely that which can be found only by trial and error, by interruption, as something intrinsically experimental—also in its representation."[54] It is here that the Denkbild flashes up. Far from presenting themselves as "models" to be imitated or as knowing "systems" to be installed everywhere, the Denkbilder of Bloch, Adorno, and their colleagues invite us to account for the irreducible materiality of language and to liberate the oppositional spirit that propels them to question any realist ideology, any supposedly transparent or self-evident mode of presentation, and any institutional or political certainties that rely on mimetic or analogous models of aesthetic ideology. What the Denkbild embodies is the precarious principle of hope: that in our infinite conversation, the last word will not have been spoken.

Mourning and the Inscriptions of Loss

One of the ways in which the Denkbild defers this last word in the moment of inscription is through its abiding emphasis on loss. This loss cannot simply be described and then categorized according to generic taxonomies but calls attention to itself *as* loss: as the loss of understanding itself and as the event of one's own non-understanding. Therefore, if my readings of the Denkbilder by Adorno, Benjamin, Bloch, and Kracauer focus on the enactment of literary, philosophical, personal, and political loss, they implicitly wish to put such losses into grammatical relation with the explication of trauma, mourning, and melancholia that Freud offers us. In "Mourning and Melancholia," for instance, Freud differentiates between two modes of responding to the trauma occasioned by the loss of a beloved person, object, idea, or ideal.[55] At first sight, Freud's model seems to privilege mourning, in which a subject gradually withdraws its libido from the lost object in order to invest it somewhere else, over melancholia, in which a subject is unable to invest its libido elsewhere because withdrawal of it from the lost object is not achieved. Yet something else reveals itself upon a closer reading of Freud's apparent binary opposition. Although melancholia can be read as a pathological deviation from the normal course of healthy mourning, it also can be understood as a refusal to lose the object a second time through the process of disengaging from it, and, by extension, as a refusal to lose one's loss. From this perspective, melancholia names a loss that is constitutive in nature and therefore cannot be compensated without undoing the ego that defines itself through this loss.

Collectively, my readings of Adorno, Benjamin, Bloch, and Kracauer—all careful readers of Freud—show that the philosophical miniatures of the Denkbild can best be understood as unfolding on the far side of an apparent binary opposition between mourning and melancholia. The Denkbild enacts a series of engagements with the constitutive loss that make a subject what it is: the loss of democracy under fascism; the loss of the certainties of the Hegelian "system"; the loss of home in displacement and exile; the loss of stable meaning and readability in modernity; and the loss of the other, such as an absent or dying friend. My readings suggest, therefore, that this genre of writing is the subterranean link that unexpectedly connects these Frankfurt School thinkers in their collective undertaking to respond to a constitutive loss and that, in turn, the Denkbild deserves to be rethought with an eye toward what it may reveal about our own sense of loss—and yet, through this very experience of loss, importantly also about our own investments in certain forms of futurity, in the as yet unthought possibilities of a transformation still to come.[56]

Among the strategies incorporated by writers of the Denkbild in their attempt to stage the unfolding that occurs on the far side of the opposition between mourning and melancholia is the effort to devise a written self that is perpetually at odds with itself by taking this self-differentiation as its very site of articulation. We could say that a Denkbild operates not unlike the philosophically invested lyric poem of which Adorno speaks in "On Lyric Poetry and Society." From such a perspective, the Denkbild "reveals itself to be most deeply grounded in society when it does not chime in with society, when it communicates nothing, when, instead, the subject whose expression is successful reaches an accord with language itself, with the inherent tendency of language." Language itself chooses the path of the writing self, a self that in the Denkbild is articulated by the otherness of language, even as the self appears to be the one through whom this language speaks. Here, "language itself speaks only when it speaks not as something alien to the subject but as the subject's own voice. When the 'I' becomes oblivious to itself in language it is fully present nevertheless; if it were not, language would become a consecrated abracadabra and succumb to reification, as it does in communicative discourse."[57] The writing self that authors a Denkbild is, therefore, non-coincident with any predetermined notion of the self that may be possessed by an other. In the same way that the Denkbild resists the binarism of mourning and melancholia, the hand that composes it elides the binarism of self and other. Rather, we may think in Levinasian terms of a "wholly other," that is, as an other not simply to this or that self, but to the very structure of self and other.[58]

The inherent difficulty in designating the Denkbild as a genre, the law that prohibits the re-marking of a particular mode of expression so that it might belong to the genre it wishes to name, can be said to intersect with the kind of mourning work that this mode of writing engages. This intersection is illuminated when we recall de Man's comments, made apropos of Baudelaire, on the relationship between generic terms and mourning:

> Generic terms such as "lyric". . . as well as pseudo-historical period terms such as "romanticism" or "classicism" are always terms of resistance and nostalgia, at the furthest remove from the materiality of actual history. If mourning is called a "chambre d'éternel deuil où vibrent de vieux râles," then this pathos of terror states in fact the desired consciousness of eternity and of temporal harmony as voice and as song. True "mourning" is less deluded. The most *it* can do is to allow for non-comprehension and enumerate non-anthropomorphic, non-elegiac, non-celebratory, non-lyrical, non-poetic, that is to say, prosaic, or, better, *historical* modes of language power.[59]

True mourning, according to this model, no longer can comprehend, but only enumerate. In the moment when de Man diagnoses the enumerative quality of mourning, his own syntax enumerates, as if in a stammer. In this double gesture, his passage performs, on a syntactical level, the concept of which it speaks and, at the same time, takes part in the activity of mourning by means of that very enumeration. The materiality of the Denkbild, along with all the historical, conceptual, and personal losses that it mourns, belongs to this mode of less deluded mourning. Because the Denkbild opens up to its non-comprehension and perpetual displacement, it refrains from celebrating its losses and thus from recuperating them in the act of writing. Whether it commemorates the experience of exile, encrypts the fallenness of modernity, or recalls dark times of state-sponsored genocide, it becomes historical only by predicating its mourning and its melancholia upon a perpetual retreat from straightforward meaning and historical transparency. This less deluded mourning that the Denkbild encrypts also sponsors the subtitle of my book, which it shares with Adorno's *Minima Moralia*, his own book of thought-images: *Reflections from Damaged Life* (*Reflexionen aus dem beschädigten Leben*). The reflections of loss and mourning, while decoupled from damaged life, nevertheless emanate from damaged life itself. Damaged life, and the senses of loss and mourning that condition it, becomes not merely the object but also the site on which dialectical thought unfolds.

The Denkbild is capable of sponsoring such a movement, if it is capable of anything at all, only by enacting its responsibility to the singular events of its occurrence as a materially textual phenomenon. It is no accident that Adorno writes to Benjamin, in a letter dated 18 March 1936, "I would not know of a better materialist program than the sentence by Mallarmé in which he defines literature not as something that is inspired but as made from words."[60] This insistence on the figural materiality of language as a truly political program is shared not only by Adorno and Benjamin but also by their fellow practitioners of the Denkbild. As a philosophical act of literature, each Denkbild demands that we respond to the otherness of its singularity, that is, to the ways in which it makes claims on us that cannot be verified by any metaphysical structure or universal certainty. The Denkbild is the textual mode par excellence that, like every work of literature worthy of its name, reminds us of the infinite task in reading literature, as Gayatri Spivak recently put it, "to learn to learn from the singular and the unverifiable."[61]

Constellations of the Singular: The Argument

Seeking to learn from the singular and the unverifiable, each of the chapters that follow proceeds by examining one or more Denkbilder composed by a particular writer associated with the Frankfurt School in relation to that writer's major theoretical texts. Thus, the first chapter places Denkbilder from Benjamin's *One-Way Street* into relation with his unfinished magnum opus, *The Arcades Project*; the second chapter situates Denkbilder on dreaming, musical experience, and non-teleological utopian longing from Bloch's *Spuren* in the context of his philosophy of music in *Spirit of Utopia* and other works; the third chapter considers Denkbilder from Kracauer's Weimar period, such as "Farewell to the Linden Arcade," in relation to the theory of extraterritoriality developed in his philosophy of history and in relation to Derrida's monolingualism of the other; and the fourth chapter analyzes Nazism and other ethico-political concerns in the Denkbilder of Adorno's *Minima Moralia* vis-à-vis his major philosophical statements in *Aesthetic Theory*, *Negative Dialectics*, and related texts. Collectively, the chapters argue that a politically charged anticipatory illumination (*Vorschein*) of a radically unknowable futurity is lodged in these

Denkbild authors' staging of an unsublatable dialectical interplay between speculative thought and aesthetic practice, an interplay that self-reflexively enacts the threat that is posed to every act of signification by the inherent instability of the representational medium in which that signification occurs. Excavating the subterranean links that connect these writers, I consider the prospects of a post-mimeticist approach to humanistic inquiry and the promise of philosophically inflected modes of literary and cultural analysis. My reading hopes to contribute to an examination of the status of literary writing in the materialist work of a reading that is still to come.

In chapter 1, "A Matter of Distance: Benjamin's *One-Way Street* through the *Arcades*," hope for the unpredictable futurity of a "coming" philosophy is shown to reside in the doubly coded gesture of a vacillation between proximity and distance, approaching and departing, motion and standstill. In these Denkbilder, Benjamin mobilizes tropes of passages, passings, crossings, and continuations alongside larger concerns of criticism and of historiographic method. I show that Benjamin's textual model of historical method, in which a constellation of Denkbilder inscribe the siblings named philosophy and literature, is illuminated by the ways in which his texts engage the difficulty of ascertaining the *rechte Abstand*, or right distance, from the visual phenomena encountered on the streets of Berlin and Paris, as well as from the very words of a text. Here, Benjamin's insistence on the value of departing from a prescribed critical course or from meta-theoretical programs, be they Marxian or messianic, gives rise to his radical poetic and methodological praxis of aberration. This non-programmatic praxis, aleatory without being arbitrary, yields an openness to the experience of undecidability and to the possibilities of the impossible.

Chapter 2, "Bloch's Dream, Music's Traces," shows that Bloch's Denkbilder give voice to a similarly transformative and non-naive utopian longing that is lodged in the peculiar dialectical tension between philosophy and music. In this chapter I argue that the hope Bloch inscribes in the "not yet" resonates on the far side of any aesthetic ideology, even as it always is mediated by the aesthetic. The figures of the dream and of music traverse, in a variety of modulations and tonalities, a substantial segment of his corpus. Focusing on the moments in his early masterpiece *Spirit of Utopia* (1918) alongside his later Denkbilder collected in *Spuren*, in which he rethinks the philosophy of music in terms of sleeping and the dream, the chapter shows how, for Bloch, one's relation to the idea of relation never can be exhausted or fulfilled. What makes Bloch's relation what it is cannot be thought in isolation from the ways in which it is always already a figure of excess and of differentiation. I suggest that two interrelated models of such thinking in Bloch's philosophy of the not-yet carry the names "music" and "dream": the music of dreams, and the dream of music. Bloch's projects in *Spuren* and *Spirit of Utopia* are linked in their rhetorical and conceptual emphasis on dreaming, sleeping, longing for the not-yet, and the attendant music of futurity. As the chapter shows, these complexly mediated terms emerge as central to the aesthetic and ethico-political impetus of his unorthodox utopian reflections.

In chapter 3, "Homeless Images: Kracauer's Extraterritoriality, Derrida's Monolingualism of the Other," Kracauer's Denkbilder are seen to gesture toward a hopeful openness to undecidability in their staging of the unsublatable dialectical interplay between belonging and homelessness, an interplay that also can be observed in the philosophical context of Derrida's monolingualism of the other. Kracauer and Derrida—one a displaced German Jew persecuted by Hitler, the other an Algerian Jew uneasily acculturated to "Frenchness"—for all their differences and singularities share a set of common concerns. Sometimes writing in languages not their "own," both Kracauer and Derrida reflect on the relation between homelessness and language, displacement and cultural identity, dispersal and community, the politics of exclusion and inclusion, and a writing that is of, from, and in the margins. Specifically, I show how the "homeless image" (*das obdachlose Bild*) of which Kracauer speaks in his 1930 Denkbild "Farewell to the Linden Arcade" names a feature that is central to the projects of both thinkers: the experience of the marginal as it disrupts the officially sanctioned discourses of a cultural system. The chapter examines the ways in which these homeless images constitute forms of Kracauer's extraterritoriality and of Derrida's monolingualism of the other. In so doing, the chapter demonstrates how, for both Kracauer and Derrida, a possible critical reading of a multiple and perpetually fractured homeless image is always yet to come. It cannot simply be assumed to be present, lest it be mistaken for having a proper home, the false home that would be present in a stable hermeneutic decoding of that image, a decoding that reduces the image to one meaning and "the one" of meaning. The homeless images that Kracauer and Derrida offer us imagine a cultural identity beyond cultural identity, a cultural practice in which one is no longer simply oneself and no longer simply one, the one who is present. Because the reality of this imagined cultural identity cannot be reduced to this or that form of presence—its desires, genealogies, contexts, overdeterminations, hidden filiations, promises, commitments, secrets, and debts always are elsewhere, invested differently, and not fully visible—we must look for its homeless images *in the future*. But this future, the chapter argues, is resistant to being programmed in advance, even by a gesture that would attempt, with the best of intentions, to install a system for reading homeless images with an eye to their futurity. Homeless images, if they do anything, challenge us to consider the ways in which they, and we, in and with them, always are still to come, even as others or as an other. Homeless images, along with the extraterritorialities and monolingualisms that they enact, are homeless precisely because they do not yet fully exist but remain to be made, thought, and read.

Then, in chapter 4, "Nazism and Negative Dialectics: Adorno's Hitler in *Minima Moralia*," we see that Adorno's Denkbilder, in their staging of a dialectical vacillation between culture and barbarism, hold out the promise of a philosophically inflected mode of literary and cultural analysis to come. The chapter argues that while *Minima Moralia* can be seen as belonging to a broad network of cultural responses in the 1930s and 1940s, from John Heartfield's Hitler photomontages and Brecht's didactic play *Arturo Ui*, to pop-cultural satires of Hitler such as those mobilized in the cartoons of Walt Disney and Dr. Seuss, to the 1940 film *The Great Dictator* by Charlie Chaplin, what distinguishes Adorno's engagement with Hitler is the way in which it theorizes the abiding threat of a critique's subterranean complicity with the structure of thought that genealogically fails to prevent the very thing it criticizes. When placed in the context of Adorno's later writings in *Negative Dialectics* and *Aesthetic Theory*, *Minima Moralia*'s engagement with Hitler refuses to foreclose the possibility that the rational structures of enlightened logic that underlie the moment of critique may not always be distinguishable from the dialectical patterns of thought that created, among other things, Hitler's Nazi Germany. Thus, even a critique of Hitler may not be immune to the dialectic of culture and barbarism that, according to the logic of Horkheimer and Adorno's *Dialectic of Enlightenment*, long precedes both Hitler and the critique. In this way, the chapter argues, *Minima Moralia* becomes a prism through which Adorno's larger concerns with Hitler, and with ethical and intellectual life "after"

Hitler, come metonymically into view. I suggest that Adorno's Hitler, including Nazi Hitlerism as well as the proper name itself, which occurs some dozen times throughout the text, sheds light on the ways in which negative dialectics strives to open up a thinking after Auschwitz that would do justice not only to the memory of the historical atrocities perpetrated in the name of Hitler, but also to its own impossibilities, to the ghostly blind spots that negative dialectics wishes not to exorcise, in an entirely understandable though ultimately misguided application of instrumental reason, but to recognize as the traces of its constitutive lack. The ruse of reason that mobilized Hitler and that gives us non-identical thinking to think, the ruse that propels us to learn to read the meaning of afterness on so many levels, also is what encourages us to find hope, not in the possibly delusional phantasmagoria of hope itself, but in the promise of the hopeless. It is from this perspective, I argue, that a negative dialectics after Hitler, fragile and elusive as it may be, still deserves to be thought.

1

A Matter of Distance:

BENJAMIN'S *ONE-WAY STREET* THROUGH THE *ARCADES*

> *Truth and goodness* are siblings *only in beauty*—the philosopher must possess just as much aesthetic power as the poet. Those without aesthetic sense are our pedantic philosophers.
> —Hegel, Hölderlin, and Schelling, "Das älteste Systemprogramm" (1796–97)
>
> Criticism is a matter of the right distance.
> —Walter Benjamin, *One-Way Street*

Thinking is a search for siblings. There can be no thinking, at least not the kind of thinking that unfolds in philosophical and poetic writing, that will not have turned upon finding a sibling. Thinking, and the thinking of thinking, is the thinking of, by, and for the sibling. It is the searching thinking that seeks connections with the sibling as the one who is related yet different, related in difference, and both the same and different in relation to the common parent whose existence both unites and divides the siblings. Thought seeks to establish relays, to articulate relations, merging with and departing from what is closest to it. It seeks a sibling to sustain it, an other who will read along even in the absence of their father's guarantees, in a gesture that also works to maintain distance between the siblings. This thought seeks to erase difference in order to join its sibling completely in a fraternal embrace while at the same time perpetuating the difference that separates it from its sibling in order to establish itself as the one who differs. No literature without siblings, no philosophy without siblings, no thinking without siblings. Thinking is a search for siblings. Yet if thinking is a search for siblings, it also depends on finding the right distance—*Abstand*—from these siblings.

"Let us suppose," Walter Benjamin writes, "that one makes the acquaintance of a person who is handsome and attractive but impenetrable, because he carries a secret with him. It would be reprehensible to want to pry. Still, it surely would be permissible to inquire whether the person has any siblings and whether his or her nature could not explain somewhat the enigmatic character of the stranger. In just this way critique seeks to discover siblings of the work of art. And all genuine works have their siblings in the realm of philosophy."[1] These words resonate with readers of his *One-Way Street* (*Einbahnstraße*), the lyrical book of paratactically assembled *Denkbilder*, albeit perhaps in the space of an overturn: while Benjamin seeks to articulate the elective affinity between literature and philosophy by progressing from a poetic form to a conceptual superstructure, a reading of his *One-Way Street* also reveals a dialectical inversion of this trajectory. If Benjamin's *Arcades Project* (*Passagen-Werk*) can be read as a philosophical system (or as a systematic non-system of the kind that the Romantic theorist Friedrich Schlegel once demanded), then *One-Way Street* can be read as the poetry that accompanies, radicalizes, and transforms it.[2] As readers of *One-Way Street*, we might therefore turn Benjamin's remarks around—reversing the direction of their one-way street—by suggesting that all genuine works of philosophy also have their siblings in the realm of literature. It is perhaps only by considering Benjamin's philosophical and literary siblings in concert that we can begin to trace the intricate and self-reflexive movement of his language that once led his friend Hannah Arendt to suggest that what is "so difficult to understand in Benjamin is that he, without being a poet, *thought poetically* [*dichterisch dachte*], and that for him metaphor had to be the greatest and most enigmatic gift of language."[3] We could say that it is this very difficulty that implicitly returns Benjamin to the siblinghood of philosophy and literature that Hegel, Hölderlin, and Schelling demanded in "Das älteste Systemprogramm" ("The Oldest System-Program"), a document they anonymously coauthored during the age of German thought to which Benjamin's doctoral dissertation is devoted.

In these pages, I wish to argue that such concerns are lodged in the language of proximity and distance, standstill and movement, approaching and leaving behind that the passages and passageways, stops and continuations, recesses and dark spaces of *One-Way Street* and of the *Arcades* conjure. Benjamin's textual model of historical method, in which the siblings named philosophy and literature are inscribed, cannot be thought in isolation from the ways in which his texts engage the question of finding and maintaining the *rechte Abstand*, or right distance, from the phenomena his gaze encounters on the rhetorical streets of Berlin and Paris.

Siblings and *Revers*: *One-Way Street* and *Arcades*

The siblinghood between the philosophy of the *Arcades Project* and the literariness of *One-Way Street* becomes visible when we recall the respective place of each in the trajectory of Benjamin's writings. In 1928 Berlin's Rowohlt Verlag published both his *Trauerspiel* study and the constellation of Denkbilder collected in *One-Way Street* that define the city and its life as a semiotically charged text to be read. Under the dust-jacket pastiche by the constructivist photographer Sascha Stone, with whom Benjamin collaborated on questions concerning the theory of photography and of reproduction in general, the Denkbilder collected in *One-Way Street* are among the most polished of Benjamin's texts. They show Benjamin as a writer. Here, the montage principle, later elaborated in the *Arcades Project*, brings together, under such suggestively cryptic titles as "Imperial Panorama," "First Aid," and "Construction Site," various reflections of philosophical, personal, and political significance, reflections that are situated in the semiotics of early-twentieth-century industrial culture. In its self-reflexively apodictic manner, this text collects some of the early Benjamin's most provocative and relentless thoughts: "When will we be ready to write books like catalogues?" "What, in the end, makes advertisement so superior to criticism? Not what the moving red neon sign says—but the fiery pool reflecting it in the asphalt."[4] These reflections, indebted to the fragments, aphorisms, and Denkbilder of Schlegel, Nietzsche, Valéry, and Kraus are printed, in the original 1928 edition, in an avant-garde typeface and page design that mirrors contemporary constructivist typology in the tradition of Jan Tschichold, Kurt Schwitters, and others.

In *One-Way Street*, the Denkbilder are not positioned in accordance with an overarching narrative principle but rather are arranged according to a systematic non-system, as if situated along a city street in which individual Denkbilder become the figurative shops, signs, buildings, and urban sites at which readers may interrupt their strolls like leisurely flaneurs on a promenade.[5] Indeed, the sixty Denkbilder or stops along *One-Way Street* can be conceptualized in visual-spatial terms, as is suggested by the architecture of Daniel Libeskind, who recently made *One-Way Street* the spatial basis of the sixty "stations of the star" in his design for an extension of the Jewish Museum in Berlin.[6] A book of streets, gas stations, advertising signs, dreams, quotidian reflections, and philosophical insights, *One-Way Street* is, as one reader puts it, no "weighty tome" or "academic monument"—it "has more of the appearance of a city plan: avenues of open space cross its pages, between compact and irregular blocks of text."[7] The Denkbilder of *One-Way Street* that act as a map of the city also may be conceived as the "heteroclite construction site of different 'moments' that constitute Benjamin's thinking," rather than as the record of a closed urban system.[8] Yet, although *One-Way Street* shares its metropolitan figures with other modernist texts that were close to Benjamin's thinking at the time, such as Louis Aragon's "Passage de l'Opéra" from *Paysan de Paris* and Alfred Döblin's *Berlin Alexanderplatz*,[9] its various philosophical investments are more nuanced. Indeed, *One-Way Street*, like so many of Benjamin's "city texts," can be read as, among other things, emerging from and transforming a specific concept of experience that is indebted to Kant and extended by Benjamin's corpus through an obsession with notions of color, the image, and the visual world more generally into the space of urban experience, the visual arts, and the siblings named philosophy and literature.[10]

The element in Benjamin's thought that works to transform the traditions of Kant and German Idealism is developed in *One-Way Street*, a text that also often is read as staging Benjamin's turn to Marxism under the troubled aegis of his lover, Asja Lacis, to whom the book is dedicated.[11] But the text also figures, as Miriam Hansen reminds us, as "part of a more general turn, around 1925, among critical intellectuals as strongly influenced by Jewish messianism and gnosticism as Benjamin, from lapsarian critiques of modernity to a more curious and less anxious look at contemporary realities, in particular the marginalized, ephemeral phenomena of everyday life and leisure culture." The book employs "textual strategies that articulate . . . the political, erotic, and aesthetic implications of the *Bahnung*, or pathway, cut by modernity, the street that entwines technological and psychic registers in the book's title trope."[12] Benjamin's style here also engages the aesthetic principles of Weimar Germany's movement of Neue Sachlichkeit, with its phenomenologically sober emphasis on things found in the object world and its interest in a cool and distanced engagement with apparently marginal appearances. This sober turn toward the marginal and the ephemeral, a turn that Benjamin shared with such friends and colleagues as Adorno, Bloch, Horkheimer, and Kracauer, is staged in the Denkbilder of *One-Way Street* as something like his poetics of historical montage, a principle that the *Arcades Project* later radicalizes. Suspicious of any form of totality, Benjamin's gaze here is directed at the marginal and forgotten, and he is fascinated with the hidden illuminating power of seemingly insignificant cultural objects such as children's books (of which he was an avid collector) and kitsch objects. Indeed, children's snow globes, as Adorno tells us, were Benjamin's favorite items.

This meticulous searching for the strange or insignificant is an eminently political gesture, not because it enacts any preconceived program of what deserves to be collected and studied and what does not, but because it refuses to accept the condition of insignificance as something natural, exposing it instead as a cultural and political construction that relies on problematic unspoken assumptions. The segment "Construction Site," for instance, describes the joy that children experience in rummaging through the debris of a construction site and the delight they take in putting into syntactical relation seemingly disparate objects to build new forms.[13] This image should be read figuratively because it is also that of Benjamin's historical materialist, the ragpicker and garbage collector of history. He looks awry, seeking his material and inspiration not in a culture's officially sanctioned venues, but in the refuse and debris that have been overlooked, repressed, or marginalized. Through a strategic poetic montage, in which the neglected debris of history is placed into a new grammatical constellation, a revolutionary image emerges. This, for Benjamin, is the image of history itself.

Most of the literary *One-Way Street*'s philosophical sibling, the *Arcades Project*, was composed not, as was the earlier text, in a setting of relative security, but during Benjamin's Parisian exile from the German fascists. As is well known, he spent his days in the great reading hall of Paris's Bibliothèque Nationale, hunched over stacks of books and file-card boxes, scribbling in and filling in his microscopic handwriting one notebook after another. Upon returning to the studies of the city and modern culture that he had begun in 1927 while working on *One-Way Street*, Benjamin shifted his gaze from the streets of Berlin to those of Paris, focusing his attention on the role that nineteenth-century Paris and writers such as Baudelaire played in the construction of modernity. In his various studies of Baudelaire in the context of Western modernity, he investigated such paradigmatic figures as the sandwich man, the whore, and the flaneur strolling through the metropolis, the elegant idleness of his pace symbolized by the turtle on a leash that he would sometimes take along. The works on Baudelaire belong to the immediate conceptual orbit of the *Arcades Project*, the massive assemblage of commentary, quotations, and observations on Parisian life, centered on the "passages" or glass-covered indoor arcades that were the early prototypes of the modern shopping mall. While Benjamin's gaze in *One-Way Street* is directed at outdoor objects in plain view, the arcades as a critical leitmotif now compel him in his studies of modernity not only because of his interest in the revolutionary aspects of glass architecture that he discovered in the work of the science-fiction writer Paul Scheerbart, but also because, in walking through them, one has the feeling of being indoors and outdoors at the same time. This double experience allows Benjamin to call into question the schism between public and private spaces upon which bourgeois ideology so heavily relies, a schism that is an object of critique in *One-Way Street* and that also is encrypted in the language of a potential revolution in his essay on "Surrealism": "To live in a glass house is a revolutionary virtue par excellence. It is also an intoxication, a moral exhibitionism, that we badly need."[14]

Because Benjamin conceives of Paris as the capital of the nineteenth century in his *Arcades Project*, he is able to discern in it the very fibers that constitute modern capitalist culture, with its commodity fetishism, its technophilia, and its political aberrations. He refers to this peculiar conceptual constellation as the "sex appeal of the inorganic." Reading everything from street lighting to iron constructions, from boredom to kitsch object, and from prostitution to world expositions, Benjamin's genealogy of modernity puts into grammatical relation a multiplicity of images barely containable even by an extended concept of Husserl's phenomenological *Lebenswelt*, or life world.[15] Benjamin, like Bloch, works to find in small and obscure objects the seeds of a radically innovative historiography that expresses philosophical rigor through the aesthetic strategies of pastiche or montage that had already been the strategy of *One-Way Street*: "Method of this project: literary montage. I have nothing to say. Only to show. I will purloin nothing valuable and appropriate no ingenious turns of phrase. But the shards, the trash: I do not wish to inventory them, but simply give them their due in the only possible way: by putting them to use."[16] Even though it remained unfinished, Benjamin hoped in his materialist work on the arcades to illuminate a powerful method of cultural analysis that relies on historical specificity, rhetorical awareness, and far-reaching political insights. The task of coming to terms with this method, that is, the task of learning to *read*, in the emphatic sense of the word, is what ultimately Benjamin wished to hand down to us. This task, for him, is always lodged in the relation of the two siblings, philosophy and literature.

The elective affinity between philosophy and literature is cast into sharper relief when we recall that, from the beginning, Benjamin conceived of *One-Way Street* and the *Arcades Project* as siblings. Because Benjamin began to make tentative plans for the contours of the *Arcades Project* as early as 1927, there is a significant temporal and conceptual overlap with *One-Way Street*. As Benjamin writes to Gershom Scholem on 30 January 1928, "Once I have, one way or another, completed the project on which I currently am working, carefully and provisionally—the highly remarkable and extremely precarious essay 'Paris Arcades: A Dialectical Fairy Play' ['Pariser Passagen: Eine dialektische Feerie']—one cycle of production, that of *One-Way Street*, will have come to a close for me, in much the same way in which the *Trauerspiel* book concluded the German cycle. The profane motifs of *One-Way Street* will march past in this project, hellishly intensified." In the same missive, Benjamin reassures himself, by assuring his friend, that his work on the Paris Arcades "is a project that will just take a few weeks," not realizing, or perhaps not admitting to himself, that the project would never be completed and that the additional twelve years he devoted to it would occupy the remainder of his life.[17] It is as though with one hand Benjamin were writing to ensure the completion of a uncompletable project while with the other hand erasing that very promise.

This double gesture enacts what *One-Way Street* ironically posits: "To great writers, finished works weigh more lightly than those fragments on which they work throughout their lives. For only the more feeble and distracted take an inimitable pleasure in closure, feeling that their lives have thereby been given back to them. For the genius, each caesura, and the heavy blows of fate, fall like gentle sleep itself into his workshop labor.

Around it he draws a charmed circle of fragments."[18] Here, *One-Way Street* acts as an explanatory supplement to the *Arcades Project* even before the latter has been written, a movement that corresponds to Benjamin's abiding attachment to the demand by Hugo von Hofmannsthal, the Austrian poet and early supporter of Benjamin, to "read what was never written."

The peculiar sibling relationship between *One-Way Street* and the *Arcades Project* figures prominently in Benjamin's interactions with his other friends. For instance, in a letter dated 10 March 1928, Benjamin thanks Kracauer for his "friendly inquiry concerning the *Arcades* [*Passagen*]," suggesting that "if it [the *Arcades*] succeeds, *One-Way Street* will present its intended form only in it."[19] Finally, Benjamin elaborates the conceptual and theoretical connection between the two projects in a February 1928 letter to Hofmannsthal:

> While *One-Way Street* was being written, I did not really feel that I could write you about it and, now that you have the actual book before you, it is even harder for me to do so. I do, however, have one request that is very close to my heart: that you not see everything striking about the book's internal and external design as a compromise with the "tenor of the age." Precisely in terms of its eccentric aspects, the book is, if not a trophy, nonetheless a document of an internal struggle. Its subject matter may be expressed as follows: to grasp timeliness as the reverse of the eternal in history [*Aktualität als den Revers des Ewigen in der Geschichte zu erfassen*] and to make an impression of this, the side of the medallion hidden from view. Otherwise, the book owes a lot to Paris, being my first attempt to come to terms with this city. I am continuing this effort in a second book called *Paris Arcades* [*Pariser Passagen*].[20]

Benjamin here articulates the methodological stance that ties the literary sentences of his thought-images in *One-Way Street* to the theoretical sentences of his *Arcades Project*. His sentences work to make visible the connection between, on the one hand, what is immediate and topical and, on the other, the larger invisible structures of historical cognition. Like the individual stops along his *One-Way Street* (gas stations, construction sites, and the Mexican embassy), the coordinates of the Arcades—the iron construction, the dream house, and the railroads—provide, through the illumination of this or that striking detail, a glimpse of the totality that these details at once contain and dissimulate. This stance, according to the *Arcades Project*, allows Benjamin "to discover in the analysis of the small individual moment the crystal of the total event," in an effort "to break with vulgar historical naturalism" and to "grasp the construction of history as such."²¹

But it is no accident that Benjamin's German mobilizes the word *Revers* to describe the methodological stance that connects his two texts. While *Revers* means "reverse side," as in the back side of a coin, it also conjures a homophonic relationship to the French *reverie*, the dreamlike meditation that is often simultaneously the method and the subject both of *One-Way Street*, as in Benjamin's "Goethe dream," and of the *Arcades Project*, with its sustained reflections on the epistemology of dreams, dream houses, and future dreams in Convolutes K, L, and elsewhere. Both siblings are books of and about dreams, of waking and sleeping, of sleepwalking and coming to terms with a history that is punctured by the urgent signal of an "alarm clock that in each minute rings for sixty seconds."²²

Yet, *Revers* interweaves the two sibling texts in a more mediated sense as well. *Revers* not only means "reverse side," it also refers to a lapel or any textile segment that is folded back at the front of a garment. If Benjamin here locates the spectral site of historical cognition, a momentary flashing up of what he later will call dialectical images, on the folds and margins of a garment, his language resonates with that of the *Arcades Project*, in which we learn that "the eternal, in any case, is far more like the ruffle on a dress [*jedenfalls eher eine Rüsche am Kleid*] than some idea."²³ As he so often does in his work, Benjamin thinks of the textile, even the most obscure textile weave, in terms of the Latin *textum*, the woven basis that gives us the word and concept "text."²⁴ To the extent that the eternal reveals itself at all, it does so only in the marginal textile-textual place of a half-superfluous ornamentation (the lapel, the ruffle) that nevertheless is aesthetically vital and philosophically charged. What reveals itself here is the flowing textual ornament that *One-Way Street*, in a gesture reminiscent of Kracauer's theory of the ornament, describes as possessing an extraordinary "density [*Dichtigkeit*] of presentation [*Darstellung*]" in which "the difference between thematic and excursive expositions falls away."²⁵ That this act of reading the weave of history as a *textum* is suffused with questions of obligation, responsibility, ethics, and their declaration is encrypted in the juridical dimension of the word *Revers*. In German, *der Revers* also denotes a written declaration of a juridical or legally binding kind, an official obligation, as in *einen Revers unterschreiben*, to sign a legal declaration or a contract. If Benjamin reads the textum as a figure in which history presents itself, albeit only fleetingly, he assumes a certain responsibility, an ethical obligation in the reading of that textum. But to whom or what, we might ask, does Benjamin assume responsibility? What is the nature of his obligation? And how might one determine whether or not justice is done to this obligation in the act of reading and writing? These questions, I wish to suggest, for the Benjamin of *One-Way Street* and the *Arcades Project* cannot be thought in isolation from methodological questions of proximity and distance.

The Threats of *Umreißen*

In our approach to the question of *Abstand*, a concept upon which Benjamin wishes us to meditate, we may turn to comments made by the earliest readers of *One-Way Street*, Benjamin's friends and collaborators. After all, from the beginning, *One-Way Street*, the only "literary" work to be published during his lifetime, was a textual meeting place for him and his writerly friends, all of whom would in time compose their own philosophical fragments and literary-philosophical Denkbilder and whose work he later cites at various points in the *Arcades Project*, especially Adorno, Bloch, and Kracauer. These friends all loitered on Benjamin's *One-Way Street*. As early as 1926, Benjamin sent a selection of the Denkbilder that were to evolve into *One-Way Street* to Kracauer, who was working for the influential newspaper *Frankfurter Zeitung*. When Kracauer arranged for a selection of them to be printed in the *Frankfurter Zeitung* later that year, he invented the title *Kleine Illumination* for them. This title, Kracauer's gift to his friend, eventually became, as *Illuminationen* in German and *Illuminations* in English, indissociable from Benjamin's name.[26] Indeed, it is on the territory opened up by *One-Way Street* that these friends find common ground. As Benjamin reports to Kracauer on 15 February 1928, "Wiesengrund [that is, Adorno] and I have seen each other quite a bit in a productive way. He has now also met Ernst Bloch."[27] It is thus hardly an accident that Benjamin's early original title for *One-Way Street* was *Plaquette für Freunde* (Booklet for Friends).[28] Significantly, Adorno, Bloch, and Kracauer all published major, but often neglected, essays about their friend's *One-Way Street*: Adorno shortly after his return to Germany from American exile after World War II, Bloch and Kracauer both in 1928, the year of its publication.

We could say that these friends already intuited the question of proximity and distance that Benjamin's work broaches. In "Revue Form in Philosophy," Bloch, whom Benjamin himself considered his most perspicacious reader, describes how the reader of *One-Way Street* enters the text's construction of houses and business establishments joyfully at first but then experiences a bewildering disorientation: "Then something starts to bother us, changes right next door, reverses directions yet again. This is how we fare in the first attempt of this kind that Benjamin has undertaken."[29] Likewise, Kracauer's review, which, to Benjamin's delight, appeared on the latter's birthday, suggests the importance of positionality for Benjamin's writerly and philosophical stance. Here, borrowing Benjamin's own language, Kracauer gestures toward the variegated phenomena that line *One-Way Street* and that spell Benjamin's writerly signature: "In Benjamin, philosophy regains the determinateness of its content; the philosopher is placed in the 'elevated position midway between researcher and artist.' Even if he does not reside within the 'realm of the living,' he retrieves from the storehouses of lived life the meanings that were deposited there and that are now awaiting a recipient."[30] Both Bloch and Kracauer sense in Benjamin's writing an abiding preoccupation with the question of positionality, that is, the notion of a writerly stance in perpetual negotiation with its own proper proximity to, or distance from, that to which it relates. This relentless negotiation is not an external imposition on a conceptual and methodological position that is already in place and secure once and for all; on the contrary, the interminable negotiation of proximity and distance is inscribed, constitutively, in the very force that first propels one to assume a stance.

After the reflections by Bloch and Kracauer, it is Adorno's essay "Walter Benjamins *Einbahnstraße*" that opens perhaps the most suggestive perspectives on a variety of levels. While Benjamin himself referred to *One-Way Street* variously as his "book of aphorisms" and his *Notizenbuch*, or notebook, he always was uneasy with this designation. As he writes to Scholem in 1926, "I am working only on the notebook that I am reluctant to call a book of aphorisms [*das ich nicht gern Aphorismenbuch nenne*]."[31] While Bloch's review already had emphasized the book's preoccupation with mobilizing a philosophy of allegorical images, it was Adorno's essay on *One-Way Street* that furnished the more apt designation of Denkbild for the short, lyrical-philosophical snapshots that are brought into a constellation by the montage technique for which the book is indebted to surrealism. *One-Way Street*, Adorno tells us, "is not, as one might at first think, a book of aphorisms but rather a collection of Denkbilder: a later series of short prose pieces by Benjamin, related in their substance to *One-Way Street*, does in fact bear that name."[32] Emphasizing the imperative to think that becomes visible in the *Denken* of these *Bilder*, Adorno points to the ways in which "for the most part, reflection is artificially excluded, and the physiognomy of things is given over to the flash—not because Benjamin the philosopher despised reason but rather because it was only through this kind of asceticism that he hoped to restore thought itself at a time when the world was preparing to expel thought from human beings." The "absurd," Adorno continues, "is presented as though it were self-evident, in order to disempower what is self-evident. The piece 'Souterrain' ['Cellar'] demonstrates this intention and at the same time, insofar as the form of philosophical robbery permits, gives an outline of it [*bezeugt ebenso diese Intention, wie es sie, soweit die Form des philosophischen Überfalls das überhaupt gestattet, einigermaßen umreißt*]."[33]

Adorno's commentary assumes significance through its performative allusions, such as its mobilization of Benjamin's "philosophical robbery" (*philosophische Räuberei*), which is an implicit reference to a line in Benjamin's Denkbild "Hardware": "Quotations in my work are like wayside robbers who leap out, armed, and relieve the idle stroller of his conviction."[34] By citing Benjamin only indirectly, that is, by citing him without citing him, Adorno reenacts the very citational robbery that is at work in Benjamin's own methodological stance. This practice of citational robbery also is the principle according to which much of the material in the *Arcades Project* was assembled into so-called convolutes.

At the same time, Adorno's word *umreißt* playfully mobilizes an important undecidability that inheres in the written form of a small group of certain German two-way prefixes. German prefixes, in general, belong to one of two categories, separable or inseparable, but two-way prefixes can belong to either category. When a two-way prefix is used separably, the verb introduced by the prefix tends to have a more literal or concrete meaning; when introduced by a prefix that is used inseparably, the same verb assumes a more abstract and figurative meaning. The difference between a two-way prefix that is used separably and one that is used inseparably can only be perceived in spoken German, where the compound word is stressed either on the opening prefix or on the verb stem, but not in a written utterance.

Thus, Adorno's word *umreißt* (*diese Intention . . . einigermaßen umreißt*) hovers undecidably between two meanings whose difference cannot be adjudicated in writing. On the one hand, the word *umreißen*, when stressed on the second syllable (*um'reißen*), can mean "to give an outline," the signification that Adorno's English translator imagined. But, on the other hand, when the stress is placed on the first syllable (*'umreißen*), the verb means "to tear down, topple, or collapse something."

It is no accident that Adorno's language plays so seriously with these meanings, because they point to a fundamental aporia lodged in Benjamin's own thought. For Benjamin, the tropological unpredictability of presentation causes the very text that enacts an author's intention to break with that intention. Insofar as the finished work resists a full expression of authorial intention, the "work is the death mask of its conception [*Das Werk ist die Totenmaske der Konzeption*]."[35] Seen in this light, the truth of a work, if there is one, is the truth that accounts for the ways in which the work itself is incommensurate with any authorial intention, an intention that itself is destabilized by this incommensurability. If *One-Way Street* here insists on a fundamental non-identity between meaning and intention, it takes up a thought that Benjamin had expressed previously in the *Trauerspiel* book. "Truth," we read there, "is the death of intention."[36] Thus, by becoming himself a cunning citational robber of a text that proclaims the method of citational robbery, Adorno mobilizes his sentences to illuminate a constellation of core concerns in his friend's writings, concerns that set the stage for our consideration of the problem of *Abstand* in Benjamin's thought. There can be no reading of the Denkbilder in which Benjamin engages matters of proximity and distance that does not also problematize the act of determining *Abstand* and its vulnerability to an irreducible difficulty: when one comes close enough to the phenomenon to outline it or to articulate its contours (*um'reißen*), one always also runs the risk of being *too* close to it, of threatening to undo and topple it in an act of misunderstanding (*'umreißen*).

Proximity and Distance

The preoccupation of *One-Way Street* with questions of proximity and distance comes even more sharply into focus in the Denkbild "These Surfaces for Rent." There, we read:

Those who lament the decay of criticism [*Kritik*] are fools. For its day is long past. Criticism is a matter of the right distance [*Kritik ist eine Sache des rechten Abstands*]. It was at home in a world where perspectives and prospects counted and where it was still possible to adopt a standpoint. But now objects have much too burningly encroached upon the body of human society. "Unself-consciousness" and "the innocent gaze" have become a lie, perhaps even the wholly naïve expression of a plain lack of purview or jurisdiction [*plane Unzuständigkeit*].[37]

In the reconfigured space of early-twentieth-century industrial culture, even the concepts by which that reconfiguration could be measured have changed. If *Kritik* conventionally relies on pronouncing its judgments from a position of epistemological and ethical security, the phenomena that are its objects have transformed this very scheme: there is no metaphysical ground to stand on, no universalization without a fissure, and no reliable grand narrative that could underwrite this or that critical pronouncement. This inability or lack calls into question the kind of epistemological privilege that, for and since Kant, enables us to tell the difference between genuinely critical and merely dogmatic philosophy. For Benjamin, criticism and critique have met with their own *Unzuständigkeit*—not because they are incompetent or wrong, but because their tools and assumptions do not apply in a locality over which they no longer have jurisdiction. This movement of critical displacement signals for Benjamin the advent of a new critical activity: that of ascertaining *den rechten Abstand*, the right distance from the phenomenal world which, in its ideological configurations, variously works to dissimulate the concept of distance either as false proximity or as radical absence.[38]

In an intertextual relay, such a reevaluation of the concept and experience of distance also informs a little-known Benjaminian fragment, written in 1923 as a sketch for *One-Way Street*, "Thoughts on an Analysis of the Condition of Central Europe." There, we learn that no community is possible without a fundamental experience of distance. Benjamin warns that the proximity brought about by suffering and social necessity may also cause distance—a condition of possibility for sober and rigorous reflection—to disappear, so "that under such circumstances more than just human distance is lost."[39] It is consequently no undiluted pleasure that modern transportation technology, for instance, has caused the existential phenomenon of distance to disappear:

On a trip through Germany, it is impossible to achieve the feeling of being on a journey. There are no more journeys in Germany. Trains serve only local traffic. Every half hour, new passengers board, ride along for a while, and make room for new ones. In this way distances, whose covering or conquering [*Überwindung*] once mediated a certain feeling of joy, crumble, breaking apart into uniform little pieces.[40]

For Benjamin, the experience of pleasure is predicated upon distance. Although this pleasure is not simply located in distance itself, it does reside in the possibilities that distance opens up. That is to say, in order for distances to be traversed or, as Benjamin says, "conquered," distance first must exist. There can be no conquering or transgression without the perpetual impetus of something to be conquered or transgressed. Through the logic of supplementarity, the continued condition of possibility for something to be undone or surpassed is firmly lodged in what is to be undone or surpassed. The movement of undoing or surpassing thus is most fully itself when its fundamental allegiance to that from which it attempts to separate itself, that in whose terms it is measured, remains visible, however faintly, in the series of traces that traverse it.

The concerns with proximity and distance in the fragment on Europe and in *One-Way Street* are explicitly staged in the opening sentences of Benjamin's "The Storyteller" (1936), an essay that connects *One-Way Street* with the *Arcades Project* in its problematization of the stance that the reflecting subject must assume as it gives experience and reflection over to language. Taking up his trope of the *rechten Abstand* from *One-Way Street*, Benjamin tells us:

The storyteller—as familiar as his name may sound to us [*so vertraut uns der Name klingt*]—is, in his living effectiveness, by no means fully present to us [*keineswegs durchaus gegenwärtig*]. He is something that already is distant from us and that is distancing itself even further [*Er ist uns etwas bereits Entferntes und weiter noch sich Entferndendes*]. To present someone like Leskov as a storyteller does not mean bringing him closer to us but, rather, increasing our distance to him [*heißt nicht, ihn uns näher bringen, heißt vielmehr den Abstand zu ihm vergrößern*]. Viewed from a certain distance [*Aus einer gewissen Entfernung betrachtet*], the great, simple outlines which define the storyteller win out in him. Better said, they come into view through him [*sie treten an ihm in Erscheinung*] just as in a rock a human head or an animal's body may appear to the observer at the proper distance and the correct angle of vision [*wie in einem Felsen für den Beschauer, der den rechten Abstand hat und den richtigen Blickwinkel, ein Menschenhaupt oder ein Tierleib erscheinen mag*]. This distance and this angle of vision are prescribed for us by an experience for which we have occasion on an almost daily basis [*Diesen Abstand und diesen Blickwinkel schreibt uns die Erfahrung vor, zu der wir fast täglich Gelegenheit haben*]. It tells us that the art of storytelling is coming to an end.[41]

In Benjamin's meditation on proximity and distance, what is most familiar to us—a concept such as the storyteller, for instance—is not actually present to us, or is familiar to us only in its distance and continued distancing. Here, we are closest to it (*vertraut sein*) when it is removed from us, when it is present, but not presently here with us (*uns keineswegs gegenwärtig*). This concept already is at a distance from us (*bereits Entferntes*) but, in its distance, becomes visible as that which continues to distance itself from us (*weiter noch sich Entfernendes*), so that its very distance is what makes its movement and behavior visible to the one from whom it departs. Were it closer to us, we might not be able to comprehend the reality of its withdrawal from us: in this proximity, it nevertheless could be withdrawing from us, but without our knowing it. This is why, for Benjamin, to present (*darstellen*) something *as* something else, the way that Leskov, for instance, is presented *as* a storyteller, means not to decrease, but to increase our distance from what is to be presented. Only by so doing can we begin to fathom the truth of that idea or object, that is, the way in which it is en route away from us. This procedure asks that we remain close to the presented object or idea by departing from it.

But one runs the risk of entirely losing sight of what is to be presented. If it is too close, then at the moment in which one wishes to trace its outline (*um'reißen*), one inadvertently topples it (*'umreißen*) and understands nothing. If one is too far removed from the object or idea in the moment of its presentation (*um'reißen*), the contours that one's outline assumes will be too coarse and too inexact, so that one's act of *um'reißen* once again will result in the destructive forces of *'umreißen*. From either perspective, one fails to perceive the essential traits that the idea or object exhibits. These traits will be brought into focus only "from a certain distance" (*einer gewissen Entfernung*). Once this *gewisse Entfernung* or proper distance—the distance that holds out the promise of hermeneutic certainty—has been assumed, we may, as Benjamin tells us, perceive a human head or an animal's body in the rock formation. This appearance is predicated upon the *rechten Abstand* and the *richtigen Blickwinkel*, two concepts with which we are confronted almost daily and which our experience "prescribes" for us, writes for us ahead of time—*schreibt uns die Erfahrung vor*—in a gesture that renders our action of perceiving a form of delayed action or retroactivity (the Freudian *Nachträglichkeit* that always arrives after the fact) in response to a writing that already is in place. A *Vorschrift* is not only a regulation, rule, or law, but also a "pre-scription" or "pre-writing," a "pre-text" that is already written and in place at the outset of any act of writing or speaking. As Jacques Derrida reminds us with regard to the arche-writing that is always already in place—that is, the general "text" of a culture or language into which one is born—writing precedes speech.

Yet what would be the *rechte Abstand*, the correct distance, and the *richtige Blickwinkel*, the proper perspective, of which Benjamin writes? Are the criteria for what would constitute such coordinates to be found within the object or idea itself, or must they be administered by an external system of reading and understanding? In the first case, would one not already have had to assume the *rechte Abstand* in order to extract from the object or idea the coordinates of the position one should assume in relation to it? In the second case, would the act of administering an external system of criteria not already constitute an act of hermeneutic violence that could not possibly do justice to the presentational singularity that a certain object or idea demands? Certainly, such an external imposition would violate a core theoretical principle of the *Arcades Project*, whose "methodological inventiveness," as Werner Hamacher reminds us, cannot be thought in separation from "its demand that history writing be reinvented for every topic and for every occasion."[42] The idea that neither option relents in its opposition to the writer's efforts is a central premise of Benjamin's thinking. From this perspective, we could even say that all of Benjamin's mature work meditates obsessively on the *rechten Abstand* in a plurality of contexts and modulations: from his readings of Kafka, Proust, and Brecht to his theory of photography, from his concept (or non-concept) of translation and his notion of reproducibility to his philosophy of the angel of history.

The abiding difficulty of these concerns is brought into sharp relief in Benjamin's aporetic examples of finding the *rechten Abstand* and the *richtigen Blickwinkel*. Thus, on the one hand, it is only through having found the right distance and the correct angle of vision that the human head and the animal body become visible to us in the rock formation.

Only here do they become a proper "text" to be read at all. On the other hand, Benjamin implicitly problematizes this scene of recognition when he decides not to tell us whether the shapes of the human head and the animal body actually exist—carved into the rock by artisans or ancient peoples, for instance. In this refusal to specify whether obtaining the correct distance and the proper angle of vision actually does give rise to the recognition of an empirical "text" or only serves to create the illusion that this text is present when it actually is not, Benjamin destabilizes the criteria by which one could differentiate between lucid perception and delusion, insight and blindness, hermeneutic success and its failure. Because the language of Benjamin's example refuses to illustrate decisively what it purports to depict on the surface, it works to strengthen the point that it seeks to make; illustrating in its own failure the way in which it fails to illustrate and exemplifying the ways in which it fails to exemplify, it succeeds in the moment of its failure. Failing successfully, it hovers once again between *um'reißen* and *'umreißen*—in an *exemplary* fashion.

If the movement of this successful failure gives us *Abstand* and *Blickwinkel* to think as concepts in which triumph cannot be thought in isolation from defeat and in which correctness is infected by its other, then Benjamin can been seen to view the phenomena in relation to which these concerns were first formulated as also gradually becoming affected by them. Here, the aporias of method are tied to the aporias of the phenomenon itself. This is why Benjamin has the art of storytelling, the very phenomenon that gave rise to his methodological concerns of *Abstand* and *Blickwinkel*, disappear: *daß es mit der Kunst des Erzählens zu Ende geht.* What experience pre-scribes for us, the letters that are spelled out in the arche-text that awaits us as the methodologically encumbered latecomers, is the writing of the disappearance of the phenomenon. What we finally read in the aporia of the *rechten Abstand* is the arche-text proclaiming that the phenomenon is always already disappearing. Neither that it already has disappeared nor that it will disappear in the future, but rather that the process of its disappearing is underway—now. Our act of reading, together with our reflections on its methods, therefore parallels the phenomenon's act of disappearing. What we are given to read are always the traces of a specific act of withdrawal.

This obsession with the liminal act of disappearing also is why, in the first sketches for *The Arcades Project*, the "Paris Arcades I," begun in mid-

1927, which overlap with *One-Way Street*, Benjamin records his fundamental methodological interest in the appearance of things in the moment when they are about to disappear, that is, "things in the moment of the 'being-no-longer' [*Dinge im Augenblick des Nicht-mehr-seins*]. Arcades are such monuments of being-no-longer . . . And nothing of them lasts except the name: *passages* . . . In the inmost recesses of these names the tearing down or the toppling is working [*Im Innersten dieser Namen arbeitet der Umsturz*]."[43] Benjamin's aporetic *Umsturz*, the violent yet barely visible undoing that is inscribed in the very heart of the phenomenon, here convenes with the logic of Adorno's undecidable *umreißen*. What makes these phenomena what they are also is the kernel of their undoing, the *Sturz* or fall, the *Umsturz* or *Umriß* of their stance. But they have not quite fallen yet—and reading them means catching them in the act of falling, in their perpetual toppling out of view. *Dinge im Augenblick des Nicht-mehr-seins*: in the wider orbit of Benjamin's writing, these ghostly phenomena not only assume anthropomorphizing names such as storyteller, translator, flaneur, prostitute, or collector, they also assume the more ephemeral names of aura, awakening, boredom, conspiracy, idleness, messianism, translation, progress, and reproducibility.

Distance and Alterity

One of the guises that the search for the right *Abstand* and *Blickwinkel* assumes in the *Arcades Project* is the question of the movement of the image, the *Bild*. What in *One-Way Street* is mobilized as the Denkbild, in the *Arcades Project* assumes the name "dialectical image" (*dialektisches Bild*). The dialectical image measures distance and proximity, angle of vision and perspective, in the traces of its own spatiotemporal positionality. As one of Benjamin's semi-concepts, intuitions that in their very movement resist a totalizing and foreclosing definition, the dialectical image is lodged in the paradox that, on the one hand, all images must "freeze" and arrest movement in order to become legible while, on the other, dialectics, in both the ancient sense of continuous disputation and in the modern Hegelian sense, by definition never can be frozen or brought to a complete standstill.[44] In this context, the dialectical image reconfigures the ways in which the image is both articulated and traversed by the past and the present. "It is not," Benjamin writes, "that what is past casts its light on what is present, or what is present its light on what is past; rather, image is that wherein what has been comes together in a flash with the now to form a constellation. In other words, image is dialectics at a standstill." He argues that "while the relation of the present to the past is a purely temporal, continuous one, the relation of what-has-been to the now is dialectical: is not progression but image, leap-like or crack-like [*sprunghaft*].—Only dialectical images are genuine images (that is, not archaic); and the place where one encounters them is language. Awakening."[45] In Benjamin's thinking, the dialectical image is a name for the articulation of a relational stance. Rather than imparting the quality of a mimetic image to what reveals itself when we simply assume that the present casts its light on the past or when the past illuminates the present, the dialectical image constitutes the scene, space, and form of a certain temporal rupture in which time and space are out of joint. This out-of-jointness is the *Sprunghaftigkeit*, possessing the qualities of leaps and cracks that characterize our relation to the past, the present, and the future, a relation that perpetually is at odds with itself.

Benjamin's word *sprunghaft* also deserves special attention here because it illustrates more generally how his concepts never are simply themselves. As Adorno reminds us, "in contrast to all other philosophers . . . Benjamin's thinking, as paradoxical as it may sound, was not one that took place in concepts. . . . He unlocked what could not be unlocked as though with a magic key."[46] That Benjamin thinks conceptually without concepts means, according to Adorno, that in his work "thought is meant to acquire the density of experience without losing any of its rigor."[47] As a consequence of this *Sprunghaftigkeit*, the thinking of any concept, for Benjamin, requires experiential density and analytic rigor. In one of the Benjaminian Denkbilder later assembled in book form by his editors in the collection by that name, he hints at the theoretical assumptions that inform this stance. There, he thematizes the moment of cognition (*Erkenntnis*) as such. In the Denkbild "Secret Signs" that belongs to the constellation "Short Shadows II," Benjamin, referring to Alfred Schuler, writes: "A word of Schuler's has been preserved for us. Every cognition [*Erkenntnis*], he said, contains a dash of nonsense, just as in ancient carpet patterns or ornamental friezes it was possible to find somewhere or other a minute deviation from the regular pattern." Benjamin continues: "In other words, what is decisive is not the progression from one cognition to the next, but the leap or crack [*Sprung*] inherent in any cognition itself. This is the inconspicuous mark of authenticity which distinguishes it from every kind of standard product that has been produced according to a scheme."[48] For Benjamin, what is significant about thinking is not its teleological progression from one certain fact of knowledge to the next, the progressive movement of covering the terrain that is to be fully thought, but rather an appreciation of the leap or crack, the blind spot without which conceptual thinking cannot occur.

It is no accident that Benjamin chooses the German word *Erkenntnis*, or cognition, here, because, unlike mere *Wissen* (knowledge) *Erkenntnis* signifies the moment and process of attempting to translate perceptual phenomena into the security of interpreted knowledge. But his thinking focuses on the ways in which the process of cognition depends in its very formation on what has not yet been fully understood. If full understanding of a phenomenon already had occurred, there would be no more process of active reading or interpretive cognition, but only the treacherous stasis of allegedly secure knowledge. Cognition, and the understanding that it promises, is thus fully itself only when non-cognition and non-understanding still reside within it. Put another way, cognition can be what it is only when it actively encounters and openly engages its abiding blind spots. These blind spots—Benjamin's leaps or cracks—constitute the defective but necessary architecture of all his concepts. And it is precisely in their "deviance" or aberration that these blind spots become authentic, an authenticity that cannot be thought apart from their implied failure as concepts. Understood from this perspective, Benjamin's notion of the dialectical image, along with his considerations of *Abstand* and *Blickwinkel*, conform to the movement that is inextricably intertwined with the cracks and fissures that traverse the ghostly scene of their conceptual appearance.

The specific temporal conceptualization that Benjamin has in mind for the dialectical image becomes more legible when we put it into syntactical relation with a parallel passage from his 1931 essay "Literary History and Literary Scholarship." Disenchanted with the state of the German academy and especially with the conservative models of reading that it propagates, Benjamin proposes a model of reading historically that breaks with received academic wisdom and that is applicable not only to literary works but also to cultural objects and social texts in the widest sense: "For with this the work transforms itself inwardly into a microcosm, or indeed a microeon. What is at stake is not to portray literary works in the context of their time, but to give over to presentation the time that perceives them—our time—in the time during which they arose. It is this that makes literature into an organon of history; to achieve this, and not to reduce literature to the material of history, is the task of literary history."[49] It is easy to misread Benjamin's movement. Our time, he argues, comes to presentation only in what it is not, that is, in the critical reading of a time that precedes it.[50] But, for Benjamin, reading historically does not simply mean arranging works in their own chronological configuration and locating in them, in a mimetic arrest, the material content necessary for the confirmation of what one already assumes to be true of a particular historical moment. Nor does it mean retroactively imposing on texts of the past the concerns and issues of the later age in which they are read. Rather, to read historically in this way means to decipher within the historicity of a text the obscure constellations that inform our own time without being reducible to it.

The condition of possibility for this undertaking is the disruption of history: both past and present are torn from their immediate contexts or, as in Benjamin's later theses on history, "exploded" out of their putative teleology. In this double rupture, the historicity of a text only may become legible subsequent to its removal from its historical embeddedness; and the present in turn only can be approached when it is contemplated through the prism of a historical time that is not its own. Thus, both past and present must first disown what properly is theirs in order to become themselves. Only subsequent to such renunciation of self-identity can they become what they are—and even then only in and as an other. For Benjamin, the space of this multiple disjunction names the historicity and spatiality of the act of reading. Only here, in the leap- or cracklike (*sprunghafte*) otherness of reading, are the proper *Abstand* and *Blickwinkel* found. They are found precisely when the displacement of various temporal categories enables them to recognize themselves in and as another. What these categorical markers recognize in their other—the present in the past and the past in the present—is the way in which they *always already* are an other, traversed by an otherness that renders their identities other, even when no other "other" is present. The dialectical image, as something *sprunghaft*, thus makes visible the fundamental encounter, in the other, with an otherness that always already speaks through and as the self. This dialectical image names the relation of phenomena in time and space that such an encounter facilitates. *Abstand* and *Blickwinkel* are articulated by this displaced relation to the other and even to otherness itself.

The *Arcades Project* further elaborates the relation of the dialectical image to history as it emerges in the scene of reading. As Benjamin tells us:

> What distinguishes images from the "essences" of phenomenology is their historical index. (Heidegger seeks in vain to rescue history for phenomenology abstractly through "historicity.") These images are to be thought of entirely apart from the categories of the "human sciences," from so-called habitus, from style, and the like. For the historical index of the images not only says that they belong to a particular time; it says, above all, that they attain to legibility only at a particular time. And, indeed, this acceding "to legibility" constitutes a specific critical point in the movement at their interior. Every present day is determined by the images that are synchronic with it: each "now" is the now of a particular recognizability. In it, truth is charged to the bursting point with time. (This point of explosion, and nothing else is the death of the *intentio*, which thus coincides with the birth of authentic historical time, the time of truth.) It is not that what is past casts its light on what is present, or what is present its light on what is past; rather, image is that wherein what has been comes together in a flash with the now to form a constellation. In other words: image is dialectics at a standstill. For while the relation of the present to the past is purely temporal, the relation of what-has-been to the now is dialectical: not temporal in nature but figural [*bildlich*]. Only dialectical images are genuinely historical—that is, not archaic—images. The image that is read—which is to say, the image in the now of its recognizability—bears to the highest degree the imprint of that critical, dangerous moment that lies at the ground of all reading [*den Stempel des kritischen, gefährlichen Momentes, welcher allem Lesen zugrunde liegt*].[51]

Amplifying his discussion of the way in which the past and the present interact with each other in the *Abstand* and *Blickwinkel* provided by a certain displacement, Benjamin here specifies what he calls the "historical index" of this displacement. Heidegger's attempt, in *Being and Time*, to "point to *temporality* [*Zeitlichkeit*] as the meaning of the Being of that entity which we call 'Dasein'"[52] relies on a phenomenon, temporality, that "has the unity of a future which makes present in the process of having been."[53] According to Heidegger, "only in so far as Dasein has the definite character of temporality, is the authentic potentiality-for-Being-a-whole of anticipatory resoluteness . . . made possible for Dasein itself. *Temporality reveals itself as the meaning of authentic care.*"54 Yet while Heidegger attempts, in Benjamin's reading, to articulate through temporality a concept of history for the sake of a phenomenological thinking that often is not fully attuned to the historicity of its phenomena and that of its own methodological assumptions, Benjamin wishes to differentiate his understanding of dialectical images from that gesture. Extending the trope of "the death of intention" from the *Trauerspiel* study through *One-Way Street* to the *Arcades Project*, he emphasizes the historical chargedness not of temporality but of the moment or event of its interruption. He names the event of this interruption "dialectics at a standstill," a designation that paradoxically perpetuates the movement of the dialectic and the cessation of that movement all at once. In so doing Benjamin displaces the relation of the present to the past—a temporal relation—onto the relation between the now and the what-has-been in a way that allows him to call it no longer temporal but figural or figurative (*bildlich*). To the extent that the relationship articulated by this dialectical image is figurative, it also enters a *spatial* dimension. The image of history that it yields is most authentic when it departs from the temporal. These figurative and spatial dimensions, even when employed in the articulation of a temporal one, hinge on the problem of *Abstand* and *Blickwinkel*, on finding the correct relation among the phenomena. But because this relation is *bildlich* to the core—figurative through and through—it only can be encountered in and as language (*und der Ort, an dem man sie antrifft, ist die Sprache*). What we awaken to is language itself.

But this encounter with the dialectical image in language, the dialectical image in whose flashes a relation that was previously thought to be temporal becomes legible in the spatial and figurative dimensions, cannot escape the treacherous act of reading itself. It is no accident that Benjamin speaks of a "critical, dangerous moment" that is the unavoidably shaky and fissured ground upon which all reading is based. This reading of what is figurative, *bildlich*, may lead one astray, and it may cause one to follow detours when one wishes to find a direct path to the proper *Abstand* and *Blickwinkel*. This is why, for Benjamin, the reading to which his method gives rise, the reading that sets out to establish the correct distance and perspective, is traversed by the ever present prospect of an aberration. This aberration unfolds on the level of both the concept and the signifier. Thus, in an often neglected methodological reflection in the *Arcades Project*, Benjamin tells us:

Comparison of other people's attempts to the undertaking of a sea voyage in which the ships are drawn off course by the magnetic North Pole. To find *this* North Pole.

What for others are aberrations, for me are the data that determine my course [*Was für die anderen Abweichungen sind, das sind für mich die Daten, die meinen Kurs bestimmen*].—On the differentials of time which, for others, disturb the "great lines" of an inquiry, I base my calculation.[55]

If Benjamin, in language that echoes the many instances of nautical rhetoric throughout the *Arcades Project*, causes his course to deviate from that of others in his welcoming of aberrations (*Abweichungen*) not merely as a threat to legibility but also as a constitutive moment of the methodological principle, then the results of the attempt to find the right *Abstand* and *Blickwinkel* may be as unpredictable as the sea itself. What sort of an *Abweichung* or aberration might we imagine is at stake here?

The C(o)urse of Aberration

I would like to suggest that an exemplary moment in a text by Paul de Man, a reader of Benjamin's who shares the latter's concerns with figural (*bildliche*) language, helps us to shed light on this question. In "Semiology and Rhetoric," de Man notoriously illustrates the tension between grammar and rhetoric by referring to the seemingly aporetic reply that the television character Archie Bunker offers to his wife's question as to whether he wishes her to lace his bowling shoes over or under: "What's the difference?" It is impossible to tell whether Archie actually hopes to learn the difference between the two ways of tying one's shoes or whether he thinks that there is no value in even considering this question. De Man concludes that the "grammatical model of the question becomes rhetorical not when we have, on the one hand, a literal meaning and on the other hand a figural meaning, but when it is impossible to decide by grammatical or other linguistic devices which of the two meanings (that can be entirely incompatible) prevails." De Man continues: "Rhetoric radically suspends logic and opens up vertiginous possibilities of referential aberration. And although it would perhaps be somewhat more remote from common usage, I would not hesitate to equate the rhetorical, figural potential of language with literature itself."[56] According to de Man's model, the turnover of the grammatical mode into the rhetorical mode does not simply occur when we have two possible meanings side by side, a figural and a literal meaning, unmediated and in isolation from one another. That is to say, the presence of more than one meaning, as these meanings are determined by various levels of concreteness or abstractness, does not yet constitute sufficient cause for the switch from grammar to rhetoric. Rather, that switch occurs *only* when it is impossible to ascertain which meaning is dominant or manifest in this or that situation. De Man's model thus is based not on a presence, but on an absence: not on the mere presence of multiple meanings, but on the absence of criteria that would enable the reader to distinguish among the meanings that are present. The argument is not that this absence reliably can be diagnosed and then designated as literature, but rather that the potential of the appearance of this absence of decidability, as a permanent threat, whether or not it is actualized, cannot be separated from the figural workings of the literary text, even from a notion of the more extended cultural and political "text" as, in some sense, literary. De Man thinks these movements as being mediated by "vertiginous possibilities," even as the logic of a "referential aberration."

But an interesting performative slippage occurs in de Man's language. It is registered by the comma in his phrase "the rhetorical, figural potentiality of language." De Man sets out to construct a model that aims to show when the transformation from grammar into rhetoric does and does not occur. He argues that this transformation does not occur simply when literal and figural meanings of a statement coexist. It does occur, he argues, when the prevailing meaning (literal or figural) cannot be discerned. But the comma in de Man's phrase seems to be of an enumerative or extending nature, assigning a status of equality to the terms "rhetorical" and "figural" when the category of the "figural" previously had been used, in opposition to the literal, to explain the occurrence of the "rhetorical" in the first place. The comma that de Man inserts between these two words thus works to equate the category with the terms in which another category is to be explained. This movement itself enacts the very point that de Man is trying to make insofar as it radicalizes, by gesturing in the direction of a tautological threat, the "vertiginous possibilities of referential aberration." After all, if even the category of the rhetorical has been tacitly collapsed with one of the categories necessary to explain it, then the undecidability of the aberration that de Man diagnoses can be extended to include rhetoric itself: the problem is not just that we cannot decide between the literal and the figurative, but that we cannot tell the difference between rhetoric and what is not rhetoric, perhaps even grammar itself. The performative nature of de Man's enigmatic comma thus enacts the trajectory of his own argumentation—it is not simply an uninteresting *mistake*, an oversight that easily could be rectified by taking recourse to some stable system of correctness, such as the code of a punctuation system from which this sentence could be said to be a mere clerical or inadvertent aberration. Rather, it is a philosophically interesting *error* to the extent that the aberration that it performs cannot easily be corrected by a truth administered by this or that system.[57] This not insignificant error performs something of the very rhetorical aberration that it itself diagnoses.

I clarify de Man's radical aberration here because it helps us to understand the stakes of Benjamin's own method of radical aberration in rhetorical terms. If the *Arcades Project* programmatically endorses aberration as its principle, then its methodology, if it has one, unfolds on the far side of any program thought to be capable of containing textual aberration. Indeed, it invites aberration as both a threat and a promise. The presence of aberration will not permit the dialectical image to be yoked to authorial intentionality of any kind, nor will it tolerate the delusional comforts of a mimetic or analogous model of political, historical, or cultural presentation. Like de Man's radical aberration, Benjamin's aberration is concerned with doing justice to the textual nature of the phenomena that are encountered "on the dangerous, critical ground" that underlies all reading. Such an aberration thus would seek its truth in the figurative elsewhere—and it is only there that the questions of *Abstand* and *Blickwinkel* meet with the uncanny rigor of their articulation. Thus, what connects the ways in which *Abstand* and *Blickwinkel* are theorized in the *Arcades Project* meets with the ways in which truth itself is mobilized in its literary sibling, *One-Way Street*, as necessary aberrations from what presents itself. As we read in the thought-image "Technical Aid":

Nothing is more miserable than a truth expressed as it was thought. Committed to writing in such a case, it is not even a bad photograph. And the truth refuses (like a child or a woman who does not love us), facing the lens of writing while we crouch under the black cloth, to keep still and look amiable. Truth wants to be startled abruptly, at one stroke, from her self-immersion, whether by uproar, music, or cries for help. Who could count the alarm signals with which the inner world of the true writer is equipped? And to "write" is nothing other than to set them into motion.[58]

For Benjamin, then, truth, at least the truth that is expressed in textual phenomena such as writing and images, can only become what it is as an aberration from itself. The truth of the truth is one that, in its expression, departs from any mimetic model. This kind of truth resists us, will never fully yield itself to us. It is something that is on its way to becoming something else—that is becoming an aberration. For Benjamin, such an aberration is what writing felicitously sets into motion. The concept of truth as aberration in writing that is poeticized in *One-Way Street* reappears in the *Arcades Project* as what escapes: "'The truth will not run away from us,' reads one of Keller's epigrams. With this, the concept of truth with which these presentations break is formulated."[59]

But this textual model of aberration does not guarantee anything, not even the aberration itself—for aberration does not always occur, and even when it does, it may not always be the same kind of aberration. For Benjamin, the *rechte Abstand* and the *richtige Blickwinkel* are knowable precisely in that moment, mediated by the Denkbild and the dialectical image, when one cannot distinguish between an aberration and a non-aberration and when one has taken leave of the delusional belief that it could be possible to decide once and for all whether an aberration or a non-aberration signals a triumph or a failure. The "correct" angle of vision that would allow us to cast an allegorical gaze on the right distance from the phenomenological world thus is to be found in aberration itself. We recall how Benjamin tells us that what "for others are aberrations, for me are the data that determine my course." The infinite deferral of a judgment as to whether these aberrations are the straight line of a one-way street or the curvy passageways of the arcades—this deferral also names Benjamin's ethico-political hope. *Abstand* here cannot be thought in isolation from *Anstand*, the ethos and practice of decency. *Abstand* and *Anstand*: these two siblings together name the thinkability of Benjamin's aberration, an aberration from any single meaning that could be imposed upon the very relationship between *Abstand* and *Anstand*. This aberration pivots on the difference of a single consonant. Benjamin's signature appears in the space in which the *Anstand* of any *Abstand* can begin to be thought as the *Abstand* from the *Anstand* that would foreclose the movement of aberration in the form of an impossible possibility. It is only in this form that Benjamin might have nothing more to which to take exception (*zu beanstanden*).

To realize that "the core of Benjamin's philosophy," as Adorno claims, is traversed by "the paradox of the impossible possibility" is to grasp that Benjamin "overcame the dream without betraying it and making himself an accomplice in that on which the philosophers have always agreed: that it shall not be." The paradox of the impossible possibility: it signals Benjamin's theoretical and political interests, and it touches all of his concepts and semi-concepts. For readers of Benjamin such as Adorno, a mode of writing like the one performed "in *One-Way Street* and that marked everything he ever wrote, originates in that paradox." Indeed, it "was nothing other than the explication and elucidation of this paradox, with the only means which philosophy has at its disposal, concepts, that drove Benjamin to immerse himself without reserve in the world of multiplicity."[60] The engagement with *Abstand* and *Blickwinkel* as forms of aberration in Benjamin's literary and philosophical sibling texts can be read as a meditation on an impossible possibility and on the political concerns that, as a question of decency, or *Anstand*, lodge this impossible possibility in the variegated linguistic movements of his signature. This impossible possibility, which, like Proust's writing under Benjamin's gaze, "is assigned a place in the heart of the impossible," names the ethico-political commitment that resists any premature closure of meaning and that retains its openness to a radical otherness.[61] This is why Benjamin can write to Scholem one year after Hitler's seizure of power, "I take as my starting point the small, nonsensical hope."[62] The cruel fate that Benjamin suffered at the hands of the Nazis just six years after writing this sentence should not deter his readers from reading, again and again, the innumerable aberrations without which the dream of the impossible possibility hardly would be dreamable. After all, for Benjamin, this dream of the impossible possibility and the possible impossibility, that is, the multiple and unacknowledged possibilities still lodged within impossibility itself, always will offer the promise and the program of a *coming* philosophy.

2

Bloch's Dream, Music's Traces

> First, there is the question of music, which, strangely, is never a question of music alone.
> —Philippe Lacoue-Labarthe, *Musica Ficta (Figures of Wagner)*
>
> For it is still empty and uncertain what is happening sonically.
> —Ernst Bloch, *Spirit of Utopia*
>
> The contentious question of whether music is capable of representing anything in particular or only is the play of sonically moved forms misses the phenomenon. Rather, these things are akin to a dream, whose form, as romanticism well knew, is so close to music.
> —Theodor W. Adorno, *Beethoven*

Musical Textures

If, as readers of an overtly "political" writer such as Ernst Bloch, our primary interest lies in the progressive use-value and utopian impulses that animate his far-reaching oeuvre, then at times it may be tempting to forget the basic fact that all his works exist in and as *language*. Indeed, to those of us concerned, for entirely understandable reasons, with the solidly political, the strictly historical, or the specifically theological trajectories of his writings—from the early *Spirit of Utopia* (1918; revised second ed. 1923) and Denkbilder in *Spuren* (*Traces*, 1930), through *Heritage of Our Times* (1933), *The Principle of Hope* (1949), and *Atheism in Christianity* (1968), to the late *Experimentum Mundi* (1975)—questions regarding the linguistic nature of his thoughts may seem at best like an afterthought to the allegedly stable content of his work, or at worst like an embarrassment to the methodological project of systematically excavating detachable truth-contents from his texts. Why linger, one might ask, with local questions of textual interpretation and the problems of form and language when one is eager to proceed in Bloch's texts to what really counts, that is, to matters of politics, history, and religion? Apart from a seemingly inconsequential ambiguity here or there, one might take for granted the general transparency and conceptual availability of his texts, as if these were not conceived at and constrained by the limits of language—in Bloch's case, a highly self-conscious, rhetorically saturated, excessive, and poetically stylized German that often betrays his early affinity with Expressionism—and the potential unreliability of meaning that such rhetorical gestures imply. But a careful rereading of Bloch's writings hardly warrants such a conclusion. In fact, Bloch himself teaches us time and again a different way of reading his texts and even supplies us with the necessary tools. In the lengthy section of *Spirit of Utopia* devoted to the philosophy of music, we read: "Only in one way, then, can one speak concretely about form: there, namely, where the formal, constructive, objectivating element is no mediation, but a concrete component itself [*keine Vermittlung, sondern ein gegenständlicher Teil selbst ist*]," that is, "as categories of their so-being [*ihres Soseins*], and generally in all art's temporal or spatially anamnestic problems."[1] For Bloch, then, the specificity of form is always something more than a mere vehicle for the transmission of a content presumed to exist independently of its specific and singular manifestation. Such an understanding of textual form is incompatible with the notion that lessons learned from a particular text can be refunctionalized so as to enable one to make sense tout court of other texts. Rather, what Bloch terms the *Sosein* of artistic form challenges one to invent interpretative strategies anew with every phenomenal form that one encounters. It is no accident, then, that Emmanuel Levinas, one of his subtler readers, suggests that "Bloch's eminent personal culture—scientific, historical, literary, musical—is at the level of the 'documents' he interprets and which he very obviously takes pleasure in interpreting, as if he were scoring, for an orchestra assembling all the geniuses of the earth, the counterpoint of the Marxist concepts."[2] Put another way, Bloch's concern with the formal specificity and singularity of every document to which he turns his attention shows his readers how to attend to the formal specificity of his own language, whether that language speaks to musical and aesthetic problems or to broader ethico-political concerns.

The importance of attending to formal specificity in the case of music, whose existence depends on the performance of its singular forms—a point illustrated by the fact that music can be cited but never paraphrased—is uncontroversial enough. However, as Edward Said reminds us, the relationship of musical notes to letters and words differs from that of spoken language in that music "is not denotative and does not share a common discursivity with language."[3] As such, music constitutes a special case of textuality that cannot be reduced to the conventionally denotative and referential functions of language. Bloch, who shares this view, even extends it in such a way as to leave no act of reading untouched in a gesture that will have enlarged the interpretative consequences of the experience of musical form into a broader realm of textuality. For him, the self-referential, nondenotative qualities of music constitute a particularly striking manifestation of the ways in which all acts of signification point to other acts of signification that exceed their adherence to any particular system of referents. Here, the question of textual signification becomes a question of *figures* and of *figuration*.[4]

According to a Denkbild in *Spuren*, "Montages of an Evening in February," "Being is full of figures, though not of fully arranged ones, with each and every thing in its fixed place. Rather, an *echo of allegorical meanings* will resound everywhere, an instructive echo sending one back and forth, reflecting ambiguously [*Das Dasein ist voller Figuren, doch nicht auch voll eingeräumter, mit allem und jedem an seinem festen Platz. Vielmehr wird überall noch ein Echo allegorischer Bedeutungen widerhallen, ein lehrreich hin und herschickendes, vieldeutig reflektierendes*]."[5] If Being is full of figures that are neither stable nor arrestable once and for all, their allegorical significations perpetually threatening to exceed the reliability of this or that predetermined meaning, then we are invited and challenged to read the world as a text. But neither Bloch's moveable figures nor Jacques Derrida's well-known formulation that "there is nothing outside the text [*il n'y a pas de hors-texte*]" should lead us to the mistaken conclusion that everything *is* a text; rather, it indicates that everything must be regarded as a textual problem of interpretation that calls upon us to decipher and make sense of it.[6] Such perpetual deciphering also recalls an incessant act of translation and recontextualization, and Derrida himself later insists that the observation that "there is nothing outside the text" is only one of the many formulations given to the realization that "there is nothing outside context."[7] The imperative to read as if our phenomena, whether textual or contextual in the stricter sense, were texts to be deciphered and understood is tied to the relentless wish to account for a potentially limitless number of possible translations, iterations, and shifting contextualizations, even as this multiplicity coalesces into this or that "individual" text. The call to perform this kind of reading may be especially urgent when a phenomenon powerfully suggests that its meaning is self-evident and natural rather than constructed, slippery, historically saturated, and therefore open to change. In this deeply historical and figurative way of reading, the concept of "text" cannot be limited to verbal or written utterances but must be extended to include a vast network of modes of signification, from the printed text of books to every kind of image, from political ideologies to religious doctrines, and from the language of dreams to that of musical sounds. Bloch's Denkbild, then, does not deny the importance of historical and political content, but rather asserts that such content, even in speculative philosophy, always is conditioned by the specific textual figures and tropes in which it is lodged. The content "itself," however, does not remain unaffected by its situatedness in figures and tropes. On the contrary, the ethico-political issues that Bloch's sentences may give us to think should be considered in terms of the figurative specificity of their enactment and, as Bloch teaches us, with an ear to the haunting "echo of allegorical meanings." Therefore, when Bloch, in his late work *Experimentum Mundi*, tells us that the "world is a singular and abiding question concerning its meaning to be excavated [*Die Welt ist eine einzige noch unablässige Frage nach ihrem herauszuschaffenden Sinn*]," this sentence can be understood as a gloss on all his sentences.[8]

The Politics of Musical Aesthetics

If the political messianism and unorthodox utopianism that once prompted Jürgen Habermas to imagine Bloch as a Marxian Schelling can be thought as a sustained and perpetually reformulated commitment to the hope of what is to come,[9] to the nameless other to what merely is, then this hope attaches both to the openness of futurity as such and to the more specific and, in each case, singular openness of signification itself, that is, an openness to the singular significations that mediate our thinking of futurity in general, not simply the futurity of this or that object or idea, but futurity itself, the futurity of futurity. For Bloch, this thinking of the futurity of futurity is invested with the hope of the "not-yet" (*das Noch-nicht*)—not a naive or childish form of wishful thinking in an administered world of reified relations in which such thinking would be utopian in the worst sense, but with an abiding intuition that the non–self-identity of thoughts and actions, their internal self-differentiation, is more than a hermeneutic or administrative problem to be overcome in the name of implementing meanings and systems. The not-yet also signals a nameless otherness that, precisely by being at odds with itself and never coming fully into its own, promises an anticipatory glimpse, the Blochian *Vorschein*, of what still remains to be thought and experienced, of what has not yet been foreclosed. As he puts it in his *Tübinger Einleitung in die Philosophie* (Tübingen Introduction to Philosophy), "If we are wandering along a street and know that, within forty-five minutes, there will be an inn, that is the vulgar not-yet. Along the street, however, along which we are wandering in this precarious world, the inn, especially the right one, has not yet been built."[10]

Given his sensitivity to matters of presentation, figuration, and interpretation, it is no accident that Bloch's preoccupation with futurity and with the nonprogrammable not-yet in the realm of the aesthetic persists throughout his writings, including the many texts on literature now collected in his *Literary Essays* and related works on aesthetic issues in architecture, the fine arts, fairy tales, the detective novel, landscape painting, and many others.[11] But perhaps nowhere do these variegated epistemological, political, and aesthetic concerns convene more forcefully than in Bloch's sustained engagement with the language of music.[12] In his study of music at university, in his early friendship with Georg Lukács, and in the modulations and tonalities that, in spite of multiple variegations, still work to sustain a recognizable signature throughout Bloch's oeuvre: the language and sound of music and musicological questions are inscribed deep in the heart of his writings. These include, in addition to the substantial section on the philosophy of music in *Spirit of Utopia*, his musico-philosophical discourses in *The Principle of Hope* (especially chapter 51) and *Experimentum Mundi*, as well as numerous essays devoted to problems of music such as the fugue, the sonata form, the funeral march, and the dialectical structure of musical performance, and to individual composers such as Richard Wagner and Anton Bruckner.[13] For instance, *Experimentum Mundi*, implicitly evoking Walter Benjamin's concept of aura, culminates in a meditation on what Bloch calls musical language's "intensive aura," which for him is figured most forcefully in Mozart's "Finally the Hour Nears" ("Giunse alfin il momento") from *The Marriage of Figaro*, Brahms's "My Slumber Grows Ever Deeper" ("Immer leiser wird mein Schlummer"), Wagner's "Dreams" ("Träume"), and Mahler's "Departure" ("Abschied") from *Song of the Earth* (*Das Lied von der Erde*).[14] As Adorno reminds us, the "sphere of music takes up more space in Bloch's thought than in that of almost any other thinker, even Schopenhauer or Nietzsche."[15] But just as it is almost impossible for Bloch to speak of anything seriously without also speaking of music, it is likewise impossible for him to speak of music without *also* speaking about something else. Bloch here enacts Philippe Lacoue-Labarthe's dictum that "the question of music" is "strangely . . . never a question of music alone."[16] To speak of music meaningfully means to translate it into a medium that it is not—for example, spoken or written language and the realm of concepts—and to find any meaning in it we must resort to concerns that are at first alien to music proper. "Only the musical note," we read in *Spirit of Utopia*, "that enigma of sensuousness, is sufficiently unencumbered by the world yet phenomenal enough to the last return," so that "whereas paint still adheres strongly to the object and can therefore also be vacated by the thing's spirit without saying a thing, the clash and resonance of sounding brass will spill over" (S 145; G 186). Music, for Bloch, is the prime sphere in which we encounter the general other-directedness of signification, an other-directedness that music shares with other forms of signification but which it stages in music-specific ways, that is, beyond any obvious model of referentiality and prestabilized norms of meaning.[17]

When Bloch's concerns with the not-yet and with the radical futurity of possibility are tied to aesthetic questions, and specifically to questions of music, they should not be understood in terms of a mimeticist model such as that of his early friend Lukács. For Bloch, music is non-mimetic in a double sense. First, it does not simply re-present what already is; it is not a mechanical reproduction or exact copy of a given reality—because such a gesture, for him, hardly would contain any utopian possibility, except perhaps that tentative and elusive possibility that may reside in the philosophical negation of that reproduced reality. Secondly, music does not simply provide a sound image of what should be, a specific and therefore closed presentation of a future world for the sake of which the present one should be discarded. Rather, music, for Bloch, invites us to think the very possibility of possibility itself. In both senses of music's nonmimesis, Bloch departs from earlier philosophers of music such as Schopenhauer, whose philosophy often depends on repressing the difference between aesthetic and empirical reality, a literalism outlined in Paul de Man's concept of aesthetic ideology in which "what we call ideology is precisely the confusion of linguistic with natural reality, of reference with phenomenalism."[18] We may say that the ideological confusion of a set of presentations with an empirical reality alleged to be external to that set is especially charged in the sphere of music because it is possible to think music as having no direct reference to the world, that is, as a structure of signification that is less able than other structures to create the powerful illusion of a transparent and stable relation between its utterances and a referential world. While musical composition, performance, and reception are materially conditioned effects of social inscriptions and historical determinations, music simultaneously stands in a nonmimetic and nontransparent relation to these governing inscriptions and determinations. If music therefore is textual without being a language in the conventionally referential sense, if it belongs to textuality without fully sharing the textual status of other textual forms, then the fissures and ruptures that it emphasizes through the schism between its significations and the idea of a relation to a referential world deserve to be exploited and radicalized as the very core of music, rather than glossed over or perfunctorily subsumed into a mimetic model of reproduction and recreation.[19]

The unexpected conceptual proximity between Bloch and de Man in this regard is highlighted by de Man's reading of the function of music in Rousseau, where de Man suggests that the "successive structure of music is . . . the direct consequence of its non-mimetic character. Music does not imitate, for its referent is the negation of its very substance."[20] He reminds us that, not "being grounded in any substance, the musical sign can never have any assurance of existence," and that "the nature of music as language" leads to a certain difficulty that is embodied in the temporality of music, to which the more synchronic experience of painting is not subjected in the same manner. "On the one hand," de Man argues, "music is condemned to exist always as a moment, as persistently frustrated intent toward meaning; on the other hand, this very frustration prevents it from remaining within the moment. Musical signs are unable to coincide: their dynamics are always oriented toward the future of their repetition, never toward the consonance of their simultaneity." Therefore, he concludes, even "the apparent harmony of the single sound, à l'unisson, has to spread itself out into a pattern of successive repetition; considered as a musical sign, the single sound is in fact the melody of its potential repetition" and music itself emerges as "the diachronic version of the pattern of non-coincidence within the moment."[21] If music therefore is, to its very core, predicated upon a temporality in which it cannot coincide with itself and in which it stages, above anything else, what we might call its ability to be repeated—its fundamental iterability—it also assumes the status of an allegory of presentational noncoincidence and of iterability as such. Unlike Schopenhauer, for whom music is privileged because it names the trajectory and force of Will itself, music for Bloch and for de Man cannot but be allegorical, unable to coincide with itself yet offering a perpetual and illuminating commentary on that very inability.[22] Expressed in utopian terms, Bloch suggests that a host of human tensions are intensified in the history and philosophy of music, in which, among other things, "melody's most remarkable attribute—that in each of its notes, the immediately following one is latently audible—lies in human anticipation and thereby in expression, which is here above all a humanized expression."[23] The humanized expression of musical unfolding is a matter of music's, and its listeners', coming to terms with the temporality and iterability that make music what it is without allowing music to come into its own once and for all. What de Man calls music's noncoincidence with itself and what Bloch imagines as a deferred and deferring musical temporality that creates a form of expression that is always yet to come, promising itself with every performance—these are the qualities that structure music's history, musical history and the history of the human ear, the qualities that turn on an irreducible series of deferred anticipations.

This history of anticipation and deferral, of noncoincidence and temporal otherness, cannot be thought in isolation from what Bloch imagines as the perpetual labor of producing sense in the world, the "singular and abiding question of its meaning, which is yet to be excavated." Indeed, the knotted relation between a textually conditioned labor of producing sense, literally of making sense, of manufacturing sense as sense itself, and the question of music and musical sense will not leave Bloch, even when he is not thinking about music alone. To grasp more fully Bloch's insistence on this perpetual and uncertain making of sense and the movement of non-coincidence in the temporality of music, we may turn to Jean-Luc Nancy's explication of the sense-producing and undoing gestures of musicality and its significations. As Nancy observes in the Denkbild "Music" in his book of Denkbilder entitled *The Sense of the World*:

> A signification is proposed, but it must be deciphered or understood . . . in accordance with the execution of its presentation, the way in which its statement is stated. Thus, the musical score (text?) including the words, whenever there are words, is inseparable from what we call, remarkably, its *interpretation*: the sense of this word oscillating then between a hermeneutics of sense and a technique of "rendering" [*rendu*]. The musical interpretation, or *execution*, the putting-into-action, or entelechy, cannot simply be "significant": what it concerns is not or not merely sense in this sense. And reciprocally, the execution cannot itself be signified without remainder: one cannot *say* what it *made* the "text" *say*. The execution can only be executed: it can *be* only as executed.

As Nancy continues:

> Further, music can only be played, including by those who only listen. The entire body is involved in this play—tensions, distances, heights, movements, rhythmical schemes, grains, and timbres—without which there is no music. The "least" song demonstrates it—and even more, no doubt, it is demonstrated by the existence of the song itself, as a permanent, polymorphic, and *worldwide* execution of musicality. That which is propagated, apportioned, and dispersed with the song, in its innumerable forms, is at the very least—and stubbornly—a playful execution of sense, a being-as-act through cadence, attack, inflection, echo, syncopation.[24]

Music, then, can be thought as the perpetual manufacturing, performance, and displacement of sense: a specific sense and the very idea of sense, sense's "senseness." It cannot simply enact a premusical, pre-presentational meaning: its presentation *is* its meaning, and its meaning *is* its performance. If there is nothing but interpretation—in music as in making sense more generally—then music and sense are exposed as those spheres in which what executes music and sense is exposed as execution itself. This being-exposed of sense, through and as music, to what executes it, to the very idea of it as something to be executed, its executedness and necessary executability, cannot, in its generality, be reduced, despite its necessarily idiomatic and singular manifestations, to a local phenomenon. It participates in a global execution of sense, of music as the execution of sense, among other things because although it must travel through the singularity of a specific form (of a particular melody, movement, set, etc., that is always tied to a local and particular material performance), this traveling of musical sense itself, whenever it is repeated in its singularity, is also one of the most general phenomena imaginable. We could say that there are only particular acts of music and *at the same time* there are only global executions of music and its mobilizations of sense. From the perspective of the worldwide execution of singularity that music occasions, it is possible to read Bloch's insistence on the world as "a singular and abiding question concerning its meaning to be excavated" as resonating, and indeed radicalizing and fulfilling itself, in his abiding preoccupation with the overly complex role of music in the making and interpreting of sense. As we shall see, the fact that this role has not yet been decided upon once and for all gestures, for Bloch, toward future possibilities and toward a commitment to a certain nonnaive hopefulness.

If the hope that Bloch lodges in the not-yet resonates on the far side of any aesthetic ideology, it likewise should not be discarded because of its apparent otherworldliness. To be sure, Bloch's project is invested in what can be thought and experienced in the form of alterities to being as it currently presents itself to us. But this does not mean that this other, or these others, to being are confined to the purely speculative and inaccessible realm of the otherworldly. Rather—and more recent thinkers of the other such as Levinas are explicitly indebted to Bloch on this point—"what exceeds being is allowed to govern our relation to being," to take up a formulation offered by Robert Bernasconi.[25] To the extent that what exceeds being can be allowed to govern our relation to being, that relation is also always a question not only of this or that relation but of relation itself, of the very idea of relation, of our relation to relation as a function of the very idea of a relation and its possibilities. In the case of Bloch, this relation to the relation can be neither fully established nor exhaustively interpreted because what makes Bloch's relation what it is cannot be thought in isolation from the ways in which it is always already a figure of excess to the other (it exceeds Being), of excess of the self (it exceeds itself by not always remaining self-identical), and of differentiation (it does not fully coincide with the precepts and demands for a relation that the world in which it unfolds would stipulate). I wish to suggest that two interlaced models of such a thinking in Bloch's philosophy of the not-yet bear the names "music" and "dream": the music of dreams, and the dream of music. More generally, I wish to argue, these complexly mediated terms are central to the aesthetic and ethico-political impetus of his unorthodox utopian reflections.

Musical Dreams, Dreams of Music

Dreams and music, of course, are not innocent or isolated concepts in Bloch's writings. These concepts traverse all of his texts in a variety of modulations and tonalities. This is not to say that every text Bloch ever wrote thematizes dreams or music overtly—although many of them do—but rather that no text of his remains unaffected by the peculiar logic and far-reaching claims that Bloch makes on behalf of these concepts. In what follows I will concentrate on his first major work, the Expressionism-suffused *Spirit of Utopia*, in conjunction with his aesthetically most accomplished text, the literary-philosophical Denkbilder collected in *Spuren*, with an eye to how both projects are connected by a rhetorical and conceptual emphasis on dreaming, sleeping, longing for the not-yet, and the attendant music of futurity. It is as though *Spirit of Utopia*, with its dreams of music and its music of dreams, were the dream text whose leitmotifs would serve as the point of departure for all subsequent texts both within Bloch's own trajectory and to a certain extent within the orbit of his friends and colleagues. As even the early Walter Benjamin relates to Ernst Schoen toward the beginning of the Weimar Republic (1919), anticipating a troubled but mutually fruitful collaboration despite some reservations, *Spirit of Utopia* is "the only book . . . against which" he could "measure" himself.[26] The same sentiment is echoed by Adorno, who, a few years before his death, recalls: "The book, Bloch's first, bearing all his later work within it, seemed to me to be one prolonged rebellion against the renunciation within thought that extends even into its purely formal character. Prior to any philosophical content, I took this motif so much as my own that I do not believe I have ever written anything without commemorating it, either implicitly or explicitly."[27]

If it is surprising that the better part of a book on the intricacies of utopian thought should be devoted, next to more likely candidates such as the phenomenon of deep astonishment or Karl Marx and socialist thought, to a philosophy of music, then it should be no less surprising that this philosophy of music begins not with a systematic exposition and clarification of some key concepts, but rather with a dream. This early dream anticipates the many theoretical modulations of dreaming that permeate Bloch's later work, such as the sustained discussion of the distinction between daydreams and night dreams that constitutes chapter 14 of *The Principle of Hope*, the essay "Dream of a Thing" in the *Philosophische Aufsätze zur objektiven Phantasie* (Philosophical Essays on the Objective Imagination), and the conversations with Bloch collected in *Tagträume vom aufrechten Gang* (Daydreams of an Upright Walk).[28] As though it were one of the Denkbilder from *Spuren*—which were largely composed between 1910 and 1929, thus overlapping with the composition of *Spirit of Utopia*—the short Denkbild entitled "Dream" functions as an enigmatic overture to Bloch's philosophy of music:

Traum

Wir hören nur uns.
  Denn wir werden allmählich blind für das Draußen.
Was wir sonst auch gestalten, führt wieder um uns herum. Es ist nicht genau so ohne weiteres ichhaft, nicht genau so dunstig, schwebend, warm, dunkel und unkörperlich wie das Gefühl, immer nur bei mir, immer nur bewußt zu sein. Es ist Stoff und fremd gebundenes Erlebnis. Aber wir gehen in den Wald und fühlen, wir sind oder könnten sein, was der Wald träumt. Wir gehen zwischen den Pfeilern seiner Stämme, klein, seelenhaft und uns selber unsichtbar, als ihr Ton, als das, was nicht wieder Wald werden könnte oder äußerer Tag und Sichtbarkeit. Wir haben es nicht, das, was dies alles um uns an Moos, sonderbaren Blumen, Wurzeln, Stämmen und Lichtstreifen ist oder bedeutet, weil wir es selbst sind und ihm zu nahe stehen, dem Gespenstischen und noch so Namenlosen des Bewußtseins oder Innerlichwerdens. Aber der Ton brennt aus uns heraus, der *gehörte* Ton, nicht er selbst oder seine Formen. Dieser aber zeigt uns ohne fremde Mittel unsern Weg, unseren geschichtlich inneren Weg, als ein Feuer, in dem nicht die schwingende Luft, sondern wir selber anfangen zu zittern und den Mantel abzuwerfen.

Dream

We hear only ourselves.
  For we are gradually becoming blind to the outside.
Whatever else we still shape leads back around us. It is not exactly as readily self-like, not exactly as hazy, hovering, warm, dark, and incorporeal as the feeling of being always only by myself, always only conscious. It is material, and an other-bound

experience. But we walk into the forest and we feel that we are or could be what the forest dreams. We walk between the tree trunks, small, soulful, and imperceptible to ourselves, as their sound, as what could never again become forest or external day and visibility. We do not have it, that is, all that which surrounds us, this moss, these strange flowers, roots, stems and shafts of light is or means—because we ourselves are it, and stand too close to it, this ghostly and yet so nameless quality of consciousness or of becoming-inward. But the sound flares out of us, the *heard* sound, not the sound itself or its forms. Yet it shows us our way without alien means, shows us our historically inner path as a flame in which not the vibrating air but we ourselves begin to tremble, and throw off our coats. (S 34; G 49)

Bloch dreams to the music of Denkbilder. His Denkbilder stage a self that is in retreat from vision ("becoming blind") and is thus on the way toward other senses, including the acoustic. The musical note, Bloch tells us, traverses our selves in an event of hearing that at once empties the self and exposes it to its own internal otherness, its self-differentiation, in which the dream can no longer simply be distinguished from the dreamer and in which the very trembling that occurs at the sound of a musical note orchestrates a gesture in which the self ex-poses itself: in the "vibrating air" of the musical note we "throw off our coats." Denuded and exposed, traversed by the otherness of the musical note, one is no longer a fully conscious, self-identical subject, but rather has become the venue for a transmutation of the dream and dreamer as each is translated into and as the other. This "ghostly" musical interpretation renders "nameless" the consciousness that designates the musical self that dreams or is dreamed—its name has not been uttered, its movements are heard and felt but not fully understood. This want of understanding is a perpetual condition for Bloch as he exposes his ear both to the otherness within itself and to the notes that penetrate it. An extensive and obsessive meditation on all the permutations of this ontological and hermeneutic lack forms a leitmotif for his entire philosophy of music.

It is therefore no accident that the section "On the Theory of Music" in *Spirit of Utopia* begins with the observation that listening "is and will remain weak enough. For too many, hearing would come more easily if one only knew how one ought to speak about it" (S 94; G 124). For Bloch, knowing how to speak about listening is the perpetual problem with which music confronts us. In fact, to the extent that knowing how to listen to music and knowing how to talk about listening to music are inextricably intertwined, the interpretive challenge we face is to translate music into an object of knowledge that remains anchored in discourse as a describable and knowable phenomenon while, at the same time, allowing it to remain an incommensurate form that refuses to yield its secret to the doctrines and efforts of conceptual language. But Bloch's philosophy is not aimed at clearing the stage for easy listening and the joyous certainty of hermeneutic closure by clarifying once and for all how one should talk about listening to music. Indeed, actually knowing how to talk about music would be the death knell of music's interpretation—just as giving up on *attempting* to learn how to talk about it also would be, because the far-reaching potential of music as an aesthetic form resides as much in its perpetual invitation to be understood as in its simultaneous refusal to be comprehended in non-musical terms.

Bloch's entire philosophy of music is predicated upon a perpetual return to the basic question of how to listen, with music emerging not only as the object of that return, but also as the agency that itself provides a ceaseless commentary on that very return. Precisely because we do not yet know how to talk about listening to it, music is a name for what remains to be thought and questioned anew with every attempted reading of that performance. According to Bloch in *The Principle of Hope*, the consequence of this perpetual deferral of meaning is that "*nobody has as yet heard Mozart, Beethoven or Bach as they really are calling, naming, and teaching.*"[29] Speaking philosophically about listening to music then always unfolds in the Kantian "as-if" mode so that we make our points about music *as if* we already knew how to speak about it.

From the perspective of having to learn how to speak about the musical experience of music as such, Bloch's reflections appear as sustained attempts that always start over one more time in their effort to speak about listening to music. These reflections compose and then abruptly abandon a wide-ranging network of discourses that might serve as the basis for generating a language for listening to music: from a historical narrative concerning the beginnings of music in antiquity and the Middle Ages, via sociological aspects of music's reception and production in the great Italian composers and in romanticism to sustained readings of a series of paradigmatic composers such as Bach, Mozart, Beethoven, Wagner, Bizet, and Brahms, from case studies of specific works such as *Missa Solemnis*, *Fidelio*, and *Carmen* all the way to a formal encounter with the more technical aspects of music, such as harmony and rhythm. Music here emerges not merely as one example to be used in more general philosophical explanations that exist independently of it, a purely illustrative sensualization of an abstract logic that just as well could find its instantiation in a very different aesthetic form. Rather, Bloch urges us to think the philosophical nature of music and the musical nature of philosophy in a way that leaves neither realm unaffected and intact. As such, the two emerge as impossible but necessary translations and perpetual transmutations of each other.

With these considerations, Bloch discovers in music many elements deserving of philosophical attention that are not to be found in the Kantian aesthetic paradigm, of which *Spirit of Utopia* is keenly aware. We recall that in paragraph 53 of the *Critique of Judgment*, in which Kant offers a "comparison of the aesthetic value of the beautiful arts among each other," music is accorded the lowest rank because it ultimately is "more pleasure than culture."[30] Kant writes that "music occupies the lowest place among the beautiful arts (just as it occupies perhaps the highest place among those that are estimated according to their agreeableness), because it merely plays with sensations [*bloß mit Empfindungen spielt*]."[31] Unlike other art forms such as poetry and painting, music cannot enter the aesthetically charged interplay in which judgment, pleasure, imagination, and intuition (*Anschauung*) perpetually interact. "Besides," Kant adds,

> there is a certain lack of urbanity in music, in that, primarily because of the character of its instruments, it extends its influence farther (into the neighborhood) than is required, and so as it were imposes itself, thus interfering with the freedom of the others, outside of the musical circle, which the arts that speak to the eyes do not do, since one need only turn one's eyes away if one would not admit their impression. It is almost the same here as in the case of the delight from a widely pervasive smell. Someone who pulls his perfumed handkerchief out of his pockets treats everyone in the vicinity to it against their will, and forces them, if they wish to breathe, to enjoy it at the same time; hence it has also gone out of fashion.[32]

Kant here articulates a devalorization of music with regard to the other arts that is shared by other writers in the eighteenth century who also frequently privilege painting, because of its presence and stability, over music, which they regard as more elusive and temporally volatile. For Kant, music cannot be connected to the realm of freedom for the following reasons: first, because it appeals primarily to the emotions and to the production and experience of pleasure alone; and second, because it imposes the opposite of freedom on those who at any given time are unattuned to its performance or who wish to be addressed by it. Music, then, for Kant, behaves somewhat like the moment of interpellation in Louis Althusser's subject of ideology, the subject that invariably turns around and feels addressed by the authority of the law when the generic "Hey, you!" is issued. Music, according to this reading, only ever says, "Hey, you there!" in a gesture of hailing that contradicts the right of nonresponse that is so deeply imbricated with the concept of freedom. Yet, at the same time, the break with freedom that music enacts is also the advent of pleasure—in response to music's appellation, the subject experiences involuntary pleasure rather than being arrested by agents of the state. It is striking that Kant's passage moves synesthetically from hearing to smelling, from one sense to another, drawing on the second sense to explicate the experience of the first. In so doing, Kant's example rhetorically performs the argument that it makes conceptually. Unlike the eye, which may close itself to block out vision, the ear has no easy defense against the intrusion of an unsolicited musical sound, in the same way in which the language that describes the experience of one sense (hearing or listening) is not immune to the intrusion of the language that describes the experience of another sense (smell and the perfumed handkerchief). The synesthetic slide from the auditory to the olfactory, from ears to noses, in the meditation on music gestures toward the idea that music cannot be thought alone—there is always something else that wishes to be thought and experienced along with music, such as music's relative promotion of freedom or unfreedom, or its relation to other sensorially mediated experiences.

Even though the Bloch of *Spirit of Utopia* proclaims himself to be closer to Kant than to Hegel, from Bloch's musicological perspective, Kant's insistence on music's allegedly narrow appeal to the emotions, its lack of urbanity, and its tendency to impinge upon the freedom of others all require qualification. To begin with, Bloch wishes to rectify what one might call a latent "ocularcentrism" that unites Kant with so many other thinkers of the eighteenth century who privileged the epistemo-critical function of the eye over the other senses (most notably hearing) by evoking an ideological tradition that regards vision as "the noblest of the senses" from Plato to Descartes via the Enlightenment and its fear of darkness all the way to Merleau-Ponty, Sartre and, ultimately, the postmodernists.[33] In a neo-Romantic gesture reminiscent of the Jena Romantics and of Novalis's polemic against the lucidity of daylight encrypted in the anti-ocularcentric, anti-Enlightenment tropes of his *Hymns to the Night*, Bloch dethrones vision as the sense that—owing to its capacity to transform the world into a modern *Weltbild*, or world image, as Heidegger later terms it in his reading of Descartes—is capable of standing metonymically for all the other senses, able to subsume the variegated perceptions that they offer under the hegemony of the eye.[34] For Bloch, in musical creation "the sound employed makes every event more acute, penetrating, sensuous. For as listeners we can also still get in close touch, as it were. The ear is, in small part, more deeply embedded in the skin than even the eyes" (S 101; G 132). Because of what Bloch sees as the ear's greater degree of embeddedness in the skin, its tactile and corporeal basis, the music that penetrates the ear cannot be thought in isolation from that organ's abiding material inscription. Among other things, the material inscription of the ear complicates the relation between sound and image. As Bloch suggests:

Therefore we bristle at having to watch a silent film image, not without reason. For here only the monochrome optical impression has been excerpted, and since it is simply given as it is, there arises in accordance with the ear's exclusion the disagreeable impression of a solar eclipse, a mute and sensuously diminished life. But then the ear assumes a peculiar function: *it serves as the representative and place holder of the remaining senses* [*es leistet die Vertretung aller übrigen Sinne*]; from things it removes alive their crackling, their friction, and from people their speech, and so the film's musical accompaniment, however vague or precise it may finally be, thus comes to be felt as the exact complement in its way to the photography. (S 101; G 132)

Here, the ear, rather than the eye, becomes the metonymic representative of all the other senses. Even when the sound that penetrates the ear is meant to "supplement" the image, that image becomes what it is only by virtue of its putatively superfluous and secondary supplement—sound. To become what it is, the photograph or "light image" (*Lichtbild*) requires the supplement of sound, not because sound "completes" an unfinished whole or pleasantly accompanies an otherwise independent visual unity, but because sound as supplement reveals that the status of that which is supplemented is always already a form of mediation and supplementation in which what is supplemented structurally shares the qualities believed to be the sole properties of the supplement itself.

Derrida explains this logic in his reading of the dangerous supplement in Rousseau as follows: "Through this sequence of supplements a necessity is announced: that of an infinite chain, ineluctably multiplying the supplementary mediations that produce the sense of the very thing they defer: the mirage of the thing itself, of immediate presence, or originary perception. Immediacy is derived."[35] As with the image of Rousseau's mother that Derrida addresses, Bloch's trope of the musical supplement of the image emphasizes differential relations, chains of signs and signifiers that are not simply the retroactive imposition of forms of presentation onto a pretextual reality in which the idea of secondary supplements and self-identical origins can be reliably upheld; instead, this trope speaks to the undoing and disappearance of a presence that powerfully creates the false impression of naturalness and self-identity, of independence from any supplements. Bloch refers to this quality as music's "photographic supplementarity," thereby emphasizing music's relation to and simultaneous break with the image while also stressing the exemplarity of music's perpetual flow as a dangerous supplement—the exemplarity of the supplement of which one would like to arrest an image, a photographic keepsake to commemorate its movement around an absence. We could say that, for Bloch, music is a photograph in notes that captures the inversion of its own status as a mere supplement to vision by delivering a commentary on its very movements of mediation and substitution.

In addition to his anti-ocularcentric, supplementarist intervention with regard to Kant's low estimation of music, Bloch also implicitly addresses the issue of freedom as it is presented in the *Critique of Judgment* by situating his discussion of music within a transformed framework. While Kant emphasizes the inscription of music in pleasure and emotion along with its attendant lack of freedom, Bloch chooses to think of music as the distant yet deeply resonant experience of what has yet to be experienced, a conceptual and aesthetico-sensual nostalgia for the future and a commemoration of what is still to come, rather than as an instantiation of freedom that has already been achieved and only needs to be expressed in notes or as the site where judgment, imagination, and aesthetic pleasure combine to yield the experience of subjective affirmation. Thus, what chiefly occupies Bloch is not the speculative complication and rehabilitation of music as aesthetic form vis-à-vis Kant or, by extension, the repetition of certain elements already present in Nietzsche's and Schopenhauer's projects. Rather, his thinking resonates in a variety of tonalities centering around the ultimate unreadability of music, the impossibility of formulating stable programs with which to speak about it, and its inseparability from (the dream of) its ethico-political promise. Bloch's project, as Christopher Norris puts it, envisioned "a new kind of listening" in which "music was the truth to which philosophy aspired but which could never reach the point of articulate understanding since language itself, and philosophical language in particular, dealt only in concepts or abstract figures of thought."[36] For Bloch, then, the truth that music is capable of imparting is the internally fissured and non-self-identical nature of all aesthetic forms, a nameless anticipatory glimpse of what always is yet to come and only just underway.

Something's Missing

The non-self-identical quality of music that inhibits the pervasive impulse to foreclose what still deserves to be thought, an elusive incompleteness that must not be casually dismissed as merely a deviation from the marching orders of a knowing system, constitutes the internally self-differentiated condition of possibility for what is yet to come. In a remarkable 1964 radio conversation with Adorno on the internal contradictions in utopian longing, Bloch draws our attention to a pertinent sentence in Bertolt Brecht: "'Something's missing [*Etwas fehlt*].' What that is, one does not know. This sentence, which is in *Mahagonny*, is one of the most profound sentences Brecht ever wrote, in two words. What is this 'something'? If it is not allowed to be cast in a picture, then I shall portray it as in the process of being. But one should not be allowed to eliminate it as if it really did not exist so that one could say about it: this is what it's all about."[37] Bloch here implicitly refers to his discussion in *Heritage of Our Times* of the sentence in scene 8 of *Mahagonny*, "Aber etwas fehlt," and that sentence's central function for a kind of thinking that is perpetually to come.[38] In Brecht's work, the character Paul Ackermann repeats this line time and again in response to the other characters' various propositions regarding what constitutes a happy and fulfilled life, from such modest thrills as smoking and swimming to more refined pleasures such as observing water or forgetting. "Aber etwas fehlt."[39] The experience of thought, and of embodied, critical thought as a form of what Husserl calls the phenomenon of our *Lebenswelt*, or life world, is inseparable from the experience of a fundamental lack or absence. Something is missing, but that something resists revelation even as a distant presence, in which it would be absent for us but present in a potentially legible *elsewhere*. Rather, "Etwas fehlt" names the aporetic and unfulfilled condition of human cognition and experience under the very circumstances that make possible an awareness of this lack and, by extension, that open up the possibility of imagining an entirely different *Lebenswelt*—a world characterized by an openness that is born of the condition of being fundamentally at odds with itself—that resembles the Lacanian real as void but is charged with an irrepressible politico-aesthetic impulse. Because "etwas fehlt," a supplement is needed to fill the void. But in assuming the form of a supplement to such charged utopian longings, music subjects itself to a state in which "etwas fehlt," that is, it becomes a supplement in need of supplementation. After all, if music embodies the aesthetic spirit of utopia, then it also must yield to the demands of cognitive analysis and to an empirically transformative potential. But because music cannot be fully grasped by conceptual means or translated fully into norms of reason in the service of an empirical struggle, it too belongs in a sphere in which "etwas fehlt." Yet it is precisely this quality of incompleteness that would be required for music to be fully translatable into the cognitive terms that might serve as a supplement to music, so that the supplement in need of supplementation becomes an allegory of the endless chain of supplementations that vex any attempt to mediate between a signifier and its absent referent, between the world of signs and notes and the sphere of what we sometimes call reality.

Bloch's logic of the musical supplement therefore situates music at the site of a struggle between the material world and aesthetic form, reason and imagination, cognition and illusion, understanding and emotion. At the same time, one may question whether the sphere of music actually constitutes an appropriate object upon which to focus such a degree of philosophical energy. Is not the elusive character of music, as it unfolds and disappears into temporality itself, absolutely other to the rigorous logical requirements of conceptual thought? With what authority, then, does a philosophy such as Bloch's take so seriously the potential truth-content of music—especially when so many philosophers, of both the Continental and the so-called analytic traditions, studiously avoid the slippery topic of musical discourse and when so many practitioners and historicist scholars of music distance themselves from philosophical speculation as though it were a tone-deaf practice contrary to the spirit of music itself? Taking Bloch's philosophy of music seriously requires that we eschew not only the use of philosophical concepts as mere tools for the description—later to be verified or rejected—of self-identical, present empirical phenomena whose more or less transparent nature allows us to evaluate the truth content of a philosophical claim, but also an approach to artworks in general, and musical works in particular, that is the hedonistic nonconceptual equivalent of slipping into a relaxing bath.[40] If the first is an unfortunate example of how to philosophize with a hammer to the sounds of Mozart, the latter reduces Bach's *Wohltemperiertes Klavier*, his *Well-Tempered Clavier*, to a *wohltemperiertes Bad*, a "well-tempered bath."

This struggle leaves no philosophy of art unaffected. Indeed, Bloch's evocation of Brecht's multiply determined "etwas fehlt" resonates even in the thought of the early Romantic critic Friedrich Schlegel, who writes: "In that which we call philosophy of art, there is usually one of two things missing: either the philosophy or the art."[41] Bloch, however, asserts that "here too the ear hears more than the concept can explain. Or, to put it differently, one senses everything and knows exactly where one is, but the light that burns in one's heart goes out when it is brought into the intellect" (S 139; G 178). Artworks, and above all music, can exist only as the embodiment of a formalized mode of resistance to the unchecked domination of reason, opening up new and unexpected conceptual spaces to allow for more playful creativity and imagination. Just as longing is predicated upon the experience that "etwas fehlt"—after all, if nothing were lacking, there would be no point in analyzing the world, in imagining it differently, or, finally, in the very act of thinking—so music depends as much on that which it is unable fully to reflect as it does on that which it is incapable of yielding fully to rational comprehension. As the Blochian supplement, then, music contains within itself the very tension that exists between nonconceptual aesthetic pleasure and the systematicity of logic and concepts. This musical tension, according to Bloch, also is deeply political.

A full consideration of the textuality of musical experience, including its aesthetic, pleasurable, cognitive, and political resonances, requires us to question the very idea that the "what" of music has been understood. "For it is still empty and uncertain," Bloch reminds us, "what is happening sonically [*was tonhaft geschieht*]." He continues:

It is hopeless to allocate music to emotions that are already exact. Not even whether a melody *can* express anger, longing, love at all unequivocally—that is, if it is these emotional contents, already experienced by us anyway, at which music aims, and where it could easily surpass a statue—is so easy to identify, once its upheavals begin to edge into one another . . . If one considers a musical piece in its technical aspect, everything is correct but says nothing, like an algebraic equation; if, on the other hand, one considers it in its poetic aspect, then it says everything and defines nothing—a strange conflict lacking any median or any equilibration accessible to the understanding, in spite of its fermenting content. Here it does no good . . . to keep to the poetic in order to force "music's infinitely blurring essence," as Wagner said, into categories which are not its categories. (S 100–101; G 131)

Challenging the notion of premusical emotional categories that are simply reflected as themselves in a musical work of art, Bloch wonders to what extent music not only performs but also invents a certain tonal system of emotional specificity and affective range that the listener, perhaps too hastily, ascribes to an extramusical world assumed to precede musical inscription. By the same token, music's resistance to assimilation by discourses such as literature can be attributed to an obedience to its own enigmatic laws such that "if I wish to communicate the essence of some musical work, I simply whistle the first theme. If, however, I am asked to narrate the essence of a literary work, then I will not cite the first sentence, but rather report the basic features of the plot or the layout of the whole" (S 104; G 135). Music always enacts itself otherwise. If music is the name for an irreducible experience of openness, an aesthetic form that has no common measure with other discourses even while sharing a common textuality, it deserves to be called a "pealing of bells in an invisible tower on high" (S 101; G 132). Its sounds penetrate us while leaving their full meaning as occluded as their source, the invisible tower whence they emanate.

The perpetually deferred meaning of music also links Bloch's "invisible tower" to broader questions of musical presentation. As Philippe Lacoue-Labarthe suggests in his commentary on Adorno's reading of Schönberg's opera *Moses and Aron*, music can be understood as an "art (of the) beyond (of) signification, which is to say (of the) beyond (of) representation." Relating music's unfolding in and as the beyond of signification to Adorno's understanding of art as a withdrawal from communication, as well as to Benjamin's concept of "pure language" and Hölderlin's caesura of "pure speech," the "ultimate paradox" for him lies in the gesture by which the echo of "the naked word—the language of signification itself—comes to tell of the impossible beyond of signification, something that Benjamin would not have denied."[42] What music gives us, then, is not simply the transmission of a communicable content, and not even the communication of its own incommunicability. Rather, music tells of its own beyondness, the persistent beyondness inscribed deep in the heart of signification itself that it simultaneously takes as its leitmotif. When Bloch therefore speaks of the experience of music as displacing by politicizing, and politicizing by displacing, the very binarism of emotive pleasure and concept-driven reason, his argument always also reverberates in a musical space beyond: as the beyond of signification and as the signification of the beyond.

Revenant Dreams

To the extent that music's performance of the beyond of signification and the signification of the beyond can be heard at all, for Bloch it is best experienced in dreams. If this musical textuality, which Bloch refers to as the uncanny "ghostly realm of music [*Geisterreich der Musik*]" (S 157; G 200), takes the form of Beethoven's "gigantic rhythmic shape, his . . . Luciferan-mystical kingdom," or of Bach's "song of the spiritual soul, shining into itself, to the great, towering organ fugue with its staircases and stories, a single self-illuminating, gigantic crystalline glory, . . . the promises of a messianic homeland beyond every expedition," then none of its instantiations can exist fully in isolation from the dream itself (S 157; G 200). As Bloch suggests: "To the latter [the metaphysics of presentiment and utopia], too, even when it stands as near as possible to us, we come near only in dreams. But it is no longer a dream recollecting the past or burrowing into the various baser passions. Rather only that yearning which brings with it what was unfulfilled, what could have absolutely no earthly fulfillment, the waking desire for what alone is right for us, which glimmers in well-correlated sound" (S 156; G 199). He concludes:

But finally, as soon as everything grows silent on this earth, within earthly action—completely dispensing with the text and even the Shakespearean world of dreams, the world of dance, masque, intoxication, and magic—then music assembles the features of the other word, the Word from another larynx and logos, the key to the inmost dream within the object's Head [*Haupt*], their own newly meaningful expression, the multiply singular, final expression of the Absolute. Now still a fervent stammering, music, with an increasingly expressive determinacy, will one day possess its own language: it aims at the word which alone can save us, which in every lived moment trembles obscurely as the *omnia ubique*: music and philosophy in their final instance intend purely toward the articulation of this fundamental mystery. (S 158; G 201)

For Bloch, the music of the dream and the dream of music are mediated by "that which is not yet; what is lost, presensed; our self-encounter concealed in the latency of every lived moment; our We-encounter, our utopia calling out to itself through goodness, music, metaphysics, but unrealizable in mundane terms" (S 158; G 201). To approach the thinkability of the possible is to encounter it in and as a dream. Bloch does not recommend a kind of wishful thinking in which unrealistic, infantile hopes are given the weight and determining momentum of the concrete. Rather, to the extent that the world deserves to be thought as that which is at odds with itself, as that which is not simply given and self-evident but articulated and historically saturated, the space in which this philosophical refusal to reconcile with the world as it currently presents itself can take place is the dream: the dream of music and the music of the dream.

In a Denkbild from *Spuren*, "Some Left-Handed Schemata," Bloch writes: "'Should one,' someone said, 'only dream when one is asleep and not at all when one is awake? . . . With open eyes one feels the air that is just as dreamlike, in which the wind blows and which is perhaps even haunted.'"[43] Not just in bed and not only when he sleeps, Bloch dreams the possibility of the impossible, a somnambulant state in which dreaming and waking are not mutually exclusive, a state in which the precepts of reason that characterize enlightened thinking are also imbricated with the less rational dimensions of thought that manifest themselves in the aberrant acts of aesthetic disenchantment. The utopian dream of music and the music of the dream that traverses Bloch's project are marked not only by an emphasis on the aesthetic dimension of dreams and thoughts but also by an emphasis on the ethico-political implications of these dreams and their compatibility with the demands of a responsibility to come. For Bloch, the philosophical negativity, the negativity with which philosophy opposes the dream names the site of a utopian vision that will not be placated with escapism or the certainty of enlightened transparency. One awakens from such a dream without betraying its insights or fully repressing the paradoxes that serve as possible objects of reflection and of experience. To be awake and asleep at the same time, in an aesthetically mediated musical space, is the condition of possibility for not resigning oneself once and for all to what announces itself as the limit of the possible. Without this wakeful dream and this dreaming wakefulness—one name for which, as Bloch suggests, may be "music"—philosophy confines itself to the affirmative. As Bloch tells us throughout his book *Thomas Münzer als Theologe der Revolution* (Thomas Münzer as Theologian of the Revolution), revolutions, even theological ones, often are ignited by those who have the courage to dream, and to hear in and through that dream, what is right: "Whoever opens himself to it, is capable also of dreaming and hearing what is right."[44] Therefore, any philosophy worthy of its name must remain faithful to the dream of the more that permeates his *Tübinger Einleitung in die Philosophie* and that casts "the dream of what is commensurate with the human" as that which "is searching for more."[45] From the perspective of this dream of the more, and even the dreamed "moreness" of the more, it is hardly a surprise that Bloch's original title for *The Principle of Hope* was *Dreams of a Better Life*.[46]

The dream, although conventionally associated with images rather than with sounds—Freud's *Interpretation of Dreams*, for instance, features an extensive index of dream images and their possible meanings but no index of dream sounds—can nevertheless be understood as a translation of sorts: one between image and sound. The link between dreaming and music so crucial to Bloch's project is addressed implicitly by Roland Barthes's meditations on music and inscription. In "Listening," Barthes writes:

> In dreams, the sense of hearing is never solicited. The dream is a strictly visual phenomenon, and it is by the sense of sight that what is addressed to the ear will be perceived: a matter, one might say, of acoustic images. Thus, in the Wolf Man's dream the wolves' "ears were cocked like those of dogs when they are alert to something." The "something" toward which the wolves' ears are cocked is obviously a sound, a noise, a cry. But, beyond this "translation" the dream makes between listening and looking, links of complementarity are formed. If little Hans is afraid of horses, it is not only that he is afraid of being bitten . . . but also [of] the noise these movements [of the horses] occasion. (The German term *Krawall* is translated as "tumult, riot, row"—all words associating visual and acoustic images.)[47]

The dream, then, can be said to create images of all kinds: visual images, sound images, perhaps even Denkbilder. Yet if the dream translates musical notes and other sounds into acoustic images, it performs the most radical translation of music, a translation that is at the same time a form of untranslatability: the dream translates music as music, that is, in terms of an otherness (the image or acoustic image) without which the music itself could not first be experienced, even when it is not being translated. If what music is or does is ultimately more then we can say—"for it is still empty and uncertain what is happening sonically," as Bloch reminds us—then any attempt at speaking and thinking about music is always already to speak of something else, even when we are speaking strictly about music. The translation of music by the dream indicates that music is that which always is en route to an elsewhere, always saying something more, less, and other than itself. It is allegorical, in the Greek sense of *allegorein* or saying something else. From this perspective, music can be understood not simply as an allegory *of* something but, because of its differential and other-directed being, as an allegory of allegory itself. Through a kind of Freudian delayed action or retroactivity (*Nachträglichkeit*) and Derridean supplementarity, the work of translation that the dream performs makes visible the other-directedness of music, the allegory of the allegory that it inherently performs.

Musical Dreams of the Denkbild

Lest his philosophical compositions be perceived as deaf to their own claims—claims regarding the dream of music and the music of dreams, the aesthetic, the musical, and the dreamlike quality of hope and a thinking of what is to come—Bloch enacts the theories of music and dreams set forth in *Spirit of Utopia* in the poetic language of *Spuren*. This collection of Denkbilder, which Bloch composed in close proximity to the literary-philosophical prose snapshots that his colleagues Adorno, Benjamin, and Kracauer each were devising at the time, gathers and deepens themes and preoccupations that Bloch had put into circulation in *Spirit of Utopia* and in the 1923 collection of essays *Durch die Wüste* (Through the Desert).[48] Although revised with the addition of numerous new Denkbilder for its 1969 republication in his collected works, the 1930 version of *Spuren* poetically condenses—under cryptic and playfully allusive literary titles such as "Sleeping," "The Gift," "Lamp and Closet," and "The Lucky Hand"—

most of the philosophical motifs from the early Bloch's intellectual orbit. Schooled in his teacher Georg Simmel's method of micrological reading, Bloch gives us a series of elusive traces to read, *Spuren*, that emerge and retreat, playing with presence and absence, meaning and its departure, and thereby enacting the poetic structure of his philosophical thought while pointing the way, like indexical footprints in the sand, toward a thinking and experiencing that has not yet been achieved, a homeland in which nobody has yet been.

In *Spuren*, we find, among the many passages that thematize dreaming and sleeping, two Denkbilder that are representative of the collection as a whole:

Sleeping

In ourselves we are still empty. Thus we easily fall asleep if there are no external stimuli. Soft pillows, darkness, silence allow us to fall asleep, the body grows dark. If one lies awake at night this is by no means wakefulness but rather a sluggish, consuming crawling around on the spot. It is then that one notices how uncomfortable it is to be with nothing other than oneself.[49]

Small Excursion

Even he who falls asleep grows lonely, though he can certainly be like someone taking a journey. When we are awake, we prefer to sit with the wall behind us, our gaze directed at the establishment. But how astonishing: when falling asleep, most turn toward the wall, even though in so doing they turn their backs to the dark room which is becoming unknown. It is as if the wall suddenly attracted, paralyzing the room, as if sleep discovered something in the wall that otherwise is the exclusive prerogative of a better death. It is as if, in addition to disturbance and strangeness, sleep too enrolled one in death; here, however, the stage appears differently, opening the dialectical semblance of a home. . . . For the pride of departure, in which the happiness and the pride of dying were already at work, is here distinctly filled with a triumph of an arrival. Especially if the ship arrives with music; then, within the Kitsch (not the petit-bourgeois kind) something of the jubilation of the (possible) resurrection of the dead conceals itself. [*Vor allem, wenn das Schiff mit Musik ankommt; dann verbirgt sich in dem Kitsch (dem nicht kleinbürgerlichen) etwas vom Jubel der (möglichen) Auferstehung aller Toten.*][50]

Sleeping, we give ourselves over to the experience of a certain multiplicity. It is while sleeping, and even more while dreaming, that we depart from the entrenched illusion structuring most of our waking hours, namely that we are no more than one. It is when we cannot sleep and dream that we become most acutely aware of the uncanny strictures that enforce a unified sense of self-identity and self-presence, when in fact the self also exists as a multitude of voices, sounds, images, and emotions that do not simply and strictly speaking amount to a single coherent self. If it is "uncomfortable to be with nothing other than oneself," as Bloch writes, then this is because a limiting and essentializing sense of self-identity prevents the self from dreaming and imagining something other than that which now dissimulates itself: defined, self-identical, and therefore, ultimately, empty. It is in the darkness of the dreamed moment—as in those rare moments when one is dreaming and knows that one is dreaming, that is, when one experiences the dissolution of the rational waking self *and at the same time* can give oneself a rational account of this dissolution even as the dissolution continues—in the darkness of this dreamed moment Freud's insistence that the ego is not master of its own house emerges not simply as a threat to the project of an ever-progressive enlightenment, but also as the uncontrollable displacement that opens the self up to its own internal contradictions and to the possibility of a world that would or could be *entirely different*. Bloch returns to this idea when he reminds us that "there is not one of us who could not also be someone else."[51]

In the Blochian sense, falling asleep also can be like embarking upon a journey. He is careful to say not simply that being asleep is like being on a journey, but that the experience of falling asleep, of being between sleeping and waking, the moment that can only be anticipated ("I am about to fall asleep") or retroactively verified ("I must have fallen asleep") but, like the moment of death itself, can never be articulated in the moment in which it occurs (one can hardly proclaim, to oneself or to another, "In this very moment, here and now, I am making the final transition from waking to sleeping and now I am sleeping"). Indeed, such a sentence only can be uttered in the uncanny temporality of literature itself, the site of the inarticulable, as when Edgar Allan Poe stages the spectral paradox of a recently deceased man reporting to us, "and now—now—*I am dead.*"[52] An erratic and unprogrammable caesura occurs, an interruption that marks a liminal space, both inside and outside consciousness, waking and sleeping, within and without the bounds of reason, here and there, departing and arriving in an arrival that is also a departure—in short, the experience of otherness and displacement as such, even if these are general functions and aspects of a self that often conceives of itself as singular.

When Bloch speaks of such an uncanny departure, from one's self and from the very idea of self-identity, as a moment of pride, he emphasizes the role that music plays in this dynamic—"especially if the ship arrives with music." The arriving ship that brings music along, that arrives *to* music and, perhaps, even *as* music, is filled not with the cargo of self-identical propositions and truth claims, but with the very hope without which the notion of redemption, the return of the dead and the restoration of all—what the Greeks called *apokatastasis*—could not even be thought. "Especially if the ship arrives with music": far from demanding a triumphalist certainty in this or that program, Bloch insists on the radical openness with which the music of the dream and the dream of music signal that non-self-identity and self-differentiation within the self and within the self's *Lebenswelt* are possible names for a certain utopian longing that is at any time radically exposed to the threat of shipwreck. If one of the names for the radically unprogrammable nature of the dream of transformation is music, then music stages the ways in which, as he says in his Tübingen lectures, "all our dreams and anticipations of a possible reality are not thereby relegated to a planning office and its designs—especially not the most important ones, among them the dream that is called freedom, leisure, and finally the terra incognita of freedom."[53] What is to come cannot be planned or programmed in advance, administered by an imaginary office for the implementation of freedom and justice, any more than one can decide what to dream about when one goes to sleep. Yet beyond the unprogrammability of this or that future system of freedom and justice—the very idea of a freedom and justice as always yet to come, as always inscribed, even if only in the traces of a weak hope—is preserved in and as the dream, as the openness and potential of what is at odds with itself, what hovers between imagination and concept, mysticism and enlightenment.

To imagine, then, a ship always about to arrive to the notes of music is to imagine Bloch as one of its passengers sleepwalking on deck, vigilantly somnambulant, waking and dreaming at the same time, analyzing relentlessly what is, yet dreaming of an absolute otherness, perhaps even of what one of his readers, Levinas, calls the wholly other—the third term that cannot be assimilated or reduced to the binary logic of self and other, remaining a wholly other not simply to any self but to *the very structure* of self and other. The absolute otherness that Bloch imagines in the dream of music and the music of the dream is sealed in what he calls "the darkness of the lived moment." As he tells us, "we do not have an organ for the I or the we, but we keep to ourselves in the blind spot, in the darkness of the lived moment, whose darkness ultimately is *our own darkness*, our being unknown, disguised, or lost, to ourselves" (S 276; G 343). The darkness of the lived moment registers the way in which experience remains at odds with itself, which is to say, it is displaced as the void that prevents the self from ever being fully conscious and awake to itself. In *The Principle of Hope* Bloch takes up this discussion when he writes that this "blind spot in the soul, this darkness of the lived moment, must nevertheless be thoroughly distinguished from the darkness of forgotten and past events." For, as he explains, if the "darkness of the lived moment . . . stays in its sleeping-chamber," then "together with its content, the lived moment itself remains essentially invisible, and in fact all the more securely, the more energetically attention is directed toward it: at this root, in the lived In-itself, in punctual immediacy, all world is still dark."[54] The lived moment, as the actuality of experience, remains a blind spot not simply because we have failed to awaken properly but because we have mistaken the imbrication of light and darkness, waking and dreaming, for absolute lucidity. To acknowledge that we are partially sleeping when we believe ourselves to be awake, and to recognize that we also are partially awake when we are sleeping, is, for Bloch, the name of a hopeful refusal: the refusal to give up on the dream that imagines modernity differently, the dream that dreams of enlightenment through and not in opposition to its own dialectic and that struggles in every moment not to forget that, for all its achieved progress and lucidity, it is always also traversed by the blind specters of barbarism and the night of its own dialectical reversal. Here, in the night of a simultaneous waking and sleeping, in perpetual fluctuation between levels of consciousness, the Blochian dream resides in a nocturnal space defined by transition and transgression "in which nothing that exists, and certainly no material that has been shaped elsewhere, makes the transition to another cosmos, [and] the categories called Mozart, Bach, and Beethoven are at home. *They are the figures of a transgression of boundaries in the spheres of sound.*"[55] The transgression of boundaries of all sorts, for which the perpetual transgression of waking and sleeping, dreaming and awakening, are privileged tropes, assumes in the sphere of music the proper names of Bach, Mozart, and Beethoven—though not as empirical composers, but as the incommensurate designation of "categories" and principles that for Bloch stage themselves musically as sound figures of transgression as such.

Although audible, the meanings of these transgressive sound figures remain deferred. Indeed, their meaning *is* deferral. Thus, Bloch argues, if the "tomorrow lives within the today," if "it is always sought," and if this tomorrow of the promise can take the form of "the trumpet call in *Fidelio*," we also must recognize that "there are so many and such heterogeneous witnesses and images, but all grouped around that which speaks for itself by still remaining silent."[56] The tomorrow encrypted in Beethoven's opera, therefore, does not promise an achieved meaning in the closed hermeneutic sense of a preprogrammed future, but promises instead to confront its own inability to address fully the futurity of the future. This inability is also its promise. The trumpet signal to which Bloch returns in many passages and contexts, the call of liberty and justice that occurs in *Fidelio* as the governor arrives, therefore belongs to those heterogeneous "witnesses" who, by speaking in many voices rather than with only a single meaning, articulate the ways in which they cannot speak transparently, and who honor what is to come by remaining silent about it.[57] Clustered around an absent center, a void that speaks of its own status as void, they point to the beyondness of signification that is the rightful territory of music and to the excessiveness to which hope attaches.

The dream of music and the music of the dream for Bloch stage the possibility of understanding our being *otherwise*. If his project is to articulate that which cannot be reduced to what merely is and to imagine that which merely is as the irreducible and non-self-identical itself, then the music he hopes one day to hear—that of Bach, Mozart, Beethoven, and others whom no one as yet has really heard—is the sound of a radical openness, mediated by what the Bloch of *Spirit of Utopia* calls "the secret" and "the form of the unconstruable question." Music is one of the forms that the unconstruable question assumes: as an irreducible otherness it resists full explication by rational argument and remains a question that must always pose itself one more time.

Anticipatory Hope

If we perceive that Bloch's ear listens to the sounds of an unorthodox Marxism that is not without transformative messianic elements even while it registers an uneasy harmony with certain forms of socialism—as, for instance, when Bloch assumed a professorship at Karl-Marx-Universität Leipzig in the German Democratic Republic upon his return in 1948 from exile in the United States—then we are in a position to grasp more fully what Bloch's project, fueled by the difficulty of aporias and paradoxes, may hope to articulate. The hope that Bloch does not wish to relinquish in his meditations on and dreams of music—indeed, the dream of music as an allegory of an entire constellation of aporetic aesthetico-political practices—is far removed from the essentializing dogma of certainty and ideological delusions of the availability of full hermeneutic meaning. Bloch's enigmatic sounds, audible in the night of his musical incantations, are closer to what recent proponents of radical democratic practice such as Ernesto Laclau and Chantal Mouffe call the "deconstructive effects in the project for a radical democracy," a "form of politics which is founded not upon dogmatic postulation of any 'essence of the social,' but, on the contrary, on affirmation of the contingency and ambiguity of every 'essence,' and on the constitutive character of social division and antagonism." Here, ultimately, the ground for any political order "exists only as a partial limiting of disorder" and "of a 'meaning' which is constructed only as excess and paradox in the face of meaninglessness."[58] The hope that resides in this recognition cannot be separated, in Bloch's conceptualization, from an incessant and productive return to the difficulties and possibilities of learning how to listen and, by extension, of learning how to read and think.

In the same way that Bloch, in *Spirit of Utopia*, speaks of an artwork's *Vorschein*, or anticipatory illumination, one also could speak of a musical *Vorklang* in describing the anticipatory sound of hope. It is in this context that Bloch advances the notion of *Hellhören*, a musically mediated, visionary listening experience or "clairaudience" that cannot be separated from the thinking of futurity itself:

In other words: clairvoyance is long extinguished. Should not however a clairaudience, a new kind of seeing from within, be imminent, which, now that the visible world has become too weak to hold the spirit, will call forth the audible world, the refuge of the light, the primacy of flaring up instead of the former primacy of seeing, whenever the hour of the language of music will have come? For this place is still empty, it only echoes obscurely back in metaphysical contexts. But there will come a time when the sound speaks. (S 163; G 297–98)

Once the visionary capabilities associated with the eye, sight, and light—and, by extension, with their Enlightenment heritage—have exhausted themselves as potentially liberatory instruments, the auditory possibilities of the ear still hold out promise. Through a kind of "visionary listening"—which also echoes in the German idiom *hellhörig werden*, to sit up and take notice—the ear attunes consciousness to the ways in which the futurity of hope has not yet been fully exhausted in the available ideologies and aesthetico-political programs that structure cognition. Without catachrestically transforming the Enlightenment into a mere "ensoundment," Bloch nevertheless wishes to invest the ear with a transformative capability that would enable the dream of the future—a dream that acknowledges the dialectically charged relation of reason and myth—to unfold also as the future of a dream from which one awakens to face the ethico-political aporias that will not permit us fully to decide whether we are dreaming or awake.

The dream of music, then, names a radical openness to what still remains to be heard and thought. As Bloch suggests:

If sound remains only allusive, unactualized, then it has surely not been put into signs, and its puzzle language does not wish to conceal from us something already resolved supernaturally; music's function is rather the most complete openness and the secret, what is comprehensible-incomprehensible. Symbolic in music is the proper object of humanity *objectively* veiling itself from itself. Sound walks with us and is We. (S 163; G 207)

The *vollste Offenheit*, or "most complete openness," that Bloch locates in the dream of music cannot be reduced to a stable meaning that has already secretly been decided elsewhere. Rather, music itself comprises this *Rätselsprache*, or abiding and enigmatic negotiation of meaning, which, in its inability to come into its own, points to a socially just way of responding to the other and to otherness itself that is still lacking. For Bloch, the human tone sings of nothing else. Standing in the service of this "most complete openness," the dream of music is inscribed in what Bloch in *Atheism in Christianity* terms "a transcending without transcendence [*ein Transzendieren ohne Transzendenz*]."[59] To locate music within the Blochian notion of transcending without transcendence is to claim for it the volatility of a process rather than the stability of a state. As a form of transcending without transcendence, music never is quite itself. Composed of a multitude of differential relations, of which those of major and minor, and harmonic and dissonant, are only among the most transparent, music is always alone even if one can speak of it only in conjunction with something else. The transcending without transcendence to which music belongs also works to keep alive a certain structure of transcending even when the concrete manifestation of that transcendence has no common measure with what, in the history of philosophy, has been associated with transcendence—such as the supersensuous, independence from consciousness, the inexperienceable, the otherworldliness in ontological thought, or the otherworldliness of God. As a transcending without transcendence, Bloch's music is both deeply historical and simultaneously at odds with its own history: it refunctionalizes the gesture of its own abandonment as a noninstrumental instrument placed in the service of a futurity that still deserves our action, hope, composition, performance, and dreaming.

Because music is composed of a process of transcending without ever reaching a final state of transcendence, its work can never be completed and, indeed, can always only have just begun. Its principles of polyphony and dissonance endlessly point to an elsewhere that is yet to come and yet to be thought. In a sense, then, to speak of "new" music would be superfluous, since music never can be anything but new. One is correct in thinking of music as a truly *modern* art, in fact, the youngest of the arts, not only because it, unlike architecture or poetry, has no known model in classical antiquity, but also because its signification as that which lies beyond signification is ever new and inexhaustible regardless of the frequency with which it is performed, heard, or dreamed. In Bloch's own words:

New music no longer has a recapitulation, with a principal key restored, on which victory could be recognized; after all, it is its greatness and its future that it no longer possesses a theme that has been placed at the beginning and that has been decided upon but that it, instead, constitutes music that is only still forming itself and that takes seriously the New and the infinity of the end [*die mit dem Neu, Unendlich des Endes Ernst macht*].[60]

For music to be serious about itself (*Ernst machen*), then, it cannot simply put to notes a pre-thought and preadministered extramusical program. The theme of music, its formal dream, which is also its leitmotif, is the thinking of the end that has no end, the end whose proper end is endlessness itself, the end that takes its own endlessness, its perpetually unfinished spectral business, seriously as the end that has not ended once and for all and that thus puts an end to the end—"mit dem . . . Unendlich des Endes Ernst macht." What Bloch ultimately gives us to learn, then, is how to hear music that is always only just forming itself ("die sich erst bildet"), a music that takes seriously, *ernst*, its own infinity by breaking with the finitude that also is a condition of its existence—*mit dem . . . Unendlich des Endes Ernst macht*. With a play, albeit a serious play, *ein ernstes Spiel*, on his own name—"*Ernst macht*"—Bloch signs the notes and sounds of his musical dream. If, as is apparent in *Heritage of Our Times*, he is concerned with the problem of how to inherit something properly, seriously, *ernsthaft* (earnestly or like an Ernst), of how to relate ethically *ernsthaft* to an inheritance and a heritage, then the heritage that he himself bequeaths to us—in and as a dream, in fact, his singular dream that nonetheless is shared and dreamed by others—is one that demands, aesthetically, ethically, and politically, that what he, in all earnestness, calls *das Unsagbare der Musik*, the "unsayable of music" (S 163; G 208), also always will remain the pleasurably sublime yet torturous music of the unsayable. Let's get serious.

3

Homeless Images:

KRACAUER'S EXTRATERRITORIALITY,
DERRIDA'S MONOLINGUALISM OF THE OTHER

> There are always holes in the wall for us to escape and the improbable to slip in.
> —Siegfried Kracauer, *History*
>
> From this shore, yes, *from this* shore or this common drift, all expatriations remain singular.
> —Jacques Derrida, *Monolingualism of the Other*

If it has a home at all, the proper home of the image, and even the thought-image or Denkbild, is homelessness. Never fully itself, the image remains at odds both with itself and with the referential burden that it is expected to carry. In its iterability, the image, which threatens to be divorced from referential functions such as time and space, tells of distance, absence, and loss, of exile and diasporic dispersal. It tells, in other words, of the states that make the image what it is and that relate it to all other images. The demand that an image be *of* something and that it faithfully and reliably re-present that something, on the one hand, and the inevitably unpredictable ways in which an image fails to comply with that demand, on the other hand, sponsor a melancholia that is shared by all images, even as it cannot but travel through the structural and historical specificity of a *singular* image. The image records an historical moment at the same time that it interrupts history, perpetuating the very thinkability of history even as it breaks with the logic of historical unfolding. As the site of multiple displacements, the image is historical when it tells us of its own departure from history, capturing time most fully when it removes itself from time, the way in which, for instance, a snapshot memorializes time by stepping outside the temporal flow. Because an image can never fully re-present, that is, present once again in exactly the same way, the vast network of traces and meanings that it first set out to arrest, it performs an *Aufhebung* that simultaneously preserves and cancels the event that once was its subject. In this double gesture, the image both forestalls and commemorates loss by recording a moment, documenting its constitutive inevitability, and making it visible as the loss that it always already was. That is to say, the image reveals the ways in which an assumed presence already was a fiction at the time when it was believed to be present. We even could say that rather than simply re-presenting its subject, the image retroactively makes visible the absence that already lay at the core of the event it set out to record.

It is the traces of these multiple displacements that connect the image with philosophical thinking—the nomadic search for a space of belonging and a sense of community where no community remains to be experienced, in short, a means of dwelling within homelessness itself—that images and philosophical thoughts share. Our task then becomes to articulate the state of homeless dwelling that occurs when the syntactical relations among building, dwelling, and thinking are caught in a perpetual *Aufbau* and *Abbau*, building and un-building, that shakes them to their very foundations, a fundamental ontological experience whose story Martin Heidegger narrates.[1] From this perspective, "philosophy," the Romantic Novalis tells us, "is actually homesickness, the desire to be at home everywhere." Georg Lukács cites Novalis's lines in 1920 in order to set the stage for his own well-known formulation of modernity's "transcendental homelessness [*transzendentalen Obdachlosigkeit*]," which he sees as the principal driving force of the novel since Romanticism and which, in turn, gives rise to a Marxian attempt at easing the suffering of this transcendental homelessness.[2] But what Novalis also gives us to think is the idea that when the homelessness in and of philosophical thought manifests itself as the desire to be at home everywhere (*überall zu Hause zu sein*), it paradoxically enforces and undoes the very idea of dwelling at home. After all, if one's home is everywhere, then it can be nowhere. This is to say that philosophical thought, not unlike the image, posits and dismantles its home, dismantling it by positing it and positing it only by dismantling it. But to say that, if one's home is everywhere, then it can be nowhere, does not erase the traces of the longing that motivates philosophy and the making and reading of images. Because "nowhere" also is the name of u-topia, the non-place, a "no-where" that may at any time enter, not into presence, but perhaps into legibility as the "now-here." Thus, the shared homelessness that binds the image to philosophical thought in a common hope that will not relinquish the idea that an absence, rather than being absolute, could remain thinkable as a distant and fractured presence—of and with a community that never can be thought or experienced *now* but always remains yet to come, in and as an infinite promise of unpredictable proportions and incalculable responsibilities.

Perhaps few modern writers are as sensitive to this imbrication of the image and of philosophical thinking in homelessness as Siegfried Kracauer and Jacques Derrida. If in these pages I place Kracauer's reflections on homelessness and its images into conceptual dialogue with those of Derrida, I wish to suggest a subterranean affinity that often is neglected. Kracauer and Derrida—one a displaced German Jew persecuted by Hitler, the other an Algerian Jew uneasily acculturated to "Frenchness"—for all their differences and singularities share a common set of concerns. Among many other things, they both are significant interpreters of Walter Benjamin, Franz Kafka, Marcel Proust, and Franz Rosenzweig; and they both share a sustained theoretical interest in themes such as waiting, writing, media technology, photography, the self-portrait, ghosts, architecture, and the philosophy of friendship. Both Kracauer and Derrida also are inclined at times to write in languages not their "own," and to reflect on the relation between homelessness and language, cultural identity and displacement, community and dispersal, the politics of inclusion and exclusion and a writing of, from, and in the margins. For Kracauer, the "homeless image" names a central aspect common to the projects of both philosophers, a spectral aspect that manifests itself in the cracks and fissures of officially sanctioned cultural discourses. From both a theoretical and a personal perspective, these ghostly homeless images sometimes are given the difficult name "extraterritoriality" (Kracauer), and other times the name "monolingualism of the other" (Derrida).

Homeless Images, Arcades, and the Terror of Territory

In a sense, the entire corpus of Kracauer's work, from the Weimar essays to his philosophy of history, speaks, implicitly or explicitly, to the problematics of homelessness, exile, and the image. That he would be so receptive to Lukács's figure of transcendental homelessness is not surprising, given the fact that his work as a whole is saturated with reflections on space, spatial relations, territoriality, and topography. Having first completed a doctorate in architecture, he discusses space, spatial relations, city streets, and other geo-topographical issues in many of his Weimar writings, including the novels *Ginster* and *Georg* and his essays in cultural criticism. Indeed, his very language often is constructed around an intricate geometry of space-specific metaphors.[3] Many of these spatial performances are microcosmically condensed in Kracauer's 1930 "Farewell to the Linden Arcade [*Abschied von der Lindenpassage*]," one of the Denkbilder from the 1920s and 30s that he later included in the book *Streets in Berlin and Elsewhere* [*Straßen in Berlin und anderswo*]). There, Kracauer speaks of the land- and cityscapes that concern him as "homeless images [*obdachlose Bilder*]." As Kracauer puts it, what he observes all around him are "homeless images, illustrations of passage-like movements that, here and there, shimmer through the cracks of the fence that surrounds us."[4] Echoing Lukács's language of ten years prior, Kracauer inscribes himself into a genealogy of homelessness by aligning his gaze with that of the homeless image.[5]

Like the photographic image, which assumes spectral dimensions in his reflections on photography, and like the workers who seek "Asylum for the Homeless [*Asyl für Obdachlose*]"—a chapter title in his 1930 book *The Salaried Masses* (*Die Angestellten*)[6]—the images that circulate through the streets of Kracauer's Weimar Germany are fleeting and elusive signifiers, divorced from any proper origin, inhabiting no permanent space. These homeless images radicalize the meaning that Gilles Deleuze and Félix Guattari later give to the concept of nomadism. Although this theoretical conceptualization of homelessness is shared by fellow members of the Frankfurt School, such as Adorno, Benjamin, and Horkheimer, Kracauer's work deepens this conceptualization with a force that mitigates against the reduction of his work to any single paradigm, even as it exhibits elective affinities with several.[7]

The image of homelessness that permeates Kracauer's thinking bespeaks a displacement that is shared by every image one may wish to read, including Kracauer's own self-portrait, which encodes a homelessness without which the signature that signs his sentences would hardly be legible. This homelessness, felt even at home, haunted Kracauer's empirical life from the beginning: born in 1889 to a middle-class Jewish family, his childhood was marred by a pronounced speech impediment that marked his mother tongue, German, as "other," even within the German context. Kracauer spoke his proper native language only as something improper and alien. Living in the schism between a disabling stutter and the refined ear that made him one of the most gifted stylists of the German language during the Weimar period, between the worlds of Jewish and non-Jewish Germans in Frankfurt, Berlin, and beyond, between what was perceived by his contemporaries as a bizarre personal appearance and the highly developed aesthetic and philosophical sense that propelled him to study architecture, philosophy, and sociology, prompted Kracauer to describe his life as "extraterritorial." The Frankfurt School's historian, Martin Jay, reminds us that although "marginality, alienation, outsiderness have been among the stock obsessions of intellectuals ever since the time of Rousseau," Kracauer's insistence on launching his thoughts and sentences from a position of extraterritoriality makes a singular demand of his readers. "Kracauer's sense of marginality," Jay continues,

> must have begun almost at birth. Physically, he was set apart from his peers by two characteristics. The first was a speech defect, a stammer which would preclude, among other things, a teaching career at any time in his life. The second was his physiognomy, whose peculiarity struck all who knew him. To Adorno, who actually used the word "extraterritorial" in describing his face, he looked as if he were from the Far East. Asja Lacis, the Latvian Marxist director who met him in the late 1920s, said he looked like an "African." To Hans Mayer, the Marxist literary critic, he was a "Japanese painted by an Expressionist." And Rudolf Arnheim, the aesthetic theoretician, remembers him as having a squashed nose that made his face "almost grotesque, but somehow beautiful."[8]

We might add that other contemporaries were more drastic and even mean-spirited. For instance, Joseph Roth spoke in a letter of Kracauer's "un-European face" and of the alleged "patience" required "to wait for half an hour before he finally stutters up his wisdom," while Harry Graf Kessler evoked a "Kracauer, to whose monstrous ugliness I cannot get accustomed."[9] For Kracauer, the marginality imposed by this extraterritoriality is not to be read as a postlapsarian state, as a fall from an original wholeness and a primordial stability of meaning from which his trajectory unfortunately has deviated. On the contrary, his otherness, inscribed by his extraterritoriality, is the very condition of possibility that makes him who he is: the one who is extraterritorial, the one who belongs to what does not belong, the one who is enjoined only by what is out of joint. For Kracauer, as for his friend Benjamin, the *Ursprung* is not merely an origin or a home but also, always, an *Ur-sprung*, a primal leap or crack.

This homeless image portrays the nomadic extraterritoriality that traverses all of his Denkbilder and, in fact, every one of his sentences.[10] Kracauer refers, directly or indirectly, to his (and others') extraterritoriality as early as his Weimar Denkbilder, and the reference continues through his last work, on the theory of history. Even his wife, Lili Kracauer, records in a letter her husband's preoccupation with extraterritoriality as a word and as a concept.[11] For Kracauer, the fact that home is not a home derives not from the state of exile from his native Germany, but from the sense that its legibility *as* a home is fundamentally predicated upon its internal division and self-differentiation, the internal otherness that reenacts, refracts, and multiplies its external otherness to the point at which the very binarism of the internal and the external dissolves. Writing in October 1958 to his similarly displaced Frankfurt School friend Leo Löwenthal in Berkeley, Kracauer registers the trauma of returning to his "home" from an extended European trip. "When we," Kracauer writes, "after a smooth flight returned to our apartment, I had a fit of claustrophobia. It is really unnatural to have a permanent residence, a so-called home; the existence as a vagabond is the only true thing. The following day I was reconciled with my life here. It is good for working and I here feel, as it were, extraterritorial."[12] The only reconciliation, for Kracauer, is the absence of reconciliation that the condition of extraterritoriality furnishes. Like Adorno, for whom *erpreßte Versöhnung*, or forced reconciliation, named the worst instincts, Kracauer can imagine reconciliation only as what refuses to be reconciled, a refusal that carries the name and the signature of the extraterritorial.

Extraterritoriality: the condition of existing in a territory beyond territory, belonging to a territory while at the same time being "extra" or superfluous to it, being outside or other to one's own or to another's territory. For someone or something to exist in a state of extraterritoriality means to depart from territory as a space and as an idea while still remaining deeply attached to it, that is, attached to it precisely in the act of departing from it. Extraterritoriality names the experience of radical insecurity in which the self encounters itself as an other. But precisely this encounter of the self with itself as an other also names the promise of possibility. As Deleuze reminds us, "The Other, as structure, is *the expression of a possible world*: it is the expressed, grasped as not yet existing outside of that which expresses it."¹³ Kracauer's extraterritoriality becomes readable not simply as the trace of a displacement, but also as the anticipatory expression of a possible world that is still to come and to be thought of as that which is not yet, as that whose territory, if it is anywhere, is always elsewhere.

Kracauer's emphasis on this experience of territoriality as extraterritoriality returns us to the very core of "territory." A territory designates that which is settled, circumscribed, defined, articulated, and distinguished—whether in geographical, political, disciplinary, juridical, national, ethno-ontological, or even anatomical terms. Territory is what underwrites the very idea of having something settled, of having established something for good. It even can carry the connotation of property and propriety, of ownership, of possessing and living in one's territory—in short, a way of being at home.

But while territory signifies a certain settlement, and the ex-perience (literally, the moving through) of that settlement, a strange tension haunts the ground of territory that suggests that the settlement of the territory also is deeply unsettling and unsettled. Indeed, the very etymology of the word territory is unsettling. While territory, as the *Oxford English Dictionary* tells us, derives from the Latin formation *territori-um*, that is, "the land around a town, a domain, district," the derivation of that formation in turn is "unsettled":

Etymology unsettled: usually taken as a deriv. of *terra* earth, land (to which it was certainly referred in popular L. when altered to *terratorium*); but the original form has suggested derivation from *terrere* to frighten, whence **territor* frightener, *territorium*? "a place from which people are warned off" (Roby *Lat. Gr.* §943). So F. *territoire* (1278 in Godef. Compl.): see also TERROIR.

Etymology unsettled: the history of territory also is the history of terror and fright. What is settled as territory is unsettled, that is, settled only as the dissimulation of what is unsettled, *heimlich* and *unheimlich* all at once. In this unsettling trajectory, that which delimits a domain or a space also de-limits it, circumscribing its limits while simultaneously abolishing them. What shelters is also what expels ("people are warned off"), and what settles is also what terrorizes. The home that the territory provides cannot be thought apart from terror itself, the terror sponsored by the threat of expulsion as much as the terror of remaining, unsettled, in the settlement. As an unsettled settlement, territory is not entirely distinguishable from what could be called a "terror-tory." What makes one feel at home also frightens one, frightens one when one feels at home and makes one feel at home only, perhaps, when one is frightened. That the homey comforts of territory cannot be distinguished from the terror that resides within it names the condition of a certain *Unheimlichkeit* that remains unsettling in any settlement.

Kracauer's emphasis on extraterritoriality now can be read as a form of experience that not only is conscious of the unsettlingly undecidable imbrication of territory and terror, but that also enacts this undecidability in the form of a meta-commentary. If territory, and the condition of territoriality that corresponds to it, work to erase any clearly delimited borders between territory and terror-tory, settlement and unsettlement, then extraterritoriality, in its "extra"-ness, its beyondness or otherness to territoriality, enacts the very distance that resists territoriality, as a word and as a concept, collapsing the competing and contradictory forces that traverse it and that will not allow it to come into its own as a legible self-identity. Extraterritoriality, then, is the condition or experience that allows for the articulation and mobilization of the ways in which territoriality is at odds with itself, a liberation of the terror that always already was hauntingly at work in territoriality, if only as a form of dissimulation. In other words, territoriality itself cannot exist without the extraterritoriality that is at work when settling and unsettling; territory and terror can no longer be distinguished reliably. Both as a condition and as a form of experience, extraterritoriality constitutes a displaced proper name for its alleged other, territoriality—but a potentially nonblinded experience that no longer takes the readability of itself and its other simply for granted. On the contrary, it invites this unreadability as a promise to be fulfilled through textual encounters—cultural, national, personal, or otherwise—whose outcome cannot be scripted in advance.

It is hardly an accident, then, that in "Farewell to the Linden Arcade," the Denkbild that mobilizes the trope of the "homeless image," Kracauer focuses on the haunted passageways (*Passagen*) of a Berlin arcade (*Passage*), placing himself into dialogue with "my friend Walter Benjamin, whose

Kracauer's Extraterritoriality, Derrida's Monolingualism 115

work has been focused for years on the arcades of Paris" and to whose "book *One-Way Street*," the collection of Denkbilder published two years prior, Kracauer's own Denkbilder respond.[14] Like Benjamin's Denkbilder of *One-Way Street* and like the fragments of his *Arcades Project*, Kracauer's Denkbild is obsessed with the arcades as a ghostly space that creates the feeling of dwelling inside and outside at the same time, a constellation in which nothing is what it appears to be:

> In the arcades, and precisely because they were arcades, the most recently created things separated themselves from living beings earlier than elsewhere, and died still warm (that is why Castan's panopticon was located in the arcade). What we had inherited and unhesitatingly called our own lay on display in the passageways as if in a morgue, exposing its extinguished grimace. In this arcade, we ourselves encountered ourselves as deceased. But we also wrested from it what belongs to us today and forever, that which glimmered there unrecognized and distorted.
>
> Now, under a new glass roof and adorned in marble, the former arcade recalls the vestibule of a department store. To be sure, the shops are still there, but its postcards are mass-produced commodities, its World Panorama has been superseded by a cinema, and its Anatomical Museum has long ceased to cause a sensation. All things have been struck dumb [*Alle Gegenstände sind mit Stummheit geschlagen*]. They huddle timidly behind the empty architecture, which, for the time being, acts completely neutral and later on will breed who knows what—perhaps fascism, perhaps nothing at all. What would be the point of an arcade [*Passage*] in a society that is itself only a passageway? [*Was sollte noch eine Passage in einer Gesellschaft, die selber nur eine Passage ist?*][15]

In Kracauer's reading, the passageways of the arcades delimit a space in which extraterritoriality is experienced, a no-man's land in which trajectories of history criss-cross and distort one another and objects become unreliable traces because the signs of the object world have ceased to speak—"alle Gegenstände sind mit Stummheit geschlagen." In fact, it is here, in the passageways of the arcades, that we encounter ourselves as another—a dead other. In this way, the arcade becomes the extraterritorial site of our encounter with ourselves as the finite other, that is, with finitude itself. But the arcade, with its homeless images, remains a hauntingly unreadable extraterritorial site. Because of the impossibility of reducing its conflicting significations in advance to this or that political program—it retreats as an illegible text—the arcades may or may not become a pretext for fascism, may or may not authorize a sociopolitical program. As a form of undecidability, its meaning is always yet to come. Coming to terms with this undecidability by facing its threat in light of the requirements that a properly political stance would demand: these are the ethical stakes of Kracauer's extraterritoriality and the homeless images in which it manifests itself. It is hardly an accident that in a 1930 review Benjamin describes Kracauer as a relentless outsider, a marginal yet revolutionary ragpicker of history, a designation of which Kracauer always remained proud. "And if we wish to gain a clear picture of him in the isolation of his trade," Benjamin writes there, "what we will see is a ragpicker, at daybreak, picking up rags of speech and verbal scraps with his stick and tossing them, grumbling and growling, a little drunk, into his cart, not without letting one or another of those faded cotton remnants—'humanity,' 'inwardness,' or 'absorption'—flutter derisively in the wind. A ragpicker, early on—at the dawn of the day of the revolution."[16]

The spatial dimension of Kracauer's extraterritoriality, as it figures in the language of the ghostly arcades passageways, is extended by a temporal component. In two 1963 letters to Adorno—missives that Kracauer, according to the literary critic Inka Mülder-Bach, privately designated as "Letters on Extraterritoriality"—Kracauer expresses his desire for "chronological anonymity": "My mode of existence literally would be put on the line if dates were roused and assaulted me from the outside." As Kracauer emphasizes, it "is not as if I were trying to appear young or younger; it is solely my fear of losing chronological anonymity by the fixation of dates and the unavoidable connotations of such a fixation."[17] What precisely would chronological anonymity mean, and just what might the "unavoidable connotations of such a fixation" be? It certainly is reasonable to suggest, with Jay, that Kracauer, on the one hand, is reflecting on his own finitude and, on the other, wishes to reject the easy compartmentalization of his work as that of yet another "Weimar intellectual," a periodization that, like all periodizations, seeks to program in advance all subsequent readings and thus to police the meanings that can be liberated from a text that ultimately will refuse to be arrested for good.[18]

But more is at stake here. Kracauer's insistence on chronological anonymity stages his own theoretical conviction that historical phenomena cannot be assimilated, without the mediation that language itself demands, to an allegedly stable and unchangeable historical context. This does not mean that Kracauer opposes the historical contextualization of phenomena—on the contrary, his preoccupation with, for instance, the historicity of everyday objects and quotidian life in the cultural text of Weimar Germany (collected in the Denkbilder of *The Mass Ornament*), his interest in the psychosocial dimension of German film (developed in his 1947 *From Caligari to Hitler*), and, indeed, his major posthumous work on the theory of history (*History: The Last Things before the Last*), all speak to his attention to genealogical issues in the reading of concepts and phenomena. But these historical contexts, for Kracauer, are never simply given or self-identical—as con-texts, they are also *textual* events whose elusiveness and ever-changing modes of resisting the historian demand to be read on their own terms.[19]

From this perspective, Kracauer shares a textual model of the historical with Benjamin. Kracauer insists on destabilizing the notion that, as he puts it in *History*, "people actually 'belong' to their period. This must not be so. Vico is an outstanding example of chronological exterritoriality; and it would be extremely difficult to derive Burckhardt's complex and ambivalent physiognomy as a historian from the conditions under which he lived and worked." Kracauer continues by arguing that like "great artists or thinkers, great historians are biological freaks: they father the time that has fathered them."[20] Here, he implicitly convenes with Benjamin, who explains in his early essay "*Trauerspiel* and Tragedy": "The time of history is infinite in every direction and unfulfilled at every moment. This means that no single empirical event is thinkable that would stand in a necessary relationship to the particular historical situation in which it was produced." Benjamin therefore argues that "the determining force of historical time cannot be fully grasped by, or wholly concentrated in, any empirical process."[21] For Benjamin, as for Kracauer, the promise of historical thinking finally is lodged in our willingness to begin to read the ways in which a historical phenomenon registers the elements of its Foucauldian episteme while at the same time breaking with that episteme. The genuinely historical event both confirms and undoes its time, confirms it by undoing it and undoes it by confirming it, in a gesture that demands our thinking of the event's singularity and materiality. Viewed in this light, Kracauer's insistence on chronological anonymity also can be read as a desire to avoid the "unavoidable connotations" of a historical "fixation" that seeks once and for all to foreclose the reading of history. From this perspective, then, the temporality of Kracauer's life, while empirical, to be sure, is empirical only *among other things* and, as such, remains open to the plurality of what always will have been other, and more, than one.

European, among Other Things

Kracauer's concern with extraterritoriality and all that it implies, both as a mode of being and as a concept, is shared by Derrida in his meditations on the relations among language, cultural particularity, and national identity. In his *Le monolinguisme de l'autre: Ou la prothèse d'origine* (1996), translated as *Monolingualism of the Other; or, The Prosthesis of Origin*, Derrida's reflections on the readability of linguistic, cultural, and national identity are inseparable from the many specters, conceptual and personal, that traverse his far-ranging oeuvre from the 1960s to the present—from such early texts as *Writing and Difference*, *Of Grammatology*, and *Margins of Philosophy*, via his "middle" phase and such works as *The Post Card*, *Glas*, and *Psyché*, to the later, more overtly ethico-political works of the 1990s and the new millennium, such as *Specters of Marx*, *On the Name*, *The Other Heading*, *The Politics of Friendship*, and *Cosmopolitanism*. His reflections in *Monolingualism of the Other* are prefigured and supplemented by earlier passages in which he, as a Jew born in El Biar, near Algiers, the capital of French-occupied Algeria, meditates on the ways in which his experience as a non-European European Jew inflects his philosophical trajectory. In a passage that echoes Kracauer's notion of "extraterritoriality," Derrida emphasizes the "exteriority" of his experience. In "There Is No One Narcissism (Autobiophotographies)," a conversation in which Derrida reflects on aspects of his Judaism, his relation to the French language and France, and his life growing up in the language of the "other" that also is that of the self (French) along the war-torn southern Mediterranean coast, we read:

There is certainly (and here I am describing naively a naive experience) a feeling of exteriority with regard to European, French, German, Greek culture. But when, as you know I do, I close myself up with it because I teach and write all the time about things that are German, Greek, French, even then it is true that I have the feeling I am doing it from another place that I do not know: an exteriority based on a place that I do not inhabit in a certain way, or that I do not identify. That is why I hesitate to call it Judaic. There is an exteriority! Some might say to me: But it's always like that, even when a German philosopher writes about the German tradition, the fact that he is questioning, writing, interrogating inscribes him in a certain outside. One always has to have a certain exteriority in order to interrogate, question, write. But perhaps beyond this exteriority, which is common to all those who philosophize and write, ask questions . . . beyond this exteriority there is perhaps something else, the feeling of *another* exteriority.[22]

What Derrida names his exteriority travels through a number of interlaced discourses: that of canonical "Western" thought (one thinks of his extensive writings and teachings on a vast number of central European writers, from Plato via Hegel to Husserl and Heidegger, from Kant and Rousseau to Kafka and Celan, from St. Augustine to Joyce and Benjamin, among so many others); that of a Judaism that is not quite Judaic, or rather, that brings to light the ways in which there never has been a single Judaism alone, in a gesture that opens up Judaism, along with the very question of "religiosity" itself, to the ways in which it differs from and with itself; and that of the critical writer who joins the community of exteriority of all those who think, write, and call into question. If, at the same time, Derrida speaks of *another* exteriority, an exteriority that is not encompassed by a prior exteriority, we can infer that this "other" exteriority is an other, perhaps, not only to the rhetoric of any interiority, but also to the very notion of exteriority as a function or even an invention of the binary code of the internal and the external. This more radical exteriority cannot be reduced to the logic of interiority and exteriority—it remains exterior to that logic. The exteriority of this "other" exteriority manifests itself, if it manifests itself at all, as the exteriority that has no interior or exterior other: it is an exteriority without and beyond exteriority. We thus could say that beyond exteriority lies exteriority, but it could only be an exteriority that already has been altered by its beyondness. It is this elusive movement of alteration of which the thought of exteriority will not cease to think.

Such a thinking of the "beyond" of exteriority is performed not for its own sake, but always in the name of something else, a something else that remains exterior and, in its radical exteriority, still to come. This is its spectral desire and its haunted promise. Derrida, in *Monolingualism of the Other*, implicitly reformulates the logic of exteriority and the desires and promises that its thinking presupposes. He imagines a desire and a promise that would unfold beyond "memory and time lost," a desire and promise inseparable from the questions that lie, in multiple formulations, at the intersection of all his work—a desire and promise, in short, that struggles to come to terms with the ethical, political, and personal implications of engaging the vexed moment in which an unveiling becomes indistinguishable from a veiling, in which every encounter with a self becomes infinitely conditioned by the specters of a non-self, an other that is an other both to the self and to itself, to itself as other, and that makes the self visible, in the other, as the other that it always already was. As Derrida writes:

> This desire and promise let all my specters loose. A desire without horizon, for that is its luck or its condition. And a promise that no longer expects what it waits for: there where, striving for what is given to come, I finally know how not to have to distinguish any longer between promise and terror.[23]

Derrida gestures toward a desire that acknowledges it is horizonless, that is, without a delimiting force of expectation that could condition in advance the telos and the unfolding of the desire and that could, by the same token, be employed as a measurement of the extent to which this or that expression of a desire has led to its fulfillment in a particular form. That this desire does not possess the comforts of a delimited space, telos, and horizon (not even, presumably, that of a Gadamerian interpretive *Erwartungshorizont*, or horizon of expectation) and that its fulfillment not only cannot be guaranteed, but also would threaten to remain unreadable even if it were to materialize—this, for Derrida, names both its "condition" (which is to say, philosophically, the condition of its possibility, but also, more negatively, the difficult condition it is in, as though it had a medical condition of sorts) and simultaneously its "luck," the accident and fortunate coincidence that bestow upon it its desirable features. Likewise, Derrida's promise is a promise that will not content itself with expecting simply what it expects; it has given up waiting for what it expects without having given up the task of expecting. This is an expectation without expectation, an expecting without expecting, in which expecting can survive only as an intransitive verb, that is, as something that takes no object and that perpetuates itself as a promise precisely in its refusal or inability to take an object, even if it can hardly be thought outside of a logic in which, if the very movement of expecting is not to be erased, one expects to expect *something* rather than nothing. This desire and this promise name the very possibility of a thinking of what is to come, of what as yet has no name but imposes itself in and as an expectation—"what is given to come." What this desire and promise occasion is itself a desire and a promise: to have learned, even as that having-learned is always in the process of being forgotten, in a formulation that echoes the imbrication of territory and terror in Kracauer, "not to have to distinguish any longer between promise and terror." It is worth noting that Derrida's desire is directed not at a learning that does "not distinguish any longer," but at one that does not "have to distinguish any longer." This gesture implies an envisioned liberation from a power or agency that would pass judgment upon, enforce, and administer matters of distinguishing and questions of distinction. Thus, what Derrida envisions is the formulation of a more radical promise, one that, rather than merely departing from the model of distinguishing once and for all between this and that, or even from the act of distinguishing itself, actually departs from the very *logic*—tied to narrowly conceived notions of reason and self-contained identity—of a system of thinking that seeks to police the horizon and the space in which the activities of distinguishing, and even the distinguishing among various distinctions, first can be performed.

These multiple movements away from the moment of distinguishing are not to be thought as a call for the abandonment of a thinking that is invested in making distinctions or of the notion of distinction itself. On the contrary, Derrida would seem to call for a new form of distinguishing, a distinguishing that distinguishes among various forms and unspoken assumptions that underlie the very idea of making distinctions and the ethico-political consequences of such acts. What his writing moves toward is the thinking of an ethics that cannot be considered in isolation from the ways in which it finds itself on unstable ground. The blind triumphalism that believes itself to have performed once and for all a stable, binding, and normative distinction between promise and terror, good and evil—and thus to be protected from it, ideologically and epistemologically—is the greatest danger of all. Derrida's writing suggests that only when we open ourselves up to the possible reversal of the one into the other, to the threat of opposing and contradictory meanings emerging within the "same" phenomenon, to the haunting prospect that a concept or phenomenon may carry its own opposite within itself, to the unsettling possibility of having to build one's house on a defective cornerstone: it is only in these aporetic moments that the promise of an ethical impulse is first articulated, because it is only here that the making of distinctions becomes an aporetic—and therefore rigorously *ethical*—experience.

That there can be no theory of this ethical mode that does not attend to its own blind spots and internal alterities also means that any ethical response to this mode must be equal to its abyssal aberrations, to the ways in which selves perpetually are made and unmade in language, even the language of the other. Derrida's imagined position, in which he "finally know[s] how not to have to distinguish any longer between promise and terror," exhibits illuminating intertextual relays to Paul de Man's project. Attempting to articulate the stakes of a certain "resistance" to theory, de Man writes:

> Nothing can overcome the resistance to theory since theory is itself this resistance. The loftier the aims and the better the methods of literary theory, the less possible it becomes. Yet literary theory is not in danger of going under; it cannot help but flourish, and the more it is resisted, the more it flourishes, since the language it speaks is the language of self-resistance. What remains impossible to decide is whether this flourishing is a triumph or a fall.[24]

Just as presumably nothing could permanently stabilize the difference between promise and terror in Derrida, so nothing could overcome the resistance to theory in de Man: theory's very condition of possibility cannot be occasioned without that which, within it, works both with and against it, enabling it and resisting it at the same time. The resistance to theory therefore would be a resistance only to resistance itself, a movement of resistance to resistance that would not work to resist resistance at all but rather to expand and to solidify it as resistance. If it remains impossible to decide whether this "flourishing" that the resistance to theory as resistance occasions is to be applauded or mourned, invited or resisted, then that impossibility itself cannot be separated from any promise it may contain. Indeed, our ability to decide once and for all between a triumph and a fall would at the same time foreclose the promise that any mode of resistance may still harbor. As in Derrida's desire and promise to learn not to have to distinguish between promise and terror in a gesture of finality, de Man's diagnosis of the impossibility of distinguishing a triumph from a fall is not the end of ethico-political thought, but rather, in its encounter with the aporia of decision, an opening up to and radicalization of such thought.

This inability to distinguish with final certainty between a triumph and a fall, between promise and terror, bespeaks a certain homelessness, even extraterritoriality, of thought in which the systematicity and reliability of thought itself cannot be fully secured. Here, thought is exposed to its homelessness. The homelessness evoked in Kracauer's homeless image is staged in Derrida's discussion of the "defective cornerstone" in de Man's reading of the Hegelian system. Problematizing Heidegger's concept of *Versammlung*, or gathering, a notion that could be understood as promoting the dangerous illusion of being at home as well as the paranoid nationalism such an illusion could inspire, Derrida elaborates upon the notion of a defective cornerstone as encrypting a home without a home, the idea of a home that conceals within itself the permanent threat of its opposite. Here, "the very condition of a deconstruction may be at work, in the work, *within* the system to be deconstructed; it may *already* be located there, already at work, not at the center but in an eccentric center, in a corner whose eccentricity assures the solid concentration of the system, participating in the construction of what it at the same time threatens to deconstruct."[25] Rather than being administered from the outside, as an external intervention, the deconstruction of the system or home occurs from within, having already occurred at the moment in which its occurrence enters into legibility. Such a defective cornerstone threatens the very foundation upon which its house rests, even while remaining a necessary and integral feature of the structure without which there would be no house in the first place. The homelessness effected by this defective cornerstone produces a being at odds with oneself, the experience of an otherness in which the dependence of the self on the voices and traces of the always already defective—but nevertheless constitutive—other become visible. Placing Kracauer and Derrida into syntactical relation through de Man, we could conceive of the defective cornerstone as a homeless image and an image of homelessness. The one who dwells in the house experiences himself as other or, more precisely, experiences himself as other and as an otherness precisely when he can no longer reliably differentiate between the cornerstone as an architectural necessity for maintaining the structure of the house and the cornerstone as the potential precipitant of the house's collapse.[26]

To emphasize the sustained and threatening logic of the defective cornerstone in Derrida's thinking also is to return it to the homelessness of his own experience, an experience that connects this logic to aspects of Kracauer's extraterritoriality within, and beyond, the Germany of his time. Born in Algeria in 1930 as a Francophone Algerian Jew, Derrida's ancestors had emigrated from Spain in the nineteenth century.[27] At the time of his move to France at age nineteen to continue the studies he had begun in Algeria, a form of identity imposed itself on him even more forcefully than before, one that was European and non-European, Jewish and non-Jewish, French and non-French, all at the same time.[28] Derrida writes of a hybridity that is at odds with itself:

> I am European, I am no doubt a European intellectual, and I like to recall this, I like to recall this to myself, and why would I deny it? In the name of what? But I am not, nor do I feel, European *in every part*, that is, European through and through. By which I mean, by which I wish to say, or *must* say: I do not want to be and must not be European through and through, European *in every part*. Being a part, belonging as "fully a part," should be incompatible with belonging "in every part." My cultural identity, that in the name of which I speak, is not only European, it is not identical to itself, and I am not "cultural" through and through, "cultural" in every part.
>
> If, to conclude, I declared that I feel European *among other things*, would this be, in this declaration, to be more or less European? Both, no doubt. Let the consequences be drawn from this. It is up to others, in any case, and up to me *among them*, to decide.[29]

Far from undoing the concept of cultural identity, Derrida brings to the fore the ways in which this identity is at odds with itself, is clustered around not a core of stable meaning, but a network of differences. Thus, to lay claim to a cultural identity such as Europeanness means to invite the ways in which the self is *plus d'un*, more than one: more than itself and no longer simply itself. Cultural identity thus becomes visible as a fractured concept in which one claims allegiance to this or that culture only among other things, that is, in and as a part of many possible and competing identities. If any one aspect of the self's cultural identity is not self-identical, we also could say that the specific ways in which that aspect is non-self-identical point to its moment of identity: the self becomes readable as the one whose identity is fractured and multiple in this or that *particular* way. Here, even the very notion of being or having something "cultural"—such as a "cultural" identity—opens up to its internal differentiations, for it is only among other things that one is or has something "cultural." Thus, not only does the self merely "possess" this or that cultural identity among others—that is, among other things and among *other* others—but even the notion of its readability as something having culture or being cultural is only one among many others, in a way that does not fetishize the ideology of culture itself, even a culture of multiplicity and difference. We could say that such guardedness with respect to the idea of the cultural corresponds to Adorno's dictum that "the greatest fetish of cultural criticism is the concept of culture as such. For no authentic work of art and no true philosophy, according to their very meaning, has ever exhausted itself in itself alone, in its being-in-itself [*An-sich-Sein*]. They have always stood in relation to the actual life-process of society from which they separated themselves [*von dem sie sich schieden*]."[30] To do justice to the ways in which the cultural departs from itself and its culture, even when it stands in relation to the culture that produced it, means to invite the specters of otherness as something constitutive of—rather than merely threatening to—any cultural identity.

This perspective is confirmed and elaborated in "A 'Madness' Must Watch Over Thinking," in which Derrida is asked by his interlocutor, "Do you mean to say that you do not want to have any identity?" To which Derrida replies: "On the contrary, I do, like everyone else. But by turning around this impossible thing, and which no doubt I also resist, the 'I' constitutes the very form of resistance." "Each time," he continues, "this identity announces itself, each time a belonging circumscribes me, if I may put it this way, someone or something cries: Look out for the trap, you're caught. Take off, get free, disengage yourself. Your engagement is elsewhere."[31] In the moment in which identity, as a form of desire, appears to manifest itself and to tighten its grip on the self, there is also a moment that resists that formation of identity. This resistance is not simply a refusal to play along, the narcissistic declining of a welcome invitation, but rather signals a commitment to what within identity remains non-identical, to what eludes identity even in the name of identity—with an eye to the incalculable and resistant future of non-self-identical subject positions.

The promise of, and desire for, the incalculable and resistant future is intertwined with the trajectory of Derrida's "own" experience, an experience of otherness that makes him singular and at the same time connects him to so many other singularities. The Algerian war, one in a series of conflicts in his native region, impressed upon the young Derrida, as we learn in "Unsealing ('The Old Language')," the "animal fashion" in which one can be displaced even within what one considers one's "most natural habitat." "Even for a child," he explains, "who was unable to analyze things, it was clear that it would all end in fire and blood. No one could escape that violence and that fear." Derrida "knew from experience that the daggers could be bared at any moment, as one left school, in the football stadium, in the midst of the racist taunts that spared no one: the Arab, the Jew, the Spaniard, the Maltese, the Italian, the Corsican. . . . Then, in 1940, the singular experience of the Algerian Jews. The persecutions, which were unlike those of Europe, were all the same unleashed in the absence of any German occupier." As Derrida elaborates:

> It is an experience that leaves nothing intact, an atmosphere one goes on breathing forever. Jewish children expulsed from school. The principal's office: You are going to go home, your parents will explain. Then the Allies landed, it was the period of the so-called two-headed government (de Gaulle—Giraud): racial laws maintained for almost six months, under a "free" French government. Friends who no longer knew you, insults, the Jewish high school with its expulsed teachers and never a whisper of protest from their colleagues. I was enrolled there but I cut school for a year. . . . From that moment, I felt—how to put it?—just as out-of-place in a closed Jewish community as I did on the other side (we called them "the Catholics"). In France, the suffering subsided. At nineteen, I naively thought that anti-Semitism had disappeared, at least there where I was living at the time. . . . Paradoxical effect, perhaps, of this brutalization: a desire for integration in the non-Jewish community, a fascinated but painful and suspicious desire, nervously vigilant, an exhausting aptitude to detect signs of racism, in its most discreet configurations or its noisiest disavowals. Symmetrically, sometimes, an impatient distance with regard to the Jewish communities, whenever I have the impression that they are closing themselves off by posing themselves as such. Whence a feeling of non-belonging I have no doubt transposed.[32]

Being homeless in one's own home, being at odds with oneself, or even being known as the one who is at odds with himself: these images of homelessness and homeless images haunt a philosophical stance or attitude that centers on cracks and fissures, on that which, within the overarching system—be it a cultural identity, a set of social codes, a geo-topographical space, or a community within a community—is extraterritorial. Here, these unpredictable shifts and displacements of identity, in which belonging can be felt only in terms of particular forms of non-belonging, are transposed onto theoretical thought itself. They, too, work to render such thought homeless, even at home.

European Headings

It is this displaced and fractured relation to the concept of cultural identity that conditions, for all their differences and singularities, both Derrida's and Kracauer's thinking and experience. Just as Derrida, an Algerian-born Francophone Jew, is fully European without being fully European, French only among so many other things, Kracauer, as a German-born Jew, was German only among other things, Jewish only among other things, and in later life, like Derrida, perhaps partially American. Writing for a prestigious German paper, the *Frankfurter Zeitung*, Kracauer experienced increasing anti-Semitism from the early 1930s on, a reduction in his salary, and, when his decidedly critical tone with regard to the overtly nationalistic films produced by the German UFA company continued, the organism of his German newspaper expelled him as though he were a foreign body. On 28 February 1933, the day after the Reichstag Fire, Kracauer and his wife escaped Germany for France and attempted to establish themselves in Paris. At age forty-four, Kracauer, whose ear has made him a distinguished stylist of German prose, was forced to live, uncomfortably and clumsily, without an ear, as it were, in the French language. His increasingly difficult Parisian exile was marked by, among other things, several internments when French authorities imprisoned Kracauer, Benjamin, and so many other people of German descent living in France, without regard to political background. After being interned and released several times, Kracauer escaped again, this time to the French port of Marseille, where by chance he reunited with his friend Benjamin, who was also attempting to flee after the Nazi invasion of France.[33] While Benjamin, in the face of severe difficulties, committed suicide at the Franco-Spanish border, Kracauer managed to leave France, traversed Portugal, and reached New York City in 1941. At age fifty-two, Kracauer learned yet another language, English—growing yet another ear, as it were—and a few years later published his first major book in English, *From Caligari to Hitler*, with Princeton University Press (1947). The last two decades of Kracauer's life were spent suspended between Europe and the United States, between languages, and even between cultural identities. Unlike his friends and colleagues such as Adorno and Horkheimer, Kracauer did not receive a call to return permanently to Germany after the war, even though, as Adorno writes in Kracauer's obituary, "he who was armored against ideologies could have done an infinite amount of good" in the cold-war world of Germany and Europe.[34] But what would it have meant for Kracauer to "return" to Europe? To whom or what would such a "return" have responded? What would his heading toward "Europe" have signified in the face of his own extraterritoriality, his desire for chronological anonymity, and the homelessness of his image(s)?

These questions, raised by the homeless image of Kracauer's extraterritoriality, especially their ethical and political dimensions, are cast into sharp relief in Derrida's elaborations of cultural identity and "Europeanness," issues that form the core of such texts as *The Other Heading: Reflections on Today's Europe* and *Monolingualism of the Other*, in which he, the Algerian Jew who, rather than being almost European, is not quite not European, reflects on the politics of having only one language, yet that language not being one's own.[35] Derrida wishes to conceptualize Europe in a post-essentialist way by rethinking facile programs of identity politics, including those of Eurocentrism as well as anti-Eurocentrism, in terms of what they simultaneously presuppose and marginalize.[36] Based on a radical respect for and openness toward the other, to the one who has as yet no name and who has not yet been subjected to a set ideological standard of evaluation—and even the self that is legible only in the other—Derrida hopes to cast into relief the spectral contours of a European democracy, a still unrealized democratic potential to come. Although this democratic promise draws on the Enlightenment's universalist principles, values of justice, and striving toward a liberal democracy, it also breaks with a certain thinking that always already will have defined—and thereby, in effect, foreclosed—what such principles in their full complexity otherwise might signify. Therefore, Derrida asks, "Is there then a completely new 'today' of Europe beyond all the exhausted programs of *Eurocentrism* and *anti-Eurocentrism*, these exhausting yet unforgettable programs? (We cannot and must not forget them since they do not forget us.)"[37] This thinking neither follows the established political and intellectual programs of the Eurocentric tradition nor blindly denounces them. Rather, what is at stake is a thinking through of the ways in which what made these programs possible is refracted and folded back onto itself in movements of thought that threaten to fail at a difficult task. This task is simultaneously to think the liberating potential of that tradition and of its violent regression, which are so often interlaced. Attending to these concerns is vital because, after all, whether one acknowledges it or not, they continue to speak through us.

This double structure of the Eurocentric tradition speaks to the ways in which "we *today* no longer want either Eurocentrism or anti-Eurocentrism.... Beyond these all too well-known programs, for what 'cultural identity' must we be responsible? And responsible before whom? Before what memory? For what promise? And is 'cultural identity' a good word for 'today'?"[38] The crux of Derrida's reflections on Europe could be condensed in the complex question of whether it is possible and desirable to be faithful to a certain Eurocentrism without Eurocentrism. That is to ask, what will it have meant to have remained loyal to a tradition of thinking by breaking with it and to reinscribe oneself in it precisely by breaking with it? And is this reinscription, predicated upon a break or radical "exscription," again to be subsumed under the programmatic impulse of the tradition itself, or does it instead make visible some of the internal breaks and fissures from which this tradition always has benefited and under which it always has suffered, the tradition upon which it has drawn and whose internal tensions it continues to foreclose?

To make possible the thinking through of such questions within the concrete borders of today, Derrida's writing revolves around the political question of the other who arrives at one's intellectual, geographic, or immediately personal border. We could think of this other, with both Derrida and Levinas, not simply as an "other," but as the "wholly other" (*tout autre*).[39] The other, by virtue of its counterdistinction from the self, is to a certain degree still comprehensible, calculable, and predictable—to the extent that it can be negatively assimilated into the available and comforting binary structure of self and other. The wholly other, by contrast, cannot be assimilated into that binarism. In its radical incomprehensibility, inscribed only in faintly legible traces but never encountered as a stable presence, it remains an other to the very structure of self and other, irreducible to any prescribed system of classification. As a triple structure or triple event, this wholly other is an other to the self, an other to the other, and an other to the self-other. Only in encountering this wholly other can certain political and ethical questions that link our response with our responsibility be posed.

By way of attempting to do justice to this structure of the wholly other, and to the responsibilities that it entails, Derrida revisits such an other in *Aporias: Dying—Awaiting (One Another at) "the Limits of Truth."* This text helps us to theorize the possibility of doing justice to the arriving other, the other that unexpectedly presents itself to us at our doorstep, at our border, the European border for example. Derrida casts this problem in the language of the *arrivant*, a term that signifies "arrival," "newcomer," or "arriving." The arrivant is the arriving other as such—an other, however, that

> does not cross a threshold separating two identifiable places, the proper and the foreign, the proper of the one and the proper of the other, as one would say that the citizen of a given identifiable country crosses the border of another country as a traveler, an émigré or a political exile, a refugee or someone who has been deported, an immigrant worker, a student or a researcher, a diplomat or a tourist. Those are all, of course, *arrivants*, but in a country that is already defined and in which the inhabitants know or think they are at home.[40]

Beyond his or its concrete manifestations, the figure of the arrivant names the political and ethical predicaments that emerge in the context of geopolitical spaces, Europe for example. The arrivant stands in as a figure for the series of displacements that its movement both triggers and describes. As Derrida explains,

> The absolute *arrivant* . . . is not even a guest. He surprises the host . . . enough to call into question, to the point of annihilating or rendering indeterminate, all the distinctive signs of a prior identity, beginning with the very border that delineated a legitimate home and assured lineage, names and language, nations, families and genealogies. The absolute *arrivant* does not yet have a name or an identity. It is not an invader or an occupier, nor is it a colonizer, even if it can also become one. This is why the *arrivant* [is] not someone or something that arrives, a subject, a person, an individual, or a living thing, even less one of the migrants. . . . It is not even a foreigner identified as a member of a foreign, determined community.

Being someone or something before or in excess of stable identity, this arrivant also transforms the site or space that it enters. Something happens during its scene of arrival to the site in which this arriving occurs. As Derrida's passage continues:

> Since the *arrivant* does not have any identity yet, its place of arrival is also de-identified: one does not yet know or one no longer knows which is the country, the place, the nation, the family, the language, and the home in general that welcomes the absolute *arrivant*. This absolute *arrivant* as such is, however, not an intruder,

an invader, or a colonizer, because invasion proposes some self-identity for the aggressor and for the victim. Nor is the *arrivant* a legislator or the discoverer of a promised land. As disarmed as a newly born child, it no more commands than is commanded by the memory of some originary event where the archaic is bound with the *final* extremity, with the finality par excellence of the *telos* or the *eskhaton*. It even exceeds the order of any determinable promise. Now the border that is ultimately most difficult to delineate, because it is always already crossed, lies in the fact that the absolute *arrivant* makes possible everything to which . . . it cannot be reduced, starting with the humanity of man, which some would be inclined to recognize in all that erases, in the *arrivant*, the characteristic of (cultural, social, or national) belonging and even metaphysical determination (ego, person, subject, consciousness, etc.). . . . This border will always keep one from discriminating among the figures of the arrivant, the dead, or the *revenant* (the ghost, he, she, or that which returns).[41]

From the perspective of a thinking of the geopolitical and theoretical notion of Europe and of a future politics that would do justice to the homeless images that traverse it, we learn in this account how the movement of the arrivant allows for the identification—as a stable subject or identity—of neither the arrivant nor the site of arrival, Europe for example. The relation between what arrives and what is arrived at always is as much in flux as are the internal shifts and movements at play within each concept or site. This means that one's relation to who or what arrives always is as much a function of one's hospitality to what is radically other as it is a function of one's critical reflection on one's own situatedness, prejudices, and evaluation of the claims to authority from which the arrival could be judged. Such critical reflection, prompted by the arrival of the arrivant, also extends to the power relations that are inscribed in any scene of hospitality—that of Europe, for example, in which, in order to share or to invite, one must remain the master of one's own space and its boundaries, installing oneself in a superior position in relation to the one who, or that which, arrives in the moment of having to respond to the event of his or her arrival. The full thinking of the scene of the arrivant is a thinking of a multitude of different relations between certain geopolitical spaces and the hope that might still be found in them. The arrivant helps us name what propels us to be open to the other, to invite it, to be hospitable to it, while respecting its potential withdrawal from meaning, that is, its irreducible otherness. Neither the languages of discrimination and nationalism nor even the rhetoric of well-meaning universalism appear adequate any longer to negotiate the transformations unfolding with and as the temporary borders between the highly differentiated site of arrival and an other who is always yet to come—even in the guise of a democracy. That the fiction of self-identity and unmediated transparency grows ever more difficult to maintain in the face of the arrivant's transgressiveness also means that questions of Eurocentrism and a new or reinvigorated sense of the political are opened up to their own self-differentiation, to the complexity that cannot be thought in isolation from their political urgency.

This opening up—which could be understood as a liberation or a making visible of what always already was the case, with a Freudian *Nachträglichkeit* that unfolds on the far side of this or that external intervention or application—this opening up also activates what already is excessive or supplemental in any French, German, or "European" cultural identity. In this sense, it could be claimed that the concept of cultural identity activates its political promise when it is transformed from within, rather than abandoned. This radical transformation from within remains necessary not because of any desire to implement its individual dogmas, but rather because it shares an irreducible elective affinity with concepts that remain undeconstructable, such as democracy and even justice itself. Thus, to remain faithful to undeconstructable concepts is also to break with them; one remains close to them by not following them. Just as nothing could be more enlightened than to criticize the Enlightenment—that is, remaining faithful to its belief in critique by radicalizing that critique and turning it against the very structure of thought and relations from which it emerged—so too no gesture of cultural identity could be more faithful than the gesture that perpetually undoes the notion of a cultural identity in a move that, rather than abandoning it, ceaselessly ushers its internal differences to the fore.

Homeless Photographs

For Derrida, as for Kracauer, questions that speak to the aporetic nature of cultural identity cannot be thought of in isolation from a consideration of the technologies of visual representation. Derrida explores these concerns in a meditation on televisual images as well as in extensive analyses of painted images and photographs,[42] while Kracauer addresses them in his theoretical works on film, in his Weimar essay "On Photography," in *Theory of Film*, and in *History*. Photography, for Kracauer, in important respects belongs to the domain of those homeless images that allow us to consider "modes of being which still lack a name."[43]

To consider the homeless image that manifests itself in Kracauer's meditations on photography is to attempt to return to that to which one can never properly return because one never can have left it fully behind: extraterritoriality. Kracauer himself theorizes the imbrication of extraterritoriality and the homeless image of photography when, in *History*, he locates them both within the "image-space" that Benjamin calls a *Bildraum*. The inability of photography to coincide with itself, its particular way of never being able fully to capture what it attempts to present, is elaborated in his Weimar essay on photography. As a spectral medium, then, photography is the name for a particular disjunction that simultaneously inscribes itself in and removes itself from history. "Ghosts," Kracauer writes, "are simultaneously comical and terrifying. . . . Now the image wanders ghost-like through the present, like the lady of a haunted castle. Spooky apparitions occur only in places where a horrible deed has been committed. The photograph becomes a ghost."[44] This haunted image of the photograph from Kracauer's Weimar essay reappears several decades later, in his discussion of the photograph in *Theory of Film* (1960), as well as in his final work, *History*. In both instances, it is the appearance of his grandmother's image that causes Marcel, the protagonist of Proust's *In Search of Lost Time*, to encounter the figure of finitude itself. There, the image of the grandmother is the homeless image of the one who, in a temporal disjunction, is both dead and going to die. In *Theory of Film*, Kracauer cites the following passage from Proust:

> I was in the room, or rather I was not yet in the room since she was not aware of my presence. . . . Of myself . . . there was present only the witness, the observer with a hat and traveling coat, the stranger who does not belong to the house, the photographer who has called to take a photograph of places which one will never see again. The process that mechanically occurred in my eyes when I caught sight of my grandmother was indeed a photograph. We never see the people who are dear to us save in the animated system, the perpetual motion of our incessant love for them. . . . How, since into the forehead, the cheeks of my grandmother I had been accustomed to read all the most delicate, the most permanent qualities of her

mind; how, since every casual glance is an act of necromancy, each face that we love is a mirror of the past, how could I have failed to overlook what in her had become dulled and changed.... I, for whom my grandmother was still myself, I who had never seen her save in my own soul... saw, sitting on the sofa, beneath the lamp, red-faced, heavy and common, sick, lost in thought, following the lines of a book with eyes that seemed hardly sane, a dejected old woman whom I did not know.[45]

Proust's Marcel encounters his grandmother as though she were a photograph—as though she had always already been a photograph. This photograph, lodged in the character's mind, reveals the writing of death, the thanatography, that is inseparable from the medium of photography. (Like Proust's recollections of the photograph of his grandmother, mobilized in Kracauer's theory of photography, Roland Barthes's reflections on photography, written about a century after Proust, pivot on a mourning of his mother, and her absent presence through a photograph that, while never shown in the text, nevertheless lies at its core.)[46] This recognition of the relation between the grandmother and death, the relation in which Proust understands that "my grandmother was still myself," also exposes him to himself as the one who is more than one, the one who exists, as a palimpsest, in the multiple and faintly visible traces of the many texts that intersect within him in order to make him who he is, even as he never can simply be "himself." Kracauer takes up this trope again in *History*: "No sooner does Marcel enter his grandmother's room," he writes there, "than his mind becomes a palimpsest, with the stranger's observations being superimposed upon the lover's temporarily effaced inscription." Continuing his spectral meditation in relation to the Proustian photograph, Kracauer writes, as if of himself, in a gesture that recalls the term "autobiophotography" from the title of one of Derrida's conversations:

> Sometimes life itself produces such palimpsests. I am thinking of the exile who as an adult person has been forced to leave his country or has left it of his own free will. As he settles elsewhere, all those loyalties, expectations, and aspirations that comprise so large a part of his being are automatically cut off from their roots. His life history is disrupted, his "natural" self relegated to the background of his mind. To be sure, his inevitable efforts to meet the challenges of an alien environment will affect his outlook, his whole mental make-up. But since the self he was continues to smolder beneath the person he is about to become, his identity is bound to be in a state of flux; and the odds are that he will never fully belong to the community to which he now in a way belongs. (Nor will its mem-

bers readily think of him as one of theirs.) In fact, he has ceased to "belong." Where then does he live? In the near vacuum of extra-territoriality, the very no-man's land which Marcel entered when he first caught sight of his grandmother. The exile's true mode of existence is that of a stranger. So he may look at his previous existence with the eyes of one "who does not belong to the house." And he is just as free to step outside the culture which was his own, he is sufficiently uncommitted to get inside the minds of the foreign people in whose midst he is living. There are great historians who owe much of their greatness to the fact that they were expatriates. . . .

It is only in this state of self-effacement, or homelessness, that the historian can commune with the material of his concern. . . . The most promising way of acquiring such knowledge is presumably for him to heed Schopenhauer's advice to the art student. Anybody looking at a picture, Schopenhauer claims, should behave as if he were in the presence of a prince and respectfully wait for what the picture may or may not wish to tell him; for were he to talk first he would only be talking to himself. Waiting in this sense amounts to a sort of active passivity on the historian's part.[47]

Among so many other things, this passage suggests how the spectrality of the photograph intersects with the homeless image that Kracauer evokes in his Denkbild "Farewell to the Linden Arcade." Here, the image of homelessness, as a homeless image, constitutes an instantiation of the state of extraterritoriality, that is, the multiple displacements of the self that are inextricably intertwined with the ways in which that self struggles to make sense of itself in relation to what it is not: the other culture, the other cultural identities, the other modes of belonging, along with all the other others who already are at work in the palimpsest we call the self. This "state of self-effacement, or homelessness" not only echoes the trope of the homeless image within the space of the photograph, it also shows that the extraterritorial inscriptions of such a homeless image can serve a critical function. Evoking Schopenhauer, Kracauer argues that rather than merely finding again and again in every image the confirmation of our previously held assumptions, we may learn to read by allowing the enigmatic image to speak to us, by allowing it to reveal and conceal its multiple secrets in its singular way. It is here, in each encounter with a never-before-seen image, that we must allow the visual text to reinvent us, assumptions, methods, and all. In this perpetual making and undoing, the photograph itself can be read as a homeless image of extraterritoriality.

In order to visualize some of the implications of the relations among extraterritoriality, photography, and homelessness, we may turn to a photographic image of Kracauer himself—a photograph that enacts his fractured self as a homeless image (see fig. 1).[48] Placing this photograph into syntactical relation with Kracauer's historical and philosophical concerns, we witness Benjamin's observation that "history [*Geschichte*] breaks down into images, not into stories [*Geschichten*]," while heeding Kracauer's methodological admonition that "the vast knowledge we possess should challenge us not to indulge in inadequate syntheses but to concentrate on close-ups and from them casually to range over the whole, assessing it in the form of aperçus. The whole may yield to such light-weight skirmishes more easily than to heavy frontal attack."[49] We could say that Kracauer's emphasis on the close-up touches both the logic of his Denkbilder and his philosophical engagement with the photographic image. His emphasis on the close-up also touches this photograph, which he made available, in partial detail, for publication in a reference book, the *Reichshandbuch der Deutschen Gesellschaft*.[50]

This extraordinary black-and-white photograph from about 1930—the year of Kracauer's Denkbild "Farewell to the Linden Arcade" and the year in which the increasing anti-Semitism of his employer, the *Frankfurter Zeitung*, forced him into an ever more decisive extraterritoriality at home—shows him sitting on his desk in half-profile, his right leg crossed over his left, wearing a shabby pinstriped suit, a light-colored shirt, and a bow tie, his melancholy gaze directed to the right. The top button of his jacket is illuminated, presumably by the photographer's flash, while the lower button appears dark, a play with light that demarcates a peculiar asymmetry along Kracauer's midline. Although we faintly perceive the black fountain pen that his left hand holds, his right hand is almost completely obscured by the shadow that hovers over the dark surface of his desk, a surface that is punctured only by the whiteness of what appears to be a slightly crumpled piece of paper in Kracauer's right hand. The windows above his head have a hauntingly distant quality about them: their white frames, which parallel the white paper on his desk, enclose dark panes that neither permit a glimpse of what lies behind them nor reflect what stands before them. These are windows that appear to belong to a no-man's land, the paradoxical visual instantiations, perhaps, of the interior of Leibniz's windowless monad. The dark, framelike space that bor-

Siegfried Kracauer. Photographic print of the surviving shards from the original glass plate (1930). Courtesy of the Kracauer Estate, Deutsches Literaturarchiv, Marbach am Neckar, Germany.

ders the photograph at the bottom and on the right contributes to this hauntingly claustrophobic effect.

The spectrality of Kracauer's photograph is augmented by the material fact that it was printed from the cracked glass plate that survived as part of his *Nachlaß*. Like the empirical Kracauer, the surviving image, a homeless image that, following a homeless life, survives the homeless one, is fractured and multiple, shattered and dispersed. Missing entire pieces, the fissured glass plate corresponds to the ruins and debris left behind by the sweep of history. The fault lines in the image effectively present Kracauer as a marionette, tied to, and manipulable by, the "strings" to which he seems to be attached. Significantly, one of these "strings" cuts through his left eye, disfiguring the face of the one whom the photograph commemorates. Here, we recall that for Kracauer it "is only in this state of self-effacement, or homelessness, that the historian can commune with the material of his concern." Indeed, the photograph, disfigured by history, works to enact this state of self-effacement and homelessness, staging its history and the history of the one whom it presents as a history of ruins and shards. As a homeless image, the photograph unwittingly stages something of Kracauer's extraterritoriality, reminiscent of Benjamin's allegory of his friend as a philosophical ragpicker who lives among the shards—the shards of the homeless image and the shards of history.

The transcendental homelessness of this homeless image, finally, also is enacted by the triangular void immediately above Kracauer's head. As if to literalize the German word for homelessness, *Obdachlosigkeit*, or rooflessness, a roof-shaped segment is missing at the top of the photograph. Is it an absent, triangular roof out of which one almost can imagine smoke rising from a chimney on the left-hand side? In the ruined image, an image shattered by the effects of time, war, displacement, and extraterritoriality, Kracauer emerges as the one who possesses no roof, only the thought of a roof, a roof that remains absent—absent either as a radical absence or as a distant presence that cannot be reached or read but that remains inscribed in his image. Its absence makes itself felt by leaving a trace—the contours of a void and the outlines of a ruined whole.

In 1927, a few years before this photograph was taken, Kracauer insisted that photography "represents what is utterly past, and yet this debris was once the present." As if commenting on the double future of his own image, Kracauer spoke to the fact that this photograph had yet to be taken and that it would survive after his death, explaining that the photograph's "ghost-like reality is *unredeemed*" and "consists of elements in space whose configuration is so far from necessary that one could just as well imagine a different organization of these elements. Those things once clung to us like our skin, and this is how our property still clings to us today. Nothing of these contains us, and the photograph gathers fragments around a nothing."[51] What the ruins of this image of photography both contain and disperse is the fragmented nature of what they record in and as history. Like the glass shards of Kracauer's melancholic image and the montage of broken fragments that once seemed to relate incontrovertibly to his skin, the photograph records the aleatory and contingent quality of any attempt to arrest the presentation of an object for good and to secure that presentation in a mimetic model of historical and subjective transparency.

Homeless Language: Only One, Not Ours

For Derrida, the roofless homelessness that Kracauer's sentences and images mobilize cannot be thought in isolation from an aporetic experience of language that opens up "the relationship among birth, language, culture, nationality, and citizenship."[52] While Kracauer engages this *Obdachlosigkeit* in the figures of multiple extraterritorialities, Derrida's nonautobiographical autobiographical reflections in *Monolingualism of the Other*, in concert with his more general concerns regarding the very possibility of autobiographical writing throughout his work,[53] consider this aporetic experience as it emerges in the tension that results from having only one language (French) without fully possessing it, from living in one's own language without being able to claim it as one's own, from speaking, reading, and writing a language that is neither native nor foreign, but both at once. Derrida offers the figure of a self in language, a self that seeks the homey comforts of speaking a language in a "severely idiomatic way, without, however, ever being at home in it."[54] The self here dwells, if it dwells at all, in a "language that fails, lastingly [*à demeure*], to reach home."[55] Taking as a point of departure his own experience of living in the French language as a non-French other, a Francophone Algerian Jew, who, along with other members of his community was stripped of French citizenship only to have it reinstated later, and who was subjected to colonialist policies—policies that marginalized "indigenous" languages such as Arabic and Berber in Algerian schools—Derrida reflects on fantasies of linguistic purity (including his own) and the ways in which one's multiply fractured relation to one's language modulates both the experience of cultural identity and its loss not simply as a lack, but also as something constitutive. In the belonging and non-belonging that language occasions, in its affiliations and exclusions, language raises questions about its own capacity to be possessed, in the double meaning of the word: "But who exactly possesses it? And whom does it possess? Is language in possession, ever a possessing or possessed possession? Possessed or possessing in exclusive possession, like a piece of personal property? What of this being-at-home [*être-chez-soi*] in language toward which we never cease returning?"[56] The openness of the question of linguistic possession also names a perpetual deferral of possessing a roof, the *Dach* of the *Obdach*.

The *Obdachlosigkeit* around which language turns cannot be thought without considering the distinction between identity and identification. As Derrida reminds us, "an identity is never given, received, or attained; only the interminable and indefinitely phantasmatic process of identification endures. Whatever the story of a return to oneself or to one's home [*chez-soi*], into the "hut" ["*case*"] of one's home (*chez* is the *casa*), no matter what an odyssey or bildungsroman it might be, in whatever manner one invents the story of a construction of the *self*, the *autos*, or the *ipse*, it is always *imagined* that the one who writes should know how to say *I*."[57] To the extent that identity has no a priori status but, rather, is invented and reinvented with every process of identification, the identity that a self possesses is subject to perpetual revision in the variegated events of identification. Indeed, the self that speaks of its cultural or linguistic identity evokes a process of identification with a particular modulation that temporarily makes it what it is. But because this self can enter legibility only in a series of identifications *with* something or someone, we may conceptualize its being, not in terms of its identity nor even in terms of its identifications, but rather in terms of its *identifications-with*. This "with-ness" of its identifications exposes the self to its dependence on the other, the one with whom or that with which it first can enter the process of identifying-with. This identifying-with—not unlike Heidegger's *Mit-Sein*, or being-with, but also not identical to it because of its refusal of all communal

Versammlung or a gathering-like convocation—tells the self that it emerges, if it emerges at all, only in and through an other, and that it will always have been affected by that encounter in as yet unforeseeable ways. As such, self and other become affirmative witnesses of each other, even of each other's aleatory nature, through the logic that links with-ness and the wit-ness.

This other can be language itself, even if that language it not fully and simply itself. What Derrida calls the "monolingualism of the other" is a form of experience and cognition that is not limited to the other inasmuch as that other is also at odds with itself and even constitutively traverses the self. The monolingualism of the other, then, which also is a monolingualism of the self, of the self in its relation to the other, marks the fact "that in any case we speak only one language—and that we do not *own* it. We only ever speak one language—and, since it returns to the other, it exists asymmetrically, always *for the other*, from the other, kept by the other. Coming from the other, remaining with the other, and returning to the other." In Derrida's own situation, "once access was barred to the language and writing of another—in this case Arabic or Berber—and to all the culture which is inseparable from it as well, the inscription of this limit could not not leave traces."[58] The traces of this monolingualism inscribe the movement by which one speaks a language, such as French, of which one also is strangely deprived, a language that one calls one's own without owning it. Monolingualism "conditions the address to the other, it gives its word, or rather it gives the possibility of giving its word, it gives the given word in the ordeal of a threatening and threatened promise: monolingualism and tautology, the absolute impossibility of metalanguage."[59] With the absolute impossibility of metalanguage—the *meta* of the with, the among, and the after—with this impossibility of the *meta*, the monolingual self, who may in fact speak more than one empirical language, is deprived of an originary identification with (a) language, an originary identification that could be called his own origin in language. To the monolingual self, there are thus only prostheses of origins, never origins "as such" or that are intact. The monolingual possesses an originary self without origin. As Derrida suggests:

The monolingual of whom I speak speaks a language of which he is *deprived*. The French language is not his. Because he is therefore deprived of *all* language, and no longer has any other recourse—neither Arabic, nor Berber, nor Hebrew, not any languages his ancestors would have spoken—because this monolingual is in a way *aphasic* (perhaps he writes because he is an aphasic), he is thrown into absolute translation, a translation without pole of reference, without an originary language, and without a source language [*langue de départ*]. For him, there are only target languages [*langues d'arrivé*], if you will, the remarkable experience being, however, that these languages just cannot manage to reach themselves because they no longer know where they are coming from, what they are speaking from and what the sense of their journey is. Languages without an itinerary and, above all, without any superhighway of goodness knows what information.[60]

Derrida continues, taking up the language of arrivals, arriving, and the arrivant that traverses his earlier reflections in *Aporias*:

As if there were only arrivals [*arrivées*], and therefore only events without arrival. From these sole "arrivals," and from these arrivals alone, desire springs forth; since desire is borne by the arrival itself, it springs forth even before the ipseity of an *I-me* that would bear it in advance; it springs forth, and even sets itself up as a desire to reconstruct, to restore, but it is really a desire to invent a *first language* that would be, rather, a *prior-to-the-first* language destined to translate that memory. But to translate the memory of what, precisely, did not take place, of what, having been (the) forbidden, ought, nevertheless, to have left a trace, a specter, the phantomic body, the phantom-member—palpable, painful, but hardly legible—of traces, marks, and scars. As if it were a matter of producing the truth of what never took place by avowing it.[61]

Hence, the experience and the event of the monolingual, understood either as an other or as a self, or as the traversal of each of these in the other, situates both the sense of homelessness that accompanies the insight into one's prosthetic—rather than originary—relation to language, native or foreign, acquired by birth or by choice, and, at the same time, the desire for an imagined dwelling, not only in an "imagined community" of others, as Benedict Anderson suggests, or in a gesture of "dissemiNation" that would mark the "liminality" of cultural identity, as Homi Bhabha imagines it, but also for an imagined dwelling in language prior to language, a first language before the first.[62] To read the self as an effect of the prosthetic status of origin—such as the original language, one's native home, one's cultural community, among many other things—is to identify the ways in which it engages in multiple *acts* of identification. These acts articulate an ever-renewed, ever-transformed self, a self that "itself" is the event of an arriving without arrival, the promise of an arrival or absolute translation to come. Here, the homeless self is itself a prosthesis. Just like the photograph of Kracauer's "spooky" lady of the haunted castle, and just like the haunted extraterritoriality encoded in the homeless image of Kracauer's own photograph, Derrida's experience of the monolingual, and all that it implies, hardly can be understood without the "spectrality of the phenomenon," which is to say, "the phantom, the double, or the ghost."[63] Phantoms and ghosts—it is these homeless images that both Kracauer and Derrida leave behind for us to learn to read.

Cultures: Transitions

The learning to read that Kracauer and Derrida ask of us is a sort of learning that transforms the very notion of cultural identity and the very thinkability of belonging, through language, birth, or blood, to this or that cultural realm. The call for this kind of learning to read connects these two thinkers to a whole constellation of other modern philosophers and writers who have meditated on these issues. To recall only those proper names that Derrida himself mentions in *Monolingualism of the Other*: Adorno, Hannah Arendt, Paul Celan, Franz Kafka, the Moroccan Abdelkebir Khatibi, Emmanuel Levinas, Franz Rosenzweig, and Gershom Scholem. While Derrida refers to Adorno's 1965 essay "On the Question: What Is German?" only in passing, Adorno's argument is well worth recalling here, not only because of his significance as a conceptual link between Kracauer and Derrida, but also because his "non-identical" thinking convenes with that of Kracauer and Derrida in a way that will prove fruitful in our engagement with the issues of language and cultural identity that dwell in the homeless images we have considered so far.

In "On the Question: 'What Is German?'" Adorno stages a careful transgression of the essentializing quest for "Germanness" and the ideology of a stable German identity. Having transgressed the ideology of a German essence, Adorno writes that it "is in the loyalty to the idea that the current state of affairs ought not to be the last—rather than in hopeless attempts to establish once and for all what is German—that the meaning this concept still may claim can be suspected to reside: in the transition to humanity [*In der Treue zur Idee, daß, wie es ist, nicht das letzte sein solle—nicht in hoffnungslosen Versuchen, festzustellen, was das Deutsche nun einmal sei, ist der Sinn zu vermuten, den dieser Begriff noch behaupten mag: im Übergang zur Menschheit.*]"[64] Adorno wishes to remain faithful to the idea ("Treue zur Idee") that the last word has not yet been spoken, that the definitive reading has not been given, that there will be an other that is yet to arrive—an other that is an other primarily to any ontologizing notion of what is German. By extension, the infinitely mediated complexity of the concept of Germanness should not be exhausted and closed off because of a delusional chase after its elusive essence in a single dominant interpretation. Such a violent positing would foreclose any faithfulness to what is to come. Adorno's transgression here consists in a double movement that opens up the concept of Germanness to difference and otherness without, however, abandoning the thinkability of that concept altogether. That is to say, he violates the concept even while remaining faithful to it. The double movement of this transgression enables him to suggest that what is German should not be posited in terms of an essential presence or a positive set of verifiable features, but rather should be sought in its fluid movement, its transition toward humanity (*im Übergang zur Menschheit*). Adorno does not advocate a transparent, communicative model of substitution, an exchange of one predetermined program for another; such a model would claim, perhaps too easily, to elevate a culture from a blemished Nazi past, for instance, to a new, higher, and Nazi-proof humanity. For Adorno, it simply would be delusional to assume that one could arrive once and for all at a stable concept or state of "humanity," a program that one easily could follow. Here, humanity, like its vital dimensions of ethics, justice, and democracy, always is still to come. In order to remain effective as the promise of a future—indeed, as the promise that there will be a future at all—these concepts never can be assumed simply to be present. Instead, Adorno locates the prospect of a future, a future Germanness, in the moment of transition itself. This new concept—if it is one—would suggest that what properly is German is its movement toward something else, rather than the programmed arrival at a secure new destination. It is most properly itself when it is on its way toward something else. This perpetual transition (*Übergang*) names the political stakes of Adorno's double reading—it is an *Übergang* that is still to be thought.

Adorno's *Übergang* helps us to imagine a subject of culture, even a cultural "self," whose identity no longer is measured by its allegiance to this or that nation-state, originary realm, or cultural space that could endow it with a determinate meaning. Rather, the cultural "self," to the extent that it becomes readable at all, migrates between cultures, the interstices of multiple cultural identifications. *Übergang* thus also names the state of being "between" cultures in a space that, on the far side of the mechanisms of assimilation that encroach upon any act of cultural recognition of otherness within a given hegemonic state or culture, first makes the gesture of recognizing cultural otherness possible.[65] This *Übergang* leads not to the promised land of cultural identity, but to the realm of extraterritoriality itself, where selves can be recognized as the ones that are gathered and dispersed in language.

Adorno's *Übergang*, his undoing of any fixed cultural identity in terms of what it is not yet and in terms of what it promises, can be thought of as setting the stage for the kind of work that Kracauer's and Derrida's texts will have asked of us. After all, what Kracauer's Denkbild of extraterritoriality and Derrida's monolingualism of the other will have asked us to consider, among so many other things, is the question of thinking and living in culture, of thinking and living culturally, even multiculturally, as a question of a certain homelessness: homeless images, homeless selves, and even homeless cultures. Both Kracauer and Derrida, each in "his" idiom and in "his" experience of expatriation, an experience that is singular at the same time that it is shared by many, invite us to expose cultural identity, even multiculturalism, to the plurality that these terms both name and exceed. That is to say, because of the internal tensions and heterogeneities in both thinkers' elaborations of the homeless—the tensions and heterogeneities that make it possible for us to speak of the promise and suffering of homelessness in the first place—these elaborations are exposed to their own multiplicities and non-self-identities. As Werner Hamacher puts it in his discussion of multiculturalism, "If the historical and structural *a priori* of every culture is its multiplication, then *one* multiculturalism cannot be enough, and there need to be *many* multiculturalisms. There must be more than one, there must be more than many, and thus, across cultures, there must be the possibility of more than that which today we still call cultures: this is the imperative of the *ac*culturations, alterculturations." For this, he continues, there "must be something other than culture and its mere multiplicity. It is the imperative of autonomization. This imperative must count, and must count many, but it cannot do so unless it exposes the countable cultures, in and beyond counting, to what cannot be counted."[66]

Without this exposure to its own alterities, even multiculturalism can be used as a concept that masks certain monocultural ideologies and colonizing gestures. If we open up Kracauer's extraterritoriality to its own internal extraterritorialities and Derrida's spectral monolingualism of the other to the plurality of monolingualisms that traverse it, there must be many extraterritorialities and many monolingualisms. Just as the autonomy that is promised by multiculturalization in order to deserve the politically charged promise of autonomy at all "cannot be only one autonomy, there would have to be many, innumerably many, and there is only one that would be too many, which would be one and only one," so there would have to be many extraterritorialities and many monolingualisms; in short, there would have to be innumerably many homeless images.[67] But such a multiple and perpetually fractured homeless image always is yet to come—it cannot simply be assumed to be present, lest it be mistaken for having a proper home, the false home that would be present in our stable hermeneutic decoding of that image, its reduction to one meaning and "the one" of meaning.

The homeless images that Kracauer's Denkbilder and Derrida's meditations offer us posit a cultural identity beyond cultural identity, a cultural practice in which one no longer is simply oneself and no longer simply one, the one who is present. Because the reality of this imagined cultural identity cannot be reduced to this or that form of presence—its desires, genealogies, contexts, overdeterminations, hidden filiations, promises, commitments, secrets, and debts always are *elsewhere*, invested differently, and not always fully visible—we must look for its homeless images *in the future*. But this future cannot be executed in advance, even by a program that would attempt to install a system of reading such homeless images with an eye to their futurity and with the best of intentions. Homeless images, if they do anything, challenge us to consider the ways in which they, and we in and with them, always are still to come, even as an other or as others. Homeless images, along with the extraterritorialities and monolingualisms that they perform, are homeless precisely because they still remain to be invented, thought, and read, again and again. *Read*: always already and always as if for the very first time.

4

Nazism and Negative Dialectics:

ADORNO'S HITLER IN *MINIMA MORALIA*

> The splinter in your eye is the best magnifying glass.
> —Theodor W. Adorno, *Minima Moralia*

One of the most painful splinters lodged in Adorno's philosophy is the specifically German version of a larger Western modernity run awry, the fascist splinter that is named National Socialism and that is brought into language metonymically through the proper name Adolf Hitler. The Denkbilder collected in *Minima Moralia: Reflections from Damaged Life* fulfill the general wish Adorno records in a letter to Walter Benjamin "not to reduce the figure of that charlatan to the dimension of the universally human" in which the "wide-meshed net of analogies proves so powerless where Hitler is concerned."[1] Rather, the fascist formation of thoughts and tropes that an annihilationist anti-Semitism facilitated in the form of Nazism needs to be thought, among other things, through the specificity of the event named "Hitler."[2] But what would be required of us—precisely beyond the self-assuringly heroic gestures of merely denouncing or even, predictably, "unmasking" Hitler—in an attempt to exceed the simplistic logic of analogy that Adorno suggests is so powerless in grasping Hitler? What would it mean for our understanding of Hitler, both politically and theoretically, to take leave of the symbolic certainty offered by the logic of analogy, moving instead toward the ironic unsettlings and figurative suspensions one encounters in radically allegorical readings? What if Adorno's confrontations with Hitler required us once again to consider the implications of the view, concisely formulated by Philippe Lacoue-Labarthe and Jean-Luc Nancy, that a "comfortable security in the certitudes of democracy and morality not only guarantees nothing" but actually may stand in the way of the ethico-political demand that an "analysis of Nazism should never be conceived as a dossier of simple accusation, but rather as one element in a general deconstruction of the history in which our provenance lies"?[3] What is it, finally, in Adorno's Hitler that makes him the emblem of a dark and singular otherness that nevertheless always already speaks in us and in our enlightened Western histories?

A text that unmasks the very gesture of unmasking, *Minima Moralia* should be read as a constellation that challenges us to think Hitler beyond the comforts of mere analogy and the secure ground of full understanding. As literary reflections from damaged life—not simply from Adorno's damaged life, but more generally out of damaged life itself: *aus dem beschädigten Leben*—the text was written in the shadow of Hitler.[4] To be sure, in the 1930s and 1940s, the phenomenon of Hitler sponsored a variety of cultural responses, from John Heartfield's Hitler photomontages and Bertolt Brecht's didactic play *Arturo Ui* to pop-cultural satires of Hitler such as those mobilized in the cartoons of Dr. Seuss and Walt Disney.[5] Perhaps most provocatively, the figure of Hitler was satirized in the 1940 film *The Great Dictator* by Charlie Chaplin, whose work occasioned theoretical reflections by his admirers Adorno and Benjamin and whom Adorno personally met at a bizarre party in Malibu.[6] But what distinguishes Adorno's engagement with Hitler from that of many others is the way in which it theorizes the abiding threat posed by every critique's subterranean complicity with the structure of thought that genealogically failed to prevent the very thing it criticizes. His engagement with Hitler therefore insists that those rational structures of enlightened logic that underlie the moment of critique may not always be distinguishable from the dialectical patterns of thought that created, among other things, Hitler's Nazi Germany. Thus, even a critique of Hitler may not reliably immunize itself against the dialectic of culture and barbarism that long preceded both Hitler and the critique.

Like *Maus*, the 1986 graphic novel that, according to its author, Art Spiegelman, was drawn "in collaboration with Hitler" even as it strove to undo the logic of Hitlerism, the Denkbilder that comprise *Minima Moralia* were written in collaboration with Hitler: composed by a German Jewish philosopher in exile, they turn on and against everything that the proper name Hitler touches.[7] One could imagine Adorno, in his complex and unorthodox engagement with Hitler, as a counter-image to the one satirized in Don DeLillo's ironic protagonist Jack Gladney, who, in the 1985 novel *White Noise*, is a professor of Hitler studies in the thriving Department of Hitler Studies at a midwestern college. Unlike DeLillo's troubled professor, Adorno engages Hitler and the speech acts and crimes authorized by that proper name in the variegated movement of language itself, that is, in a textual model of the political and the historical. Thus, Hitler, as a proper name and as a concept, traverses in a variety of modulations a significant part of Adorno's corpus (consisting of close to 15,000 printed pages published to date)—from his musicological writings to his *Notes to Literature*; from *Negative Dialectics* to his studies of contemporary culture; from his sociological analyses to his works on Kierkegaard, Hegel, and Kant; and from *Aesthetic Theory* to his extensive lecture notes, now being published, on metaphysics, moral philosophy, the theory of musical reproduction, and the concept of freedom. But perhaps nowhere is the immediate impact of Hitler on Adorno's thinking and being articulated more complexly than in *Minima Moralia*, written during and immediately after Hitler's dictatorship. Hitler inscribes himself into this work with singular force as an image of perpetual reflection. *Minima Moralia* performs, among other things, an obsessive meditation on Hitler as a political and theoretical category, a category that never left Adorno's writing after the fateful day of twin events, 30 January 1933, when Adorno's first book, on Kierkegaard, appeared in Germany and Hitler assumed chancellorship of the Reich. In this way, *Minima Moralia* becomes a prism through which Adorno's larger concerns with Hitler, and with ethical and intellectual life "after" Hitler, come metonymically into view.

I wish to suggest that Adorno's Hitler (both the Nazis' Hitlerism and the proper name itself that occurs some dozen times in the text) sheds light on the ways in which negative dialectics strives to open up a thinking after Auschwitz, that is, a thinking that would do justice not only to the memory of the atrocities perpetrated in Hitler's name, but also to the impossibility of its own undertaking by obsessively attending to the ghostly blind spots that negative dialectics wishes to recognize as the traces of its constitutive lack rather than to exorcise in an entirely understandable though ultimately misguided application of instrumental reason. I will therefore proceed in this chapter to advance my argument not by taking recourse to the teleology of a putatively stable narrative linearity, but rather by placing a series of excessive excursuses and obsessive digressions into a strategic constellation where they may illuminate each other in a number of relations that perpetually realign themselves. In short, this chapter performs its arguments through an Adornean parataxis.

From *Magna* to *Minima*: Questions of Language

Because *Minima Moralia* engages political and philosophical issues in a literary or poetic language, it is inscribed in the broader relations between poetry and philosophy, rhetoric and logic, that traverse Adorno's work. Before tracking Hitler in *Minima Moralia*, then, it will be helpful first to situate the politico-philosophical concerns of that specific text in the more general constellation of traces that are Adorno's signature.

Like Benjamin's siblings, Adorno's siblings—the siblings that answer to the names "philosophy" and "poetry," the rigorous logic of a conceptual system and the rhetorical flourish of aesthetic form—cannot be thought in isolation from each other. Because "aesthetic form is sedimented content," as his *Aesthetic Theory* puts it, any reading of Adorno's philosophical claims must necessarily travel through the paths of his tropes and the rhetorical *Holzwege*, or wrong tracks, that may lead us astray.[8] These paths of poetic presentation, curvy and unpredictable, may at times also lead the way to long-forgotten siblings who were considered hopelessly estranged, but whose projects, for all their irreducible otherness, still exhibit some subterranean affinities. Thus, for all Adorno's skepticism with regard to the logical positivism of the Vienna Circle's philosophy in general, and that of his contemporary Ludwig Wittgenstein in particular,[9] *Minima Moralia* nevertheless can be said to enact Wittgenstein's suggestion that "philosophy ought really to be written only as a form of poetry [*Philosophie dürfte man eigentlich nur dichten*]."[10] By theorizing aesthetic concerns in a language that is *itself* aesthetic, *Minima Moralia* enacts Adorno's double reading of the concept of *aesthetic* theory—without, however, claiming that philosophical and literary language are identical.[11]

In the expansive orbit of Adorno's oeuvre, *Minima Moralia* is especially sensitive to the imbrication of literary and philosophical language.

While it is traditionally read as a theoretically inflected autobiographical document, there is much to be said for also reading it as a poetic text that stages in its artistic movements the peculiar relationship between literary language and philosophy.[12] After all, perhaps more than any of Adorno's other texts, *Minima Moralia* defies the certainty offered by generic categorizations, self-consciously mobilizing literary devices and tropes, poetic figures, and artistic compositions that not only seek to transmit a conceptual content but self-consciously wrestle with their own status *as* language. *Minima Moralia* stages something of a narrative voice that is not always simply the author's. Like Nietzsche's ironic philosophical voices, the narrator of *Minima Moralia* inflects the text's sentences in such a way that one is tempted to read them *as if* they were spoken by a character. In this "as-if" mode, the text's rhetorical nature reveals itself. The language of *Minima Moralia* belongs to, among other things, the peculiarly philosophical realm of literature that Adorno describes in "On Lyric Poetry and Society." Like a lyric poem, *Minima Moralia* "reveals itself to be most deeply grounded in society when it does not chime in with society, when it communicates nothing, when, instead, the subject whose expression is successful reaches an accord with language itself, with the inherent tendency of language." It is here, on the path that language chooses for the speaking subject, that this subject encounters itself as an other in the otherness of language, an otherness that it itself speaks. In this philosophically charged "literary" moment, "language itself speaks only when it speaks not as something alien to the subject but as the subject's own voice. When the 'I' becomes oblivious to itself in language it is fully present nevertheless; if it were not, language would become a consecrated abracadabra and succumb to reification, as it does in communicative discourse."[13] Unfolding on the far side of mere communication, the lyrical sentences of *Minima Moralia* present the scene of a narrative voice that cannot simply come into its own, either in itself or in another.

To suggest that *Minima Moralia* conforms to Adorno's larger concerns regarding the imbrication of the conceptual and the literary is not to diminish its philosophical standing. On the contrary, the text enacts the kind of compositional principle that Adorno later explicitly demands of philosophy in *Negative Dialectics*. Emphasizing philosophy's "presentation in language," Adorno argues that "the presentation of philosophy is not an external matter of indifference to it but immanent to its idea [*der Philosphie ihre Darstellung nicht gleichgültig und äußerlich ist sondern ihrer Idee immanent*].[14] Adorno elaborates this idea when he suggests that

> philosophy, instead of reducing itself to categories, would in a sense have to compose itself first. Its course must be a ceaseless self-renewal, by its own strength as well as in friction with whatever standard it may have. The crux is what happens in it, not a thesis or a position—the texture, not the deductive or inductive course of a one-track movement of thought. Therefore, philosophy is essentially not expoundable [*referierbar*]. Otherwise it would be superfluous; the fact that most of it can be expounded speaks against it.[15]

In the attention to its own compositional principles, the perpetual weaving and unweaving of thoughts, and the abiding resistance to paraphrase that keeps all its thoughts and theses in strategic flux, *Minima Moralia* can be understood as Adorno's attempt to compose, as if in quasi-musical notes of the kind that structure his *Notes to Literature*, a new kind of philosophical stance in the unreliable language of the literary. This stance would be characterized, as Adorno puts it in "Words from Abroad," by "compactness and conciseness as the ideal of presentation, the renunciation of things that are self-evident, silence about what is already compellingly contained in the thought and should therefore not be repeated."[16]

In their self-reflexive attention to figuration and to questions of presentation, the tropes of *Minima Moralia* therefore show themselves responsive to Adorno's view that in "artworks nothing is literal, least of all their words."[17] Disregarding this view only "creates the illusion that what is said is immediately equivalent to what is meant," a mimeticist or referential fallacy from which Adorno's aesthetics, in theory and in praxis, works to depart.[18] "In its dependence on texts," Adorno reminds us, "philosophy admits its linguistic essence [*sprachliches Wesen*] which the ideal of method leads it to deny in vain. This essence has been tabooed in recent philosophical history, as rhetoric.... In philosophy, rhetoric represents that which cannot be thought except in language."[19] For Adorno, therefore, in philosophical thought "nothing is meant entirely literally," so that whatever conceptual work is performed, there is a rhetorical remainder that resists full assimilation into the logic and pure rationality of science and scholarship—*ein in Wissenschaft nicht gänzlich Transformierbares*. For those who regard the nonliteral or figurative qualities of language only as an embarrassment to logical thought that must be repressed or expelled, the "scientistic ridicule by the adults of what they consider mere 'thought-music' only serves to drown out the creaking of their moveable filing cabinets into which they deposit their questionnaires, the traffic noises of pure literalness."[20] On the far side of the mere transmission of this or that content, Adorno's own sentences thus work to enact the way in which, as we read in his *Aesthetic Theory*, "all artworks are writing, not just those that are obviously such; they are hieroglyphs for which the code has been lost, a loss that plays into their content." *Minima Moralia*, as a work of art, thus enacts the ways in which for Adorno "artworks are language only as writing."[21] The specific elusiveness of the text's figures and tropes cannot be separated from its aesthetic, cultural, philosophical, historico-political, and personal investments. As a philosophical and literary artwork, *Minima Moralia* therefore belongs to those aesthetic forms that, for Adorno, possess a cognitive content with a nonpropositional character.[22]

A poetic and fragmentary transcript of philosophical, cultural, and personal displacement, written in exile in Los Angeles between 1944 and 1947 and first published in 1951 upon Adorno's return to Frankfurt, *Minima Moralia* is a paratactical book of ruins: the ruins of life and the ruins of understanding. In 153 Denkbilder that interlace the reflection of personal experiences with meditations of philosophical and political importance, *Minima Moralia* convenes with the Denkbilder of Adorno's friends Benjamin, Bloch, and Kracauer, who by the time Adorno composed his text had already mobilized this aphoristic philosophical form in print. Just as in the writings of his friends, which also attempt to connect the most general philosophical reflection with the specificity of subjective experience, the textual and conceptual movement of *Minima Moralia* serves to enact Adorno's idea of micrological thinking. Indeed, in its textual movements, the book *is* micro-logical.[23] These textual movements circle around an absent center that they nevertheless refuse to relinquish. In this gesture of abiding renunciation and perpetual affirmation, they enact the sense that, as Helmut Schnädelbach writes, "Adorno's philosophy in truth consists of one single thought that, however, cannot be expressed in a sentence."[24]

Perhaps even more obsessively than in the other major works that Adorno completed in California—among them *Philosophy of Modern Music*, *Dialectic of Enlightenment* (with Max Horkheimer), and *Composing for the Films* (with Hanns Eisler)—Adorno's narrative persona in *Minima Moralia* assumes the voice of a radical negativity that appears to circle obsessively around the maxim, "There is no right life in the false one [*Es gibt kein richtiges Leben im falschen*]."[25] Despite the fact that *Minima Moralia* remains by far Adorno's best-selling and most widely read book, this negativity has from the beginning worked to divide its readers—at least those who refuse to make the refractory and slippery rhetorical specificity of *Minima Moralia* disappear, with Hans Robert Jauss, into a vague "literary process of modernism."[26] Thus, on the one hand, there are those who recognize in the work the inscription of the traces of Adorno's struggle with the Hegelian thinking of the System, a struggle with the ways in which the idea of universality threatens to do injustice to the individual while at the same time remaining indispensable as a category. As a representative of these readers, even Jürgen Habermas, Adorno's former assistant, who is not usually known for his openness to fragmentation and playful experimentation in form and thought, suggests that *Minima Moralia* wrestles with the idea of systematicity from within, ultimately resisting it in its fragmented, nontotalizing form, in a main work that resists the very idea of a main work: "With his *Minima Moralia*, Adorno constructed a worthy monument to this effect. For that which those who misunderstand him could consider an insult to him is a sign of honor: His main work is a collection of aphorisms. It is admissible to study it as though it were a *summa*."[27] On the other hand, *Minima Moralia* has upset many of those readers who wish for more hopeful or reassuring perspectives in the text's dark world of alienation, in which every last recess of resistance to a fully "administered world" seems to be always already co-opted and empty. In this regard, the commentary of one of the earliest readers of *Minima Moralia*, Thomas Mann, with whom Adorno collaborated in his California exile on the musicological dimensions of his novel *Doctor Faustus*, is representative of many readers' experience.[28] Although Mann considered *Minima Moralia* "magnificent,"[29] as he announced to Adorno in August 1951, he also added, writing from Pacific Palisades, a suburb of Los Angeles, in January 1952:

I have held on to your book magnetically for several days; it makes, day after day, for fascinating reading, though it can only be enjoyed in small gulps, as it is the most concentrated nourishment. It is said that the companion of the planet Sirius, which is of white color, is made of such dense matter that a cubic inch of it would, with us, weigh a ton. This is why it has such an extraordinarily strong field of gravity, similar to the one that surrounds your book. And all this in the face of the homey and inviting titles above your breathtaking figures of thought. No sooner has one said to oneself, "That's quite enough for today!," than along comes such a nice fairytale-like heading that one delves into a new adventure.[30]

By October 1952, the daily doses of Adorno's dark Denkbilder have left even a reader such as Mann, generally strengthened by the asceticism of relentless irony, craving some affirmative grounding: "If there were only ever a positive word from you, my revered one, that would permit as much as a glimpse of the true society to be postulated! Your reflections from damaged life too were lacking in this, and only in this. What is, what would be, the right thing [*das Rechte*]?"[31] Adorno's response to Mann, formulated in December 1952 in Santa Monica, illuminates the ways in which Adorno hopes to situate, ethico-politically and aesthetically, *Minima Moralia* and, by extension, his entire mature work to come:

I am less adroit at responding to your fundamental objection, the question concerning what is positive, and here I really have little else to say but that only a trickster gives more than he himself has. If anything has penetrated my flesh and blood from Hegel and those who put him on his feet, it is the ascetic stance regarding the unmediated expression of the positive. This is truly an ascesis for me, believe me, since the other, the more unrestrained expression of hope, would be much closer to my nature. But I always have the feeling that, if one fails to persist in the negative or moves too quickly into the positive, one plays into the hands of the untrue.

Citing as examples Stefan George and Nietzsche, both of whom, according to Adorno, were finally unable to persist in negativity, Adorno continues:

Now, I do not wish to push the twilight of the idols so far as to fetishize determined negation itself, and, if it is true that the powers of the positive have moved into the negative, then it is no less true that negation is justified only by means of the powers of the positive. I cannot tell whether these powers can even be articulated as such in our times, as it would have to happen, or whether ascesis has the last word, as much as I have grown accustomed, in the course of my life, to staring into darkness; in one corner of my heart I still believe that it will be possible.

Adorno concludes by calling into question the very binarism of positivity and negativity:

But in the meantime I would like to raise the question whether in the end the whole issue of the positive and the negative is inhabited by a *pseudos*, by something overproportioned that for the sake of its abstractness allows what is most important to slip away. After all, utopia is the concrete rather than being itself a general theory or a concise instruction for praxis, and every truly saturated contemplation, to which conceptual being certainly belongs, is the guarantee of precisely what is ground up between the principles. Telling you, the artist, about this means carrying owls to Athens [*Eulen nach Athen tragen*] who begin their flight at dusk.[32]

If Hegel, along with his readers Marx and Engels, instructed Adorno in the ascetic hesitation to endorse this or that counter-system even in the moment of critique, then it would be his task to articulate the ways in which negativity can be marshaled in the service of something that even a radical concept of critique is not prepared to renounce. But unlike Aristotle's *Magna Moralia*, whose title it both conjures and inverts, *Minima Moralia* does not wish to present a "great ethics" or a normatively inflected system that could objectively instruct one in the ideas of the virtues and in how to conduct one's life. Rather, it focuses on the remnants of thinking and on the possibilities of ethical behavior after the collapse of metaphysics and after the traumas of Nazism. It is a "small ethics" in that it does not seek its ethical stance in a normative system grounded in universal certainty, but rather investigates the way in which the remnants of ethics can be mobilized only in the ruins of thought itself, that is, in terms of the possibilities that only the impossible may still offer. The notion that "es gibt kein richtiges Leben im falschen" thus presents an aporetic situation through which any ethics after Hitler must travel—much as for Nietzsche, to whom Adorno's formulation is indebted, an erroneous view of life is not only inseparable from a correct view of life but is even a necessity.[33] What interlaces the historical and the structural reading of Adorno's sentence (that is, its evocation of Nazism and its implicit reference to Nietzsche's aphorisms) is the sense that although there is no correct way of living in a system that is corrupt to its very core, this difficult impasse also opens up the possibility for future thinking and for the perpetual reevaluation of the possibilities for a life that does not yet exist but remains always yet to come.

The very impetus that propels Adorno to diagnose this state of affairs in *Minima Moralia* testifies to the future possibilities inscribed in the current impossibility. Adorno refrains from triumphalist gestures of optimism decidedly enough to be able to write the most exquisite prose of his oeuvre, without giving in to the pessimism that would have precluded the writing of *Minima Moralia* entirely. After all, if there were no hope inscribed in the hopeless, there would have been no reason for Adorno to record this hopelessness so elaborately.[34] Rather, the act of writing *Minima Moralia* in a mode and mood of relentless negativity is performed in the name of something else, something unnamable that is yet to come, and as such embodies the hope that inscribes itself with every act of writing, with the very idea of writing. This is why Adorno writes "Es gibt kein richtiges Leben im falschen" (There is no right life in the false one) rather than "Es kann kein richtiges Leben im falschen geben" (There can be no right life in the false one)—the constative dimension of Adorno's formulation retains the weak echoes of a certain Benjaminian messianism and a Blochian "not yet." In this vein, his statement can be understood not merely as a form of resignation, but also as an implicit call to think the conditions of possibility for a transformation of the "false life" into something else, in which *richtiges Leben*, which itself remains to be thought on the far side of any attempts at *erpreßte Versöhnung*, the forced reconciliation that he so abhors, could theoretically become legible.[35]

Minima Moralia applies its philosophical stance—a kind of Hegelianism without Hegel, a Marxism without Marx—to two historico-cultural siblings of what Adorno calls the administered world: the Hitlerian political system that had driven him from Germany and the American culture industry as he witnessed it first in New York and later in California.[36] For Adorno, the relationship of these siblings, the political violence and propaganda-driven terror of German fascism and the amusement-based, distraction-oriented mechanisms of the culture industry in which thought is prevented from coming into its own, are related, among other things, in their careful manipulation of the consciousness of the masses. This manipulation of the masses, *Minima Moralia* tells us, "drove the prospective victims of Hitler's régime to buy, in paralyzed greed, the newspapers in which stood the measures announcing their own doom. Fascism was the absolute sensation: in a statement at the time of the first pogroms, Goebbels boasted that at least the National Socialists were not boring. In the Third Reich the abstract horror of news and rumor was enjoyed as the only stimulus sufficient to incite a momentary glow in the weakened sensorium of the masses" (*MM* 237; 271). Adorno suggests that the common father of these siblings, German fascism and the culture industry, was a fateful misreading or even repression of a certain dialectic of enlightenment, a misreading that failed to appreciate the ways in which the regressive and barbaric potential of even the most enlightened thought is always the dark underbelly of what is enacted in the name of reason. The failure fathered by this misreading is not simply the inability to engage in a putatively reliable diagnosis: *here* the application of reason is palatable and just, *there* it is misguided and regressive. Rather, the stakes of this failure of and in reading are so high because this misreading fails to reflect upon the ways in which the very possibility—whether realized or not, it matters little—of a dialectical turnover of reason into reason's opposite informs the ways in which we think about enlightened reason in the first place. That is to say, this specific misreading of enlightened thought dissimulates the more general question concerning the extent to which a threat not only threatens what it threatens but also transforms the thinkability of what it threatens. It forecloses reflection on the extent to which this very threat does not simply remain a threat that signifies the potential loss of something but, rather, can also be thought as a constitutive threat, as something that not only threatens but also enables the very existence of what it threatens. The forgetting or repression of the threat as a dialectical moment that hovers uncontainably between its status as an aberration from the norm and as a constitutive category of loss is the predicament of modernity. It is this predicament—inflected poetically, philosophically, politically, historically, and personally—that names the space in which the reflections of *Minima Moralia* find their subtitle: *Reflections from Damaged Life*.

To the extent that all the sentences of *Minima Moralia* are touched by this damage, they can be read, as Jacques Derrida suggests, as those sites in which dreams, even the most beautiful or hopeful ones, are touched by a negativity that will not let them persist.[37] We might add that Adorno's Denkbilder from damaged life not only bespeak or mourn damage, they are also dependent upon damage for their existence—no Denkbilder without damage. That is to say, just as the threat of reason, understood in this double coding of the genitive preposition "of," is to be read as both endangering and enabling the thinking of reason, damage should be understood as both an injurious loss and as the condition of possibility for writing. Indeed, what is to be transformed or compensated by the writing of *Minima Moralia*, the pain of damaged life, is also what first makes this writing possible. The pain inflicted by traumatic damage, though not reducible to the use-value of instrumentality that Adorno rejects in his denunciation of modernity's instrumental reason, is nevertheless a pedagogical tool, the tool of a pedagogy that unfolds on the far side of pedagogy: "The splinter in your eye is the best magnifying glass" (*MM* 50; 55). The splinter names a painful damage to the eye, since ancient philosophy the instrument of vision, understanding, and insight, and then, since the eighteenth century at the latest, the symbol of enlightened knowledge. It is precisely when vision and insight are interrupted by pain, when enlightenment is pricked by its blinding and spectral other, that this very interruption makes more visible what is to be seen and interpreted. The painful splinter damages the eye without destroying it completely. The splinter serves dialectically as one of Adorno's prisms.[38]

Minima Moralia here convenes with another book of aphoristic Denkbilder, Maurice Blanchot's *The Writing of the Disaster*. Blanchot, Adorno's contemporary and fellow theorist of the disaster of Hitlerism, reflecting on the world after Auschwitz and its terror beyond words, admonishes us: "*Learn to think with pain.*"[39] Just as Adorno's splintered eye continues to see even when it is in pain, Blanchot's imperative records the necessity of learning to think even when one is in pain, the pain of both personal and historico-political traumas. At the same time, learning to think with pain also means learning to think along with pain, to learn as one would from a teacher, to adopt the thinking that pain performs on its own, even when it is not with the one who suffers from it or who attempts to learn from it. To learn to think with pain would thus mean to tolerate and to emulate it all at once, to continue in one's own thinking even when that thinking is interrupted by the otherness of pain and at the same time to learn that other way of thinking, to think the way that pain thinks both when it traumatizes us and when it is off on its own. Blanchot's propaedeutic demand—the learning that is needed in order to learn how to learn—illuminates the meanings of Adorno's splinter in the conceptual realm of their common experiential space, that is, damaged life and the writing of the disaster that this damage engenders. Without the pain of this splinter, Adorno could hardly have read, thought, or written.

Dedications and Interruptions

In the context of this pain, Hitler becomes the name of a principle. "If an émigré doctor says: 'For me, Adolf Hitler is a pathological case,' his pronouncement may ultimately be confirmed by clinical findings, but its incongruity with the objective calamity visited on the world in the name of that paranoiac renders the diagnosis ridiculous," Adorno tells us. He continues: "Perhaps Hitler is 'in-himself' a pathological case, but certainly not 'for-him'. . . . People thinking in the form of free, detached, disinterested appraisal were unable to accommodate within those forms the experience of violence which in reality annuls such thinking. The almost insoluble task is to let neither the power of others, nor our own powerlessness, stupefy us" (57; 63). In order, then, for us to have the ability to resist both the existence of external power and the absence of internal power, that is, to resist the ways in which they work to render us stupid, it must be predicated upon our recognizing Hitler not simply as a singular aberration but as a principle and, by extension, upon our ability and willingness not simply to attempt to work through this Hitlerist principle but also to trace the ways in which it constantly threatens to undermine the very apparatus that would first enable such a reflective coming-to-understand. This task is *almost*, but not entirely, impossible (Adorno speaks of a *fast unlösbare Aufgabe*), even while the category of the possible—absent as such but intimated by that of the only "almost" impossible, that is, absent only as a distant presence—is not guaranteed by any political or epistemological program that could predict its implementation in advance. In *Minima Moralia*, one of the privileged names for this lack of a guarantee is the proper name Hitler.

One way of situating Adorno's mobilization of Hitler in *Minima Moralia* is to read it in the context of the often-overlooked introductory dedication of this book.[40] Several pages long, this "Zueignung," or dedication, places the book in the hands of his friend and collaborator Max Horkheimer. The dedication is preceded by another, a short dedication in the more conventional sense. The dedication before the dedication, this dedication that is dedicated to the dedication that follows it, the primal dedication, this dedication before all others, the dedication that thus encapsulates the very idea of "dedicatedness," reads:

> Für Max
> als Dank und Versprechen

This dedication to the proper name of a friend, Max, even to the first name of the friend, is a most intimate and personal gesture, even though it

Adorno's Hitler in Minima Moralia   161

is made at the beginning of a publication, the most general and public forum. It is as though Adorno perhaps wished silently to object, in the space of language, to the memory of the unsavory coincidence that will forever have tied the day of the publication of his first book to Hitler's takeover of Germany in 1933, by dedicating *Minima Moralia* to his friend's birthday. He writes: "The immediate occasion for writing this book was Max Horkheimer's fiftieth birthday, February 14th, 1945" (18). This is also Valentine's Day.

Adorno's English translator, Jephcott, has a difficult time rendering the subtleties of Adorno's dedication when he writes:

For Max
in gratitude
and promise

The misleading replacement of the conjunction "als" (as) with a preposition ("in") is more than a grammatical infidelity. It elides much of what *Minima Moralia* wishes to enact. Adorno's predicative conjunction "als" suggests that the Denkbilder to follow are offered to the friend both in terms of something ("als" describing the characteristics) and in the place of something ("als" describing that for which the text is meant as a substitute). Introduced and connected by what could be called a performative conjunction, the two terms, *Dank* and *Versprechen*, both open the text and remain operative throughout it. They situate the temporality of the act of writing precisely by removing it from the logic of temporality inscribed in the act of writing the dedication: writing here takes places both in and for the past (that for which *Dank* is due and which thus must already have occurred) and in and for the future (that for which the following book is a *Versprechen*, or promise). Thus, while the dedication looks both backward and forward, it can be said to unfold in a kind of interruption of time, the literary space that opens up in and to writing when it takes stock while at the same time offering a promise.

But *Dank* and *Versprechen* signify even more in Adorno's dedication. *Versprechen* in German means both to promise and to misspeak, and Adorno signals the uneasy ways in which promising and misspeaking are hauntingly interlaced. The promise may not be confirmable by a future repetition or reaffirmation, especially if that future repetition or reaffirmation must be made under the sign and proper name of Hitler.

At the same time, Adorno's dedication to his philosopher friend mobilizes the relationship in German between *Denken* and *Danken*, thinking and thanking, that first enabled *Minima Moralia* to be thought and thanked for. In order to appreciate the imbrication of the two words and concepts, distinguished only by a vowel, we may recall Martin Heidegger's discussion of them. As early as his 1929 inaugural lecture "What Is Metaphysics?" Heidegger thematizes the connection between *Denken* and *Danken* in the realm of poetic writing (*Dichten*). There, speculating on the ways in which being can be thought to be imbricated in the shifting constellation of *Dichten, Denken,* and *Danken,* he suggests that "*Danken* and *Dichten,* in different ways, probably stem from primordial thinking, which they require but without being capable of being a *Denken* in themselves."[41] Later, in his interpretation of Hölderlin's poetry, which is also informed by the nexus of *Dichten, Denken,* and *Danken,*[42] and in "What Is Called Thinking?" ("Was heißt Denken?"), Heidegger returns to these concerns. In his 1951–52 lecture "What Is Called Thinking?," held in the same year *Minima Moralia* was published, Heidegger elaborates on the ways in which *Denken* and *Danken* enable and illuminate each other. He asks: "What is it that is named with the words 'Denken,' 'Gedachtes,' 'Gedanke'? Toward what sphere of what is spoken do they point?" Heidegger continues: "Is *Denken* a *Danken*? What does *Danken* mean here? Or does *Dank* rest in *Denken*? What does *Denken* mean here? Is memory no more than a container for the *Gedachte* of *Denken,* or does *Denken* itself reside in *Gedächtnis*? How does *Dank* relate to *Gedächtnis*?"[43] By situating thought (*der Gedanke*) and thanks (*der Dank*) in their shared etymological ancestor *der Gedanc,* we also hear the echoes of *Gedächtnis,* or memory.

We could say that Heidegger here implicitly echoes Hegel's distinction between *Gedächtnis* and *Erinnerung,* that is, between memory as a kind of reflective thinking (encrypted in the aspect of *Gedächtnis* that relates to *Gedanke* and *Denken*) and memory as a nonthinking interiorization (*Erinnerung* as the mnemonic act of the one who interiorizes, *er innert*). In Heidegger's model, *Dank* is the gift that *Denken* presents, insofar as something that requires thanks always refers to something that comes from an other, something that is given (*geben, gegeben*) by the other as a gift (*Gabe*). It is here—in the gift that comes from the other, the gift that reaches us from the outside and that thus requires us to acknowledge the other—that we are presented with the thought of our own dependence on, and fundamental relatedness to, the other. When we experience this thinking form of thanking that the other inspires in us, then—in the act of receiving the other's gift, the gift that is the other—we remark the ways in which we are called upon by the idea of the other more generally. That is to say, in and through the other, we experience our fundamental relatedness to the other as our thinking opens onto the idea of relation itself. In this moment, we can begin to think the thanks that are due for the talent with which our existence has been gifted, our personal *Begabung* that becomes visible in the *Gabe* when it illuminates the relation of *Denken* and *Danken* in the act of *Dichten*. Heidegger's intuitions about the inexorable imbrication of thinking, thanking, writing, and memorializing that dwells in language help us to understand the debts that Adorno's *Dichtung*, *Minima Moralia*, owes to the thinking and thanking that Horkheimer's gift occasioned. *Für Max als Dank*.

To the extent that this relation of *Denken* and *Danken* is responsible for the *Dichtung* of the text, it can be said to take place in an interruption: the interruption of work, but also the work of interruption, an interruption that can hardly be thought in isolation from Hitler. This constellation of interrupted relations becomes recognizable if one recalls the circumstances of the text's production. "The major part of this book was written during the war," Adorno explains, "under conditions of contemplation. The violence that expelled me simultaneously denied me full knowledge of it" (*MM* 18; 16). Adorno tells us that the book's "composition took place in a phase when, bowing to outward circumstances, we had to interrupt our work together. This book wishes to demonstrate gratitude and loyalty by refusing to acknowledge the interruption. It bears witness to a *dialogue intérieur*: there is not a motif in it that does not belong as much to Horkheimer as to him who found the time to formulate it" (*MM* 18; 17). The interruption of which Adorno speaks is thus operative on more than one level: it marks the interruption that the writing of the poetic Denkbilder in *Minima Moralia* introduced into the production circle of his more sober philosophical treatises, it registers the general interruption that Hitler introduced into the working of the Frankfurt Institute for Social Research, and it encrypts the interruption of Horkheimer's and Adorno's shared work—especially the writing of the *Dialectic of Enlightenment*, out of whose final fragments Adorno partly drew his inspiration for *Minima Moralia*—by Horkheimer's serious illness.

Minima Moralia thus owes its existence to interruption, and its language could not have unfolded without the felt impact of this interruption. Even if the writing of these Denkbilder is predicated upon an ignoring of the interruption, this enabling ignoring depends on what it ignores, the interruption itself—because there can be no ignoring without something to be ignored. If every sentence in these Denkbilder is shared language, if every word belongs as much to Horkheimer, who did not write any one of them, as it does to Adorno, who did, then these words belong to an author who is more than one and no longer one. If Adorno tells us that the sentences in *Minima Moralia* are the transcripts of an interior dialogue, rather than a monologue or an external or actual dialogue with his friend, they belong to the ghostly conversation with a friend that takes place in the author, with a friend not as he "really" is but as he appears in the author in the form of an image, a multiplicity, and an other. Adorno thus acknowledges the ghostly ways in which the other speaks in, through, and as him, the ways in which the other always already speaks even when the self is not placing quotation marks around the voice that emanates from it. All of these mechanisms are triggered by the work of interruption.

If the common work of Adorno and Horkheimer—the work, for instance, that led them to coauthor, during the Hitler regime, *Dialectics of Enlightenment*—first needs to be interrupted to bring these two friends closer, if this interruption first makes possible the "specific approach of *Minima Moralia*, the attempt to present aspects of our shared philosophy" (*MM* 18; 17), and if, finally, Adorno mourns the writerly absence of his friend from his work by making the voice of the friend part of a ghostly dialogue and the structuring principle of the entire work, then Adorno's textual gesture points to the notion by which every friendship is permeated: the awareness of finitude.[44] That is to say, the friendship may come to an end, it may die. And even if it does not die, then the two friends will continue their friendship in the knowledge that one of the two will die first, and that even if they should die at the same time, they cannot die together. The experience of the singularity of their respective deaths both connects and divides them. One of the two friends will be left to himself, having to mourn the other's death. This is the mourning that is fundamentally inscribed in friendship, and in all *Denken* and *Danken*. In fact, Adorno eventually did die first, and Horkheimer was compelled to mourn at his friend's grave in Frankfurt. Speaking a few days after Adorno's death in August 1969, Horkheimer recalls how his friend "always spoke of his longing for the 'other,' without using words such as heaven, eternity, or beauty. And I even believe that it is the greatness of his project that he, by inquiring into the world, in the end meant the 'other.' Yet he was convinced that this 'other' could not be grasped by describing it, but rather by depicting the world, such as it is, with an eye to showing that it is not the only thing, and not the only thing to which our thoughts are directed."[45] We could say that in *Minima Moralia*, Adorno mourns his own future death in the guise of the possibility of the death of the elusive other for whom and for which he so deeply cares. Reading the lines of his dedication today, we see an Adorno of whom we can say that he is dead and that he is going to die, in the strange epistemo-grammaticological conflation of the past and the future tense that we encounter when looking at the image of a person who has died since his picture was captured.[46]

If interruption thus works both to connect and to divide these friends, making their writing and their thinking possible, then it is the work of interruption too that struggles, however obliquely, against a certain injustice. As a perpetual disruption of injustice, interruption sponsors a work of Denkbilder, *Minima Moralia*, in which damaged life can be reflected and in which the friend can be mourned as the other who will remain forever absent, even before his actual absence. Interruption, for Adorno, inaugurates the written attempt to "atone in some part for the injustice whereby one alone continued to perform the task that can only be accomplished by both, and that we do not forsake" (*MM* 18; 17). In the face of interruption, this refusal to forsake forever ties the speaking voice to the mute voice of the absent friend who nevertheless speaks through it, and the writing self is the I who becomes visible as the one who is always more than one, as the spectral "we."

Hitler, then, is a threat to the enabling interruption of *Minima Moralia* not merely because he interrupts in the wrong way, with brutal means and in the name of the wrong ideology, but because the uncontainability of the interruption—our inability to predict in advance how it will function, whether it will enable or inhibit or both—is itself interrupted. Hitler interrupts the interruption by imposing on it the stability of a single, monolithic meaning—the ideology of fascism—and he suspends the suspension created by the undecidability of the interruption by claiming to resolve its aporetic character.

Hitler: Genealogies of a Signifier

Adorno's Hitler is a signifier that threatens to cause a suspension, and even an interruption, of the interruption precisely in the moment when that signifier is assigned the stable meaning of a singular historical aberration alone. Adorno therefore argues that the "claim that Hitler has destroyed German culture is no more than an advertising stunt of those who want to rebuild it from their telephone desks. Such art and thought as were exterminated by Hitler had long been leading a severed and apocryphal existence, whose last hideouts fascism swept out" (*MM* 57; 63–64). Suggesting the genealogical imbrications of Hitler's barbarism, Adorno speaks of "a fatal confusion. Hitler eradicated culture, Hitler drove Mr. X into exile, therefore Mr. X is culture. He is indeed. A glance at the literary output of those émigrés who, by discipline and a sharp separation of spheres of influence, performed the feat of representing the German mind, shows what is to be expected of a happy reconstruction: the introduction of Broadway methods on the Kurfürstendamm, which differed from the former already in the Twenties only through its lesser means, not its better goals." Adorno therefore concludes: "Those who wish to oppose cultural fascism should start with Weimar" (*MM* 57–58; 64). For Adorno, aspects of the Weimar Republic become signs of the sibling-like imbrication of German fascism and the culture industry, but also the emblem of a certain genealogical continuity of the dialectic of barbarism and culture that defenders of a more triumphalist emplotment of the history of Western modernity have sought systematically to dissimulate. The task of reading this dissimulation turns in significant ways on our ability to read the signifier Hitler in terms of a dialectic of interruption and continuity. This dialectic of interruption and continuity is also the formal and theoretical principle that informs *Minima Moralia* as a whole.

The task of reading Hitler as a signifier that cannot be thought in isolation from the work of the dissimulation in which it participates also leads Adorno to trace some of the possible conceptual chains of substitutions and displacements that are genealogically encoded in this signifier. For instance, as Adorno tells us in the Denkbild "A Word for Morality": "If Cesare Borgia were resurrected today, he would look like David Friedrich Strauss and his name would be Adolf Hitler" (*MM* 97; 109). Borgia, Renaissance prototype of the highly gifted man of violence, an Italian adventurer whose father became pope and whose methods of obtaining and exerting power were considered more brutally unscrupulous but also more shrewd that those of comparable military leaders, here figures as the undead, the resurrected zombie. As a zombie, Borgia returns to reinstall his ferocious regime—a regime that significantly imbricates a will to power, political cunning, relentless brutality, Italy (later one of the so-called Axis powers), and the church—but in the guise of a new, split morphology. First, Borgia's outward appearance is that of David Friedrich Strauss, the nineteenth-century Hegelian philosopher who supported Bismarck and, in his critique of the Bible, argued for the substitution of Christianity by a new ideology of Darwinian evolutionism, an ideology whose application to concepts of race and nation were palatable to Hitler; second, in addition to this new Straussian body, Borgia would answer to the name Adolf Hitler, the signifier that can be said to encode within itself the history of a certain brutal ideological genealogy. The task of reading Hitler's dissimulations would thus also require the genealogical reading of the multiple cultural and political dissimulations in which this signifier is inscribed.

Just as, for Adorno, Hitler is not merely himself but can be thought in terms of interwoven ideological trajectories, Hitler does not necessarily need to be present for certain of the authoritarian elements of Hitlerism to find fertile ground. In the Denkbild "Second Harvest," we learn that certain rhetorical gestures in themselves may already contain the thinkability of Hitler's seizure of power: "The phrase 'Kommt überhaupt gar nicht in Frage' ['it's completely and utterly out of the question'], which probably came into use in Berlin in the twenties, is already potentially [Hitler's] seizure of power. For it pretends that private will, founded sometimes on real rights but usually on mere impertinence, immediately represents an objective necessity that admits no objection" (*MM* 110; 124). When the contingency of a subjective assertion assumes the rhetoric of objectivity, the guise of necessity works to legitimate the violence perpetrated in its name. Reading Hitler would thus require an infinitely close unweaving not only of the rhetorical structures that are produced by him and in his name, but also of all those more general aberrations of the rhetoric of persuasion and domination for which Hitler stands, figuratively, as a prosopopeia—the voice or mask of an absent or dead speaker.

If reading the signifier Hitler, whether in terms of a genealogy of violence or in terms of specific rhetorical gestures, requires a meditation on the epistemological principles underlying any such act of reading, then the view of history in which such readings are inscribed also deserves to be rethought. From this perspective, Adorno wishes to reconsider the validity of the Hegelian system, the very systematicity of the system, in the shadow of Hitler. Just as the dedication renders Hegel's presence in these Denkbilder ghostly, that is, conceptualizes Hegel as the one "whose method schooled that of *Minima Moralia*" but whose dialectical theory is also called into question by the same *Minima Moralia*, unfolding in "opposition to Hegel's practice yet in accordance with his thought" (*MM* 16; 15), so Adorno emphasizes the moment of radical negativity that threatens elements of the Hegelian system in a movement of critique that was first enabled by that very system. Thus, in a Denkbild entitled "Out of the Firing-Line" and carefully dated "Autumn 1944," Adorno writes of Hegel, Hitler, and Nazi technology:

Had Hegel's philosophy of history embraced this age [*Hätte Hegels Geschichtsphilosophie diese Zeit eingeschlossen*], Hitler's robot-bombs would have found their place beside the early death of Alexander and similar images, as one of the selected empirical facts by which the state of the world-spirit manifests itself directly in symbols. Like fascism itself, the robots career without a subject. Like it, they combine utmost technical perfection with total blindness. And like it, they arouse mortal terror and are wholly futile. "I have seen the world spirit," not on horseback, but on wings and without a head, and that refutes, at the same stroke, Hegel's philosophy of history. (*MM* 55; 61)

Adorno alludes to the section in Hegel's lectures on the philosophy of history that discusses the means by which the idea of the world-spirit of history finds its realization. There, Hegel offers three human examples of the realization of the idea of the world-spirit: Alexander, Caesar, and Napoleon. The idea of the realization of the world-spirit was facilitated by these historical leaders, Hegel says, and the respective ends these figures met offer versions of the ways in which these facilitators were discarded by history after they had performed their task: "They die young like Alexander, are murdered like Caesar, or are deported to St. Helen like Napoleon."[47] By adding Hitler's robot-bombs to Hegel's arsenal of historical figurations of the world-spirit, Adorno ironically calls into question the very notion of a world-spirit that is facilitated by great military individuals. While Hegel's model of the manifestation of the world-spirit depends on the idea of a subjectless subject, that is, the idea of a great human subject that is not the source but merely the subjective medium through which the dialectically operating world-spirit travels in order to manifest itself in objective terms, Adorno uses the image of Hitler's robot-bombs to problematize Hegel's model in deeply ironic terms: Hitler's robot-bombs can be read as the ultimate subjectless subject, the radicalized and fully technologized manifestation of the militarized world-spirit that, headless and blind, technically perfected yet utterly unseeing, serves to enforce the ideology of German fascism. That the militarized world-spirit can no longer be seen riding a mere horse—an allusion to Hegel's reported exclamation, upon seeing Napoleon, "I have seen the world-spirit on horseback"—but, rather more like Benjamin's tortured angel of history, is seen winged and disfigured, suggests that the age of the world-spirit came to an end with Hitler.

Finally, this logic, inseparable from the very idea of Hitler, is cast into sharper relief in the final section of *Negative Dialectics*, the meditations on metaphysics "after Auschwitz." There, Adorno tells us that a "new categorical imperative has been imposed by Hitler upon unfree mankind: to arrange their thoughts and actions so that Auschwitz will not repeat itself, so that nothing similar will happen. When we want to find reasons for it, this imperative is as refractory as the given one of Kant was once upon a time. Dealing discursively with it would be an outrage, for the new imperative gives us a bodily sensation of the moral addendum."[48] Referring to the difficulties associated with Kant's view, developed in the *Groundwork for the Metaphysics of Morals* (1785) and the *Critique of Practical Reason* (1788), that to the extent to which I wish to act in accordance with the requirements of the moral law, I must act in such a manner that the maxim of my individual action could and should become the articulation and formalization of a universal law, Adorno does not wish simply to depart from Kant's normative requirement that we attempt, in a necessarily infinite gesture, to ground our actions in such a way that they could become universal maxims of morality; instead, he wishes to raise awareness of the difficult impulse in post-Hitlerian thinking of seeking a universalizable morality of action even when we have no secure metaphysical or universal ground on which to stand.[49]

This impulse—the impulse that will not relinquish ethicality even in the face of its ungroundedness—is both ethically necessary and potentially impossible. This is why Adorno writes not of the abolition of the categorical imperative after Hitler, but of its transformation into a new, refracted form. This transformation would push the imperative to the limits of its own possibility and, indeed, would take the threats of its own limitations not as a mitigating embarrassment to the claims of his ethical relevance but as its precarious condition of possibility. Spelled out, the new categorical imperative would read something like this: Act only according to a maxim through which you can simultaneously will that it should become an expression of the universal law that Auschwitz or anything like it should not and will not happen again. That this new categorical imperative, in the moment it wishes to provide universal justifications for the claims made by the acts committed in its name and authority, proves as "refractory" as Kant's suggests that a thinking of that new categorical imperative should be sensitive to the demands made by its own blind spots and insufficiencies—not to eradicate them in the name of inaugurating a new universal principle of superior moral rationality, but rather to accept and invite these blind spots and slippages as constitutive and enabling categories of thought and action after Hitler.

"True" Thoughts After the *Muselmann*

The movement of thought that was opened up for Adorno with regard to the relation between Nazism and negative dialectics by the proper name Hitler takes its cue from a reappropriation not only of Kant, but also—in a reappropriation that can always only have just begun—of such other proper names as Hegel, Marx, Benjamin, and even Kafka, all of whom strive to think, in very different terms, a metaphysical system in the moment when it ceases to be metaphysical, when its very metaphysicality not only informs but also undoes it, a system that is, finally, both necessary and superfluous. "The innervation that metaphysics might win only by discarding itself," Adorno writes, "applies to such other truth, and it is not the last among the motivations for the passage to materialism. We can trace the leaning to it from the Hegelian Marx to Benjamin's rescue of induction; Kafka's work may be the apotheosis of the trend." Writing in the shadow of the proper name Hitler requires learning to read these other proper names, among so many others, and the materialist transition toward a metaphysics that strives to overcome itself as corrupt and outdated, even while theorizing why it is unable to do so. Therefore, Adorno argues: "If negative dialectics calls for the self-reflection of thinking, the tangible implication is that if thinking is to be true—if it is to be true today, in any case—it must also be a thinking against itself." It is here, in the thinking that faces its own aporias, the thinking that remembers not what, but that and why, it has forgotten—not in the synthesizing security offered by a reductive reading of the Hegelian Absolute, but in the perpetual cracks and fissures that traverse it—that the stakes of reading Adorno's Hitler are so high.[50] Therefore, if "thought is not measured by the extremity that eludes the concept, it is from the outset in the nature of the musical accompaniment with which the SS liked to drown out the screams of its victims."[51]

In light of the imperative to think a negative dialectics after Hitler, *Minima Moralia* therefore offers us the following one-sentence Denkbild: "True are only those thoughts that do not understand themselves [*Wahr sind nur die Gedanken, die sich selber nicht verstehen*] (*MM* 192; 218). If truth resides in a thought, for Adorno it is lodged in a moment of non-understanding. This true thought—is it a thought that shows the truth or is it true in the precise ways in which it fails to show the truth?—does not understand itself. Indeed, Adorno's sentence hovers between two possibilities of non-understanding. On the one hand, the sentence could be read to mean that thought does not understand itself because it is defective in one of two ways: either there is something that could be understood, but the thought fails to do so; or the thought's failure to understand results from the failure of something else to be understandable, in which case non-understanding is not the failure of the thought. On the other hand, although a true thought cannot be understood by itself, it is possible that it could be understood by someone or something else. After all, how could thought be expected to understand itself without recourse to a subject performing the understanding of the thought that the thought itself is incapable of performing? Vacillating undecidably between these various levels of meaning, the truth of thoughts is, for Adorno, inseparable from non-understanding. In other words, thoughts that could understand themselves would be untrue. If Adorno aligns the truth of thoughts with non-understanding and, by implication, the untruth of thoughts with understanding, then we might say that one of the reasons for this alignment resides in his wish to understand understanding and to inquire into the ways in which the simple arrest of understanding, along with the stability of meaning and the positive facts of knowledge that allegedly underwrite it, also threatens one's ability to question understanding. For, once understanding is achieved, the activities that lead to it, reading and interpretation, die. Understanding would thus be the death of reading and interpretation, just as in *One-Way Street*, the book of Denkbilder by Benjamin, the "work is the death mask of its conception."[52]

In a cultural situation determined by Hitler's fascism and the culture industry, in which a facile sense of having understood marginalizes the critical and theoretically infinite activities that may lead to understanding, there is little room for the thought that thinks understanding: "Only what they do not need first to understand, they consider understandable; only the word coined by commerce, and really alienated, touches them as familiar. Few things contribute so much to the demoralization of the intellectuals. Those who would escape it must recognize the advocates of communicability as traitors to what they communicate" (*MM* 101; 114). If we can understand Adorno's reflections on incomprehensibility, among other things, in light of the first sentence of this last statement, then, for him, what is to remain alive is the truth of the thought that is perpetually in need of understanding. Truth in this sense can be understood only as the perpetual deferral and keeping open of itself, as the suspension of all uncovered and stable truths. Such thoughts would be unusable for the concept machines of Hitlerism.

Adorno's maxim about true thoughts that do not understand themselves, thoughts that find their truth only in and as what they are not, convenes with the epigrams for the three parts of *Minima Moralia*. Each of these short lines or sentences enacts some of the movements of such true thoughts and the thoughts of truth that they evoke. In their textual "in-betweenness" these three mottoes simultaneously connect and divide the three parts of *Minima Moralia*, in much the same way that punctuation marks, on which Adorno so eloquently wrote, serve both to connect and to separate. As liminal yet terse interruptions that also work to facilitate, these mottoes can be read, both generically and conceptually, as condensed Denkbilder of the very thought of the Denkbild. They hover undecidably between different readings and stage some of what Adorno's "true" thoughts, those that are at odd with themselves, engender.

The epigram for part 1 of *Minima Moralia*, supplied by the nineteenth-century Austrian poet Ferdinand Kürnberger, enacts such a textual movement: "Life does not live" or "Life is not alive [*Das Leben lebt nicht*]" (*MM* 19; 20). Similar to the true thought that does not understand itself, the image of a life that does not live could mean, on the one hand, that this life is defective; it fails to do what it is supposed to do, that is, live, and instead may be dead. This would be a deceptive life, a life that has perhaps masked its failure to live or to be alive, because in order for it to earn the continued designation "life" it must surely be thought to live. On the other hand, the sentence could also mean not that it is life that performs the activity of living, but rather that this activity is performed by those who are alive, that is, those who have life, rather than by life itself. Instead of valorizing a certain side-by-side-ness of the possibilities, Adorno's method would ask us to consider the ways in which one reading can hardly be thought in the absence of the other, in an effort to think through the transformations that these competing meanings of life will not cease to inscribe in our life-world.[53]

It is also necessary to read Adorno's citation of Kürnberger's "Das Leben lebt nicht" with regard to the reconceptualizations of the ideas of life and death that Hitler has forced upon us. After Auschwitz, during whose time the part of *Minima Moralia* that Kürnberger's sentence introduces was largely composed, the relation of culture and death cannot be thought of in isolation from a violent convulsion. Therefore, as Giorgio Agamben suggests, the "ambiguity of our culture's relation to death reaches its paroxysm after Auschwitz. This is particularly evident in Adorno, who wanted to make Auschwitz into a kind of historical watershed."[54] To help us think of this paroxysm, Agamben ambivalently takes recourse to *Minima Moralia*: "On the one hand," he writes,

> Adorno seems to share Arendt's and Heidegger's considerations . . . regarding the "fabrication of corpses"; thus he speaks of a "mass, low cost production of death." But on the other hand, he scornfully denounces Rilke's (and Heidegger's) claims for a proper death. "Rilke's prayer for 'one's own death,'" we read in *Minima Moralia*, "is a piteous way to conceal the fact that nowadays people merely snuff out."

Agamben argues that this "oscillation betrays reason's incapacity to identify the specific crime of Auschwitz with certainty. Auschwitz stands accused on two apparently contradictory grounds: on the one hand, of having realized the unconditional triumph of death against life; on the other, of having degraded and debased death." Therefore,

> neither of these charges—perhaps like every charge, which is always a genuinely legal gesture—succeeded in exhausting Auschwitz's offense, in defining its case in point. It is as if there were in Auschwitz something like a Gorgon's head, which one cannot—and does not want to—see at any cost, something so unprecedented that one tries to make it comprehensible by bringing it back to categories that are extreme and absolutely familiar: life and death, dignity and indignity.

Agamben suggests that one example of this category is the *Muselmann*, the one who is meant to remain invisible, who "wavers without finding a definitive position," and "who is inscribed in every survivor's testimony as a lacuna."[55] The term *Muselmann* was used in Hitler's extermination camps for those prisoners who had been traumatized physically and psychologically to such a degree that they had surrendered to their destiny of a slow death. A Muselmann would, for lack of nutrition, waste away and experience severe musculoskeletal decline. His respiration slowed down, and his ability to move so much as a limb gradually vanished. Vulnerable to abscesses and edema, a Muselmann, with brittle hair and an empty gaze, would often stink and be covered in dirt. In more ways than one, he was a living corpse in whom the line of demarcation between life and death was itself almost suspended. As Agamben writes:

> He is truly the larva that our memory cannot succeed in burying, the unforgettable with whom we must reckon. In one case, he appears as the non-living, as the being whose life is not truly life; in the other, as he whose death cannot be called death, but only the production of a corpse—as the inscription of life in a dead area and, in death, in a living area. In both cases, what is called into question is the very humanity of man, since man observes the fragmentation of his privileged tie to what constitutes him as human, that is, the sacredness of death and life. The *Muselmann* is the non-human who obstinately appears as human; he is the human that cannot be told apart from the inhuman.[56]

To the extent that the Muselmann suspends the certainty by which we can differentiate between the human and the nonhuman, between death as death and death as nondeath, that is, our ability to think these terms in a meaningful and determined relation to human experience, the haunting idea of the Muselmann cannot be separated from our general struggle to think after Auschwitz. Agamben's general reflections thus help us to liberate a further layer of signification in Adorno's citation. For if, as Agamben suggests, our ability to bear witness and to receive testimony after Auschwitz depends on our ability to think the paradoxical figure of the Muselmann—of the one who was present to witness yet could not bear witness, the one whose act of witnessing was inseparable from his own death and thus also the undoing of that very act—then we can suggest that Adorno's mobilization of Kürnberger's sentence encrypts within itself the challenges that the Muselmann places on thinking and living after Auschwitz. After Hitler, the words "Das Leben lebt nicht," it seems, can only be uttered and thought in the Muselmann's continuing wake.

If Adorno, through the voice of Kürnberger, places the rhetoric of life and death at odds with itself in order to help us think after Hitler, the motto that introduces part 2 of *Minima Moralia* takes a similarly self-destabilizing turn. Here, Adorno cites, in English even in the German text, a sentence by the British philosopher F. H. Bradley, who, like Adorno, finished by writing both with and against Hegel: "Where everything is bad it must be good to know the worst" (*MM* 83; 94). At first, this sentence seems to authorize a reading that focuses on the idea that, in a situation where everything is bad, it must be good to know the worst—perhaps because one can then think oneself prepared for experiencing the worst that one expects might come to pass in this bad situation, or, if one has experienced the worst already, one at least has the consolation that it cannot get any worse than what one already knows. However, if one knows the worst, then not everything in fact is bad—some things are in fact singularly the worst, not simply garden-variety bad. In that case, the truth upon which the first presupposition of the sentence relies, that everything is bad or that we are thinking about a place where everything is bad, is called into question. Likewise, if, where everything is bad, it is in fact good to know the worst, then everything no longer is bad there: if knowing the worst is actually good, then that knowledge renders the condition ("where everything is bad") something other than what it is said to be (bad). This excess of meaning is intensified by the undecidability as to whether the phrase "must be" is a constative, an imperative, or a speculative form, that is, if it makes a general truth claim ("it is always like this"), issues a command ("make it so!"), or imagines a possibility ("it is thinkable that it may be so"). Hovering among mutually exclusive readings, Adorno mobilizes Bradley's sentence to suggest the performativity of his own Denkbilder and their truth—a truth that is only true if it is at odds with itself. It is perhaps no accident that Adorno dates this part of *Minima Moralia* "1945": it sets the tone for learning to think in the wake of Hitler's defeat and "after Auschwitz."

The idea of a time of thinking and living in the wake of Hitler becomes concrete in part 3, dated 1946–47. That part is introduced by a quotation from Baudelaire's poem "Le goût du néant": "Avalanche, veux-tu m'emporter dans ta chute?" (*MM* 159; 182). By citing the French poet, Adorno implicitly returns to the sometimes heated debates over the significance of Baudelaire as a dialectical cipher of modernity that he conducted with Benjamin, for whom Baudelaire was the modern emblem of cultural production and decay in the Parisian arcades of nineteenth-century capitalism. By installing Baudelaire's line as the epigram for part 3 of *Minima Moralia*, Adorno not only continues a ghostly conversation with his dead friend, he also lodges the future prospects of thinking after the trauma of Hitler's fascism in the double movement of a rhetorical question. The questioning voice inquires of an avalanche, a natural phenomenon that here becomes a personified and thus addressable catastrophe, if it wishes to carry away the voice and its bearer in the movements of its fall and tumble, but also in its ruinous downfall and disaster. Here, the "veux-tu," the "will you" or "do you wish to" of the lyrical I, appears to hover between an anxious inquiry (please do not take me with you in your downfall) and an active request (please do). Adorno locates life after Hitler precisely here, on the slippery edge between the suicidal temptation of giving oneself over to the disaster and the wish to continue life in order, perhaps, to write—even if only to write the writing of the disaster.

Adorno's Innkeeper: Hitler's Barbarism, Freud's Rats

To elaborate what thinking true thoughts after Hitler, according to *Minima Moralia*, may ultimately require of us, Adorno offers, in *Negative Dialectics*, a disturbing story about a child and an innkeeper named Adam:

> A child, fond of an innkeeper named Adam, watched him club the rats pouring out of holes in the courtyard; it was in his image that the child made its own image of the first man. That this has been forgotten, that we no longer know what we used to feel before the dogcatcher's van, is both the triumph of culture

Adorno's Hitler in Minima Moralia   177

and its failure. Culture, which keeps emulating old Adam, cannot bear to be reminded of that zone, and precisely this is not to be reconciled with the conception that culture has of itself. It abhors stench because it stinks—because, as Brecht put it in a magnificent line, its mansion is built of dogshit. Years after that line was written, Auschwitz demonstrated irrefutably that culture has failed.[57]

The innkeeper's story requires that we linger over it, because it is not at first sight obvious how it illustrates the stance that Adorno has taken in his argument. At first glance, the utter brutality and violence perpetrated by the innkeeper, of whom the child is so fond, repulses us, and the thought that the child might model its image of man after this violent, club-swinging innkeeper—Adam, the first man, the prototype of mankind—may be justifiably disturbing. One may wonder about the extent to which this repulsive scene of execution influences the child and whether the witnessing of the innkeeper's killing spree may not also diminish the high esteem in which the child holds the innkeeper. It is possible that the child will henceforth live with a postlapsarian image of the innkeeper, the image of a man who has fallen and who is damaged by his own violence. At the same time, however, the temporality or causality of this scene of violence remains somewhat occluded. It is impossible to tell whether the child's witnessing of the innkeeper's violence is an aberration from the innkeeper's previously observed admirable behavior or whether the violence is a regular aspect of the child's fondness for him, in which case the scene of clubbing the animals to death is constitutive of the innkeeper's lovability. Either way, one may imagine a line of defense for the innkeeper's violence that would point to his legal and moral right to club these rats. After all, they are a pest intruding upon his property, carrying diseases with them and threatening his establishment. What is more, the innkeeper also has a responsibility to his guests, who in turn have a right to look to him as the proprietor for the maintenance of a safe and pest-free environment. Likewise, the dogcatcher's van—and Adorno's startling tropological shift from rats to dogs should be investigated, and investigated in a way that probes beyond its figurative preparation for Brecht's dogshit metaphor—the dogcatcher's van rounds up stray dogs in order finally to execute them, an exercise both brutally violent and inscribed in the culturally sanctioned program of urban order and cleanliness.

But Adorno does not decide either for or against the innkeeper, for or against the dogcatcher's van—or rather, he decides not to decide. Instead, he tells us, the fact that we have forgotten what we used to feel at the sight of the innkeeper's clubbing and the dogcatcher's van is "both the triumph of culture and its failure." One might ask, then, what precisely it was that we once felt at these sights, and why our failure to remember is not only the failure of culture but also its triumph.

To delimit this question with respect to Adorno's reading of Hitler and German fascism, it is useful to appreciate the ways in which his figure of the rat-clubbing innkeeper is deeply inscribed in a psychoanalytic dynamic. Adorno is acutely aware of the point that the mature Freud consistently argues, namely that there is a fundamental antagonism between culture and the economy of our libidinal and aggressive drives. These repressed drives need to be sublimated in order for a subject to participate in any construction of culture. There can be no culture without the sublimation of drives into what they are not: institutions, artworks, legal systems, social codes, and so on. But, once sublimated, these drives return to haunt, and in their aggressive and libidinal forms, they leave no cultural product or activity unaffected. The sublimated drives, according to the Freudian model, leave behind the traces of a perpetual *Unbehagen*, or unease, in our cultured selves. Indeed, just as throughout *Civilization and Its Discontents* (*Das Unbehagen in der Kultur*) the aggressive and libidinal forms of the sublimated drives perpetually threaten to return to haunt us, the rats keep returning to the innkeeper.[58] While the innkeeper Adam in this primal scene of the establishment of culture, owes the existence of his cultural institution to the elimination of rats, these rats cannot be repressed or sublimated for good: as uncontrollable waves of filth, they may return to rear their ugly heads at any moment.

It is hardly an accident that both Freud and Adorno take recourse to the image of the rat, and it is worth remaining with this image for a while in order to appreciate Adorno's negatively dialectical reading of Hitler. As early as 1909, some twenty years before *Das Unbehagen in der Kultur*, Freud emphasizes the significance of the figure of the rat in psychoanalytic interpretation. In his *Notes upon a Case of Obsessional Neurosis*, a case study that has come to be known as that of the Rat Man, Freud reminds us of the idea that "the rat is a dirty animal, feeding upon excrement and living in sewers," and of the fact that the "notion of a rat is inseparably bound up with the fact that it has sharp teeth with which it gnaws and bites. But rats cannot be sharp-toothed, greedy and dirty with impunity; they are cruelly persecuted and mercilessly clubbed to death by man, as the patient had often observed with horror. . . . He had often pitied the poor creatures."[59] The obsessional neurosis of Freud's patient revolves around a peculiar sanction called the "rat punishment," in which a person sits down naked on a bucket filled with live rats that crawl into the transgressor's anus to live and gnaw. In the course of Freud's extended analyses of his patient, we learn that the latter's rat delusion is a complex knot in which ideas of guilt, punishment, fiscal and psychological compensation, compulsive masturbation, Oedipal struggles, anal eroticism, and various infantile theories of sexuality are intertwined.

If these analyses at times seem like a bit of interpretive exaggeration on Freud's part, we may recall Adorno's admonition in *Minima Moralia* that in "psychoanalysis nothing is true except the exaggerations [*an der Psychoanalyse ist nichts wahr als ihre Übertreibungen*]" (*MM* 49; 54), and that there may even exist an essential and structurally necessary rapport between the very thought of a negative dialectic and the philosophical moment of exaggeration.[60] Through a series of bold metonymic links, Freud relates the patient's rat idea to a disturbed masturbatory response to his father's death; to the occurrence of the patient having bitten someone in his household as a young child; to his father's gambling debts (he was a *Spielratte*) and to the resulting relays between *Raten* and *Ratten* (interest rates and rats); the patient's quest for *Rat* (advice) and his trepidations about *heiraten* (getting married); to the fear, rampant among the patient's military cohorts, of syphilitic infection through the penis (as a filthy rat) inserted into the anus; to the penis-rat as a figurative extension of the anal autoeroticism that the patient experienced as an adolescent when he inserted worms into his anus for stimulation; and even to the idea of rats as uncultured children. For, reinscribing the imagery of Ibsen's Rat-Wife and of the Pied Piper (*Rattenfänger*) of Hamelin on which Ibsen's character is based, Freud relates the scene of the Rat Man as a young person at his father's grave: "Once when the patient was visiting his father's grave he had seen a big animal, which he had taken to be a rat, flitting by the grave. He assumed that it had actually come out of his father's grave, and had just been having a meal off his corpse [*und hätten soeben ihre Mahlzeit von seinem Leichnam eingenommen*]." This image of the rats gnawing at his father's corpse is significant because the patient "himself had been just such a disgusting, dirty little fellow, who was apt to bite people when he was in a rage, and had been fearsomely punished for doing so." Freud continues, citing a phrase from Goethe: "He could truly be said to find 'a living likeness of himself' in the rat. . . . According, then, to his earliest and most momentous experiences, rats were children."[61] Freud here refers to scene 3 of part 1 of *Faust*, in which Goethe has Mephistopheles say: "But to break through the magic of this threshold / I need a rat's tooth. [He conjures up a rat.] . . . Another bite, and it is done! [*Doch dieser Schwelle Zauber zu zerspalten / Bedarf ich eines Rattenzahns. . . . Noch einen Biss, so ist's geschehen!*]. Goethe's rhetoric of the rat reappears in the scene in Auerbach's Cellar, where we read, "For in the bloated rat he sees / A living likeness of himself [*Er sieht in der geschwollenen Ratte / Sein ganz natürlich Ebenbild*]." If Freud's Rat Man sees himself as the living likeness of the rat, then he situates within his obsessional psyche the perpetual conflict between the cultural demands made by the superego and the libidinal-aggressive transgressions lodged in the id that cannot be eradicated. Even without sharing the particular obsessional manifestations of Freud's neurotic patient, in the struggle of the relentless violence of our drives with the culture-building trajectories of our infinite sublimations, we are all rat men.

Adorno echoes the language of Freud's psychoanalytic rats in order to inscribe them into his own dialectical model of culture and barbarism, which turns on the name and concept of Hitler. Just as for Freud there can be no culture without the violent repression and sublimation of drives, for Adorno no culture can remain unaffected by the moment of violence on which it is always already founded. Indeed, for Adorno there is a constitutive moment of violence that resides in culture, an element of barbarism that is always already at odds even with the attempts to undo barbarism that a culture may profess on the surface.[62] Thus, the failure to remember what we used to feel before the innkeeper's clubbings and the dogcatcher's van is a failure to remember and to commemorate the interminable dialectic of culture and barbarism.

Yet, this forgetting is also a successful failure, the most successful failure of culture: it is only in the forgetting of the threat posed to its logic by its own interminably dialectical core that culture can keep its own other at bay long enough to establish itself as culture. After all, the radical dialectic of culture and barbarism cannot be "reconciled with the conception that culture has of itself," which is to say, the conception of a benevolent, enlightened culture that has overcome barbarism. It is not the fact that we have carelessly forgotten or simply failed to remember, with the best of intentions, that signals our fall, but rather that we have forgotten to remember how and why we have forgotten the violent dialectic of culture and barbarism. That is to say, in Adorno's model, the categorical imperative that Hitler imposed upon us after Auschwitz cannot be thought in isolation from our ability and willingness to remember that we have forgotten why our forgetting of the brutal dialectic of culture and barbarism is both a triumph and a defeat, both the condition of possibility and the utter bankruptcy, of our cultural system. Western culture has become Brecht's palace built of dogshit when it no longer can account for why it has neglected to attend to the essential impossibility of distinguishing fully between a triumph and a defeat. Brecht's dogshit is the stench left behind by the inmates of Adorno's dogcatcher's van.

It is because of this particular failure to fail successfully, that is, to fail in a way that would remain open to the ways in which failure is both a threat to success and its condition of possibility, that Adorno locates culture after Hitler:

> That this could happen in the midst of the traditions of philosophy, of art, and of the enlightening sciences says more than that these traditions and their spirit lacked the power to take hold of men and work a change in them. There is untruth in those fields themselves, in the autarky that is emphatically claimed for them. All post-Auschwitz culture, including its urgent critique, is garbage. In restoring itself after the things that happened without resistance in its own countryside, culture has turned entirely into the ideology it had been potentially—had been ever since it presumed, in opposition to material existence, to inspire that existence with the light denied it by the separation of the mind from manual labor. Whoever pleads for the maintenance of this radically culpable and shabby culture becomes its accomplice, while the man who says no to culture is directly furthering the barbarism which our culture showed itself to be.[63]

Here, Adorno does not simply give away what for him, *pace* Alfred Sohn-Rethel, belongs to the ur-sins of humanity, the separation of intellectual from manual labor. The garbage of which Adorno speaks, that is, both the food and the home of rats as well as the cultural remnants of what Hitler has left behind, cannot be merely disposed of, the way that the innkeeper rids his guests of rats or the dogcatcher's van raids our streets. To endorse culture after Hitler and to reject it wholesale are equally nonviable options, because both fail to do justice to the new categorical imperative, imposed upon us, as Adorno says, by Hitler—that is, that Auschwitz, or anything like it, must not repeat itself. This new categorical imperative would travel through the commemoration of the ways in which we have failed to remember why and how we have forgotten the brutal dialectic of culture and barbarism.

From this perspective, Adorno's famous and notoriously misunderstood lines, written in 1949, two years after *Minima Moralia* and, like *Minima Moralia*, published in 1951 in the essay "Cultural Criticism and Society," the lines that connect *Minima Moralia* and the later *Negative Dialectics*, are illuminated in a different light:

> The more total society becomes, the greater the reification of the mind and the more paradoxical its effort to escape reification on its own. Even the most extreme consciousness of doom threatens to degenerate into idle chatter. Cultural criticism finds itself faced with the final stage of the dialectic of culture and barbarism. To write poetry after Auschwitz is barbaric, and this gnaws even at the cognition [*und das frißt auch die Erkenntnis an*] of why it has become impossible to write poetry today. Absolute reification, which presupposed intellectual progress as one of its elements, is now preparing to absorb the mind entirely. Critical intelligence cannot be equal to this challenge as long as it confines itself to self-satisfied contemplation.[64]

It is conceptually important to note that the published English translation of Adorno's essay renders the phrase "das frißt auch die Erkenntnis an" as "this corrodes even the knowledge." But the language of corrosion is today mainly reserved for chemical processes; it succeeds in capturing the gnawing and biting of Adorno's *anfressen* only if one reliteralizes its figurative qualities by tracing "to corrode" back, via the Middle English *corroden*, to the Latin *corrodere*—"to gnaw away." In the context of our discussion, it is hardly an accident that Adorno takes recourse to the gnawing and biting language of *anfressen—fressen*, a biting and gnawing that, in contrast to the human activity of eating, *essen*, is reserved to animals—in order to make his point. Just as the rats of the innkeeper return to subvert his cultural establishment, and just as the rats figure as Freud's image of choice for the struggle between drives and culture, the rhetoric of gnawing and biting here stages the potential threat to which any cognition is exposed. For Adorno, cognition is gnawed at by the rats, just like the corpse of the Rat Man's father. There can be no cognition without this perpetual gnawing and undermining. (*Rats!*)

Rather than claiming that Auschwitz has made writing poetry barbaric and that it thus no longer ought to be practiced—a tenacious misreading, made for entirely understandable political reasons—Adorno suggests that Hitler and the genocide that his dictatorship facilitated are the "final stage" of a dialectic of culture and barbarism. This view implies that this dialectic preceded Hitler; the rats had been at work all along. Adorno argues that writing poetry after Auschwitz, that is, producing art, is barbaric—but *not* that it should not be practiced. If the dialectic of culture and barbarism goes back long before Hitler—indeed, as far back as the innkeeper named Adam—then the writing of poetry has always been barbaric. What changed after Auschwitz was that the dialectic of culture and barbarism, and the reification of the mind whose sibling forms are German fascism and the culture industry, could no longer be so effectively and so violently dissimulated. Hitler, then, was not simply an interruption of cultural tradition, but also the interruption of a dissimulation that worked to hide a brutal dialectic. Just as Marx and Engels, in the *Communist Manifesto* and elsewhere, saw in capitalism the distasteful yet potentially revelatory force that robbed the power mechanisms of greed, exploitation, and the oppression of one group by the hegemony of another once and for all of their pretenses of serving a higher good (such as religion), so Adorno's Hitler serves as a violent supplement that makes visible, after the fact and with a kind of Freudian *Nachträglichkeit*, the dialectic of culture and barbarism that long preceded it.[65] As such, Hitler not only interrupts both a certain cultural tradition and the kind of enabling interruption that underlies *Minima Moralia*, he is himself the object of an interruption insofar as his intended unilateral or one-dimensional interruption is itself interrupted to yield a variety of uncontainable interruptions, including the one that may interrupt the dissimulation of a brutal cultural dialectic.

Adorno gives us a Hitler to think who is ultimately both radically singular and historically inscribed: historically inscribed in that he belongs to the brutal and genocidal human history of the dialectic of culture and barbarism, singular in that he made visible the workings of this larger dialectic in specific and formerly unknown ways (we think, for instance, of Nazism's special brand of modern state-sponsored industrial killing, the efficient systematicity of its annihilationist anti-Semitism, its intricate network of advanced killing camps, of its strategic genocide of the Germans' Central European neighbors, its brutal liquidationist programs that were mediated by an especially aberrant form of techno-fetishism, its highly self-conscious aestheticization of politics to achieve its goals, among many other things.) To say, then, that *Minima Moralia* is informed by the thinking of an uncontainable dialectic of interruption and continuity is to say that it wrestles with the very idea of Hitler's Nazi Germany as both a singular event and as a genealogically inscribed phenomenon that shares certain aspects with other catastrophes. If Adorno's project strategically decides not to decide once and for all between reading Hitler exclusively as a singular aberration and understanding him as a symptom of the larger dialectic that, for Adorno, long preceded Nazism, it nonetheless attempts to show itself responsible to the aporetic historical demand that the particularity of the phenomena, their event-structure, be given its due, but that at the same time their common measure with what preceded them not be repressed—as though the event, however catastrophic, had suddenly erupted one fine morning in an ahistorical vacuum. The stakes of such a double demand are high. For, as Berel Lang elegantly puts it, "one way to make something disappear is to place it, like a grain of sand in the desert, in a mass of supposed likeness."[66] Thus, a gesture of comparison that was initially meant to affirm specificity and singularity by emphasizing difference from comparable others may at any time have the opposite effect, the undoing of singularity through excessive comparison. In *Minima Moralia*, the signifier "Hitler" names precisely this larger perpetual historico-theoretical struggle.

"Hitler's Stupidity Was a Ruse of Reason": Between *Sturz* and *Fall*

Minima Moralia's Denkbild "Little Folk"—which contextualizes Hitler in, among other things, the shortcomings of Germany's industry in international competition, the failures of a "liberal" society for which even the Führer's consciousness was too "liberal," and the politico-cultural stupidity for which Hitler was but a symptom—ends with the apodictic statement: "Hitler's stupidity was a ruse of reason [*Die Dummheit Hitlers war eine List der Vernunft*]" (*MM* 106; 120). Hitler's stupidity, the violent stupidity without which there could have been no National Socialism and no Jewish genocide, was the ultimate act of barbarism. Thought in terms of a negative dialectic, however (that is, in terms of a dialectic that knows it properly was always already negative), Hitler's stupidity was non-identical with itself.[67] In spite of itself, it caused the "final stage" (that is, the most recent and perhaps most traumatizing modern version) of the dialectic of culture and barbarism—the dialectic that finds its articulation in an undialectically conceived administered world of instrumental reason—to become visible. Reason thus instrumentalized Hitler's stupidity to unveil its own dissimulations; but it did so in the mediation of a triple gesture: it used itself both in the name of and against itself; it did so in the very gesture of the instrumentalization that this unveiling eventually worked to undo; and it did so even in the form of itself as an other (that is, in the form not of itself but that of a ruse), which is to say that reason, usually said to be self-identical by its undialectial defenders, comes into its own in the place and in the appearance of what it is not (a ruse).

This triple mediation through which reason mobilizes Hitler as a ruse in order to affirm and undo itself constitutes one dimension of Adorno's reading of Hegel after the fall: after the fall of Hegel and after the fall of Western metaphysics after Auschwitz. To appreciate Adorno's strategy, we must recall that Hegel introduces the concept of "the ruse of reason" (*die List der Vernunft*) in his lectures on the philosophy of history. There, Hegel argues that the universal (*das Allgemeine*) results from the negation triggered by the encounter of the particular (*das Besondere*) and the determined (*das Bestimmte*). When particulars struggle with each other, exposing themselves to dangers that threaten their respective existences, the result of these struggles is the universal itself. Thus, the universal, and the very idea of the universal, are not threatened for Hegel, even as the struggles of the particulars, that is, the condition of possibility for the universal, are. For Hegel, the idea of the universal "keeps in the background, unthreatened and unharmed [*hält sich unangegriffen und unbeschädigt im Hintergrund*]," while the particulars engage in struggle. The process by which what enabled the general idea of the universal suffers damage or is lost once it has performed its task can be called "the ruse of reason."[68] Although for Hegel's philosophy of history, the idea of reason, anchored in the universal, is never threatened by the potentially violent struggles among the particulars and the individualities that give rise to it—this is, after all, its ruse—the ruse of Adorno's reason works *for* reason, stabilizing it so that it can manifest itself, but also causes itself to be decisively transformed. If

Hitler is the ruse of reason, then what occurred in his name and under his authority did not leave reason itself unaffected. On the contrary, the ruse that was Hitler unmasked the violent dialectic of culture and barbarism that, once made fully visible and subjected to a decisive reflection, cannot leave the idea of reason itself untouched. If we live and think "after Auschwitz" and if Hitler was a ruse of reason, then reason still is alive—but it has metamorphosed. As Jean-François Lyotard once wrote, "After philosophy comes philosophy. But it is altered by the after."[69] In the case of Adorno's uneasy image of Hitler as a ruse of reason, we could say that after reason comes reason. But it is altered by the after.

Adorno's writing about and after Hitler could be conceptualized as a ceaseless attempt to articulate the various modulations of the afterness of this after. It inquires into the ways in which the afterness of reason, and the thinking in which it finds its form, becomes its sedimented content. Indeed, many of Adorno's post-Hitler studies of the 1950s and 1960s, such as "Education after Auschwitz," "On the Question: What Is German?" "The Meaning of Working Through the Past," and "Why Still Philosophy?" all work to bring into momentary focus the question of this afterness.[70] What this afterness, brought about by Hitler as a ruse of reason, entails is the thinking of a fall. Neither simply a thinking of how and why the fall occurred, nor simply a diagnosis of fallenness, but the falling itself—a suspended and perpetual falling, as it were, the interruption of the model of departure and arrival, the blind spot in time that is named by the void between tripping and landing.

This perpetual falling, I wish to suggest, and the figure of Hitler as the ruse of reason that is responsible for it, motivates the thinking that unfolds in the crucial and enigmatic final sentences of *Negative Dialectics*. There, Adorno argues that "the need in thinking is what makes us think. It asks to be negated by thinking; it must disappear in thought if it is to be really satisfied; and in this negation it survives. Represented in the inmost cell of thought is that which is unlike thought." For Adorno, the "smallest intramundane traits would be of relevance to the absolute, for the micrological view cracks the shell of what, measured by the subsuming cover concept, is helplessly isolated and explodes its identity, the delusion that it is but a specimen. There is solidarity between such thinking and metaphysics at the time of its fall [*Metaphysik im Augenblick ihres Sturzes*]."[71] The radically non-identical thinking, the thinking that self-reflexively thinks the manners in which it is non-identical with both identity and non-identity, shows solidarity in that *Augenblick*, or blink of the eye, that catches a glimpse of metaphysics falling. The solidarity of this radical thinking of non-identical thinking and metaphysics in the blink of the eye during which it falls consists precisely in their common suspension of the teleology of departing and arriving, of the binarism of leaving behind and entering, and of the violent and false choice between full presence and remainderless absence. Rather, Adorno is concerned with the thinking of an afterness after Hitler that will not remain itself, that has departed from itself but has not yet arrived as something completely different. This attempt at a departing from metaphysics while acknowledging that departure cannot be fully achieved, this attempt at thinking non-identically while remaining open to the threat of thinking identically, that is, this attempt at thinking a negative dialectics that threatens to remain attached to dialectics—this is where Adorno hopes to posit any consideration of afterness, even as his thinking struggles to acknowledge that this very act of positing, to the extent that it runs the risk of becoming or even merely repeating metaphysical programs of positing, may itself already be an act that suspends the very suspension that it hopes to posit.

This is to say that the radically non-identical thinking that Adorno proposes would have to be aware of the difference between falling as a real *Sturz* and falling as a mere *Fall*, as in the threat of the *Rückfall*, or regressive falling back, that *Minima Moralia* stages at and as its end.[72] "The threatening relapse [*Der drohende Rückfall*] of reflection into unreflectedness," Adorno writes, "gives itself away by the facility with which the dialectical procedure shuttles its arguments, as if it were itself that immediate knowledge of the whole which the very principle of the dialectic precludes." Such a thinking works "violently to break off the movement of concepts, to arrest the dialectic by pointing to the insuperable inertia of facts." When this happens, we learn, "the thinker uses the dialectic instead of giving himself up to it. In this way thought, masterfully dialectical, reverts to the pre-dialectical stage: the serene demonstration of the fact that there are two sides to everything" (*MM* 246–47; 282–83). If the radically non-identical thinking of a negative dialectics, in the after of its own afterness, fails to differentiate between a *Sturz* and a *Fall* as a *Rückfall*, between, we might say, a lapse and a relapse, then it fails to progress, even with the best of intentions, beyond the kind of empirical positivism that, wherever it turns, sees only the simultaneity of various possibilities and that is incapable of theorizing, dialectically, its own cracks. Adorno's point is not that thought ought to construct a safeguard against this threat, a warning system or program that could tell us at any given time the difference between lapse and relapse, between truly non-identical and merely self-identical thinking. The proposal of any such system would be precluded by the very non-systematicity and openness to non–self-identity that it would be intended to propagate. Rather, the point is to think about the ways in which our knowledge of our perpetual inability to tell a lapse from a relapse, a *Sturz* from a *(Rück)fall*, inflects the ways in which we approach the very idea of non-identical thinking in the first place. That is to say, rather than viewing our inability systematically to ward off the intrusion of models of thought—a thought that we considered discarded and superseded for good—as a threat to the negative dialectics of non-identical thinking after Hitler, we might struggle to appreciate, in a nonprogrammatic and necessarily tentative way, how such a threat or difficulty becomes the very condition of possibility for any new thinking. Rather than seeing this failure as a mere (undialectical) failure, that is, rather than regarding our inability to decide between the suspending powers of *Sturz* and the regressive tendencies of *(Rück)fall* as a threat to our ability to think, we might invite it as a constitutive failure, a failure whose existence first makes our new thinking of non-identity thinkable.

That we cannot reliably tell a lapse from a relapse is the difficulty that opens up a new form of aporetic thinking, one that shows itself responsible to its own irresponsibilities and that seeks its possibilities precisely in the impossible. That non-identical thinking organizes itself around an openness to these threats names its singularity. If it failed to do so, then the thinking of non-identity would itself become a mere thinking of the identity of non-identical thinking and thus, as another form of a thinking of identity, cancel that which precisely resists identity in the non-identical.

The further consequences of this non-identical thinking were to be the subject of an intended continuation of *Minima Moralia*. While *Minima Moralia: Reflections from Damaged Life* spans the time of Adorno's experiences in exile from Hitler, the counterpart was to be a series of Denkbilder that centered on reflections from damaged life after his return to Germany.[73] This continuation of *Minima Moralia*, to be entitled *Graeculus*, never was completed, though numerous sketches and extensive drafts survive in the collection of his philosophical notebooks now housed in the Adorno archive. The projected title suggests how Adorno wished his teachings to be understood in the aftermath of the after. A Graeculus was a member of the Graeculi or "little Greeks," the tutors and teachers of the Roman ruling classes in the first century B.C. who were ridiculed by the likes of Cicero and Juvenal for even speaking about things of which they knew little. But Adorno wished to rehabilitate the Graeculi as those whose wisdom and classical erudition first made possible the education of privileged Romans. Thus, even though they no longer belonged to the fallen empire of Greece, revered by Romans as the unattainable and long-lost ideal of cultural and intellectual sophistication, the Graeculi, even as *little* Greeks, facilitated the attainment of a level of knowledge and reflection that otherwise would not have been available to Roman culture. As with the little Greeks, Adorno is one whose "little ethics" enact on the stage of culture after Hitler the difficulties and possibilities of thinking, even if this teaching offers no more than an uneasy thinking of non-identical thinking itself. But as with the Graeculi, Adorno as the Graeculus can be read in the ironic light in which Albert Einstein, upon arriving in Princeton, is reputed to have observed that thinkers and scholars were tolerated as Graeculi by the well-meaning local barbarians. Either way, the tentative lesson of Adorno as the Graeculus after Hitler, if there is one, concerns the relentless and elusive reading of an afterness, an afterness that includes the sense in which the Graeculi, as the teachers of an afterness, themselves are inscribed and implicated in that afterness—precisely to the extent that they themselves come *after* the original Greeks.

The ruse of reason that mobilized Hitler and that gives us non-identical thinking to think, the ruse that propels us to learn to read the meaning of afterness on so many different levels, is also what encourages us to find hope, not in the possibly delusional phantasmagoria of hope itself, but in the promise of the hopeless. According to the final Denkbild of *Minima Moralia*, the "only philosophy which can be responsibly practiced in the face of despair is the attempt to contemplate all things as they would present themselves from the standpoint of redemption" (*MM* 247; 283). The non-identical gaze cast upon these objects fastens not on how they present themselves now, but, in the conditional as-if mode, on how they would appear in an unpredictable futurity. The standpoint that now is out of reach and that dictates our reading and experience of the objects inhabiting the damaged life along with us is transformed, not in actuality, but by the non-identical thinking that thinks this standpoint of thinking as what it is not, that is, as something that both presents itself as itself now and as something that will be reread from a different perspective, as a different and evolving text, in an unnamable and hypothetical futurity. Therefore, the "more passionately a thought denies its conditionality for the sake of the unconditional, the more unconsciously, and so calamitously, it is delivered up to the world. Even its own impossibility it must at last comprehend for the sake of the possible. But beside the demand thus placed on thought, the question of the reality or unreality of redemption itself is almost irrelevant [*fast gleichgültig*]" (*MM* 247; 283). If thought thinks its own impossibility in the name of a possibility that refuses to remain unthinkable even when it presents itself as impossible, then the movement of thought that enables this thinking is facilitated by the hypothetical idea of redemption. From the standpoint of the thought-enabling function of redemption, its actual manifestation or "reality" would not seem to matter: it works to set thought into motion even when that thought seems to have been arrested for good.

Almost. After all, Adorno refuses to write simply that the reality of redemption is irrelevant—he writes that it is *almost* irrelevant or equally valid—*fast gleichgültig*. That this "almost" remains perpetually open, that it never is the last word but, literally and figuratively, the second to last word, not *das letzte Wort* but, as in *Minima Moralia*, *das vorletzte Wort*—this names the fragile promise of any negative dialectics after Hitler. Almost.

Coda

Always a reflection from damaged life, the Denkbild names our response to the constitutive loss that makes us who we are, an acknowledgment of our finitude. These friends, whose complex personal relations to each other were modulated by the genre of the Denkbild, shared this experience of finitude in their collective effort to articulate a new form of speculative writing that would reconceptualize critical theory. The Denkbilder that they wrote with, through, and for each other thus can also be read as miniature memorials, small gravestones that commemorate, even before the other's passing, the mourning to which all friendship is exposed. That friends can die at the same time but ultimately not together, that every friendship is inflected, from its inception and even before, by the futurity of finitude tinges these friends' Denkbilder with sadness. Perhaps each Denkbild is, among so many other things, also a tear of mourning. As Jacques Derrida writes on the occasion of the passing of a friend, all friendship is touched by such a tear:

To have a friend, to look at him, to follow him with your eyes, to admire him in friendship, is to know in a more intense way, already injured, always insistent, and more and more unforgettable, that one of the two of you will inevitably see the other die. One of us, each says to himself, the day will come when one of the two of us will see himself no longer seeing the other and so will carry the other within him a while longer, his eyes following without seeing, the world suspended by some unique tear, each time unique, through which everything from then on, through which the world itself—and this day will come—will come to be reflected quivering, reflecting disappearance itself: the world, the whole world, the world itself, for death takes from us not only some particular life within the world, some moment that belongs to us, but, each time, without limit, someone through whom the world, and first of all our own world, will have opened up in a both finite and infinite—mortally infinite—way. That is the blurred and transparent testimony borne by this tear, this small, infinitely small, tear, which the mourning of friends passes through and endures even before death, and always singularly so, always irreplaceably.[1]

For Derrida, the law of friendship also is the law of mourning and the law of the tear. As such, our friendships always will have been conditioned by the future absence of the other, even of the self in the other, and by the fact that one or the other inevitably will be left behind—as in 1940, when Adorno received news of Benjamin's suicide during the latter's escape from the Nazis; as in November 1966, when Adorno, Bloch, and Horkheimer, all in Germany, learned of Kracauer's unexpected death in New York from a lung infection; as in August 1969, when Horkheimer spoke at the graveside of Adorno; and as in July 1973, when reports of Horkheimer's death reached Bloch.[2] While Derrida works to formulate a series of axioms and laws that respond to the structure of friendship as mourning and finitude, he never fails to remind us that each death of a friend is singular, as he puts it, each time, the end of the world. Our friends, whether dead or alive, are absolutely singular and, at the same time, connected to each other and to us through the prospect of their and our shared finitude, a finitude that, sooner or later, will give rise to the tear of mourning and commemoration.

Like the friend who responds to loss with a mournful writing that cannot quite relinquish the hope that attaches to the writing of loss—after all, whoever writes has not quite given up, even when the writing occurs in a hopeless register—the Denkbild names the experience of finitude that will not relinquish the struggle for an otherness that is still to come and in whose unknown name the experience of thinking, reading, and writing from damaged life occurs. The Denkbild gives us the freedom of thought itself to think—in the aesthetic moment when it shows this freedom already to be at work.

Notes

A note on citations and translations: Wherever two references to an individual text are given, the first refers to an English edition, the second to a German edition. Where only a German source is cited, the translation is my own. I have modified existing translations where necessary in order to enhance their fidelity to the original.

INTRODUCTION

1. Jacques Derrida, *Positions*, trans. Alan Bass (Chicago: University of Chicago Press, 1982), 71.

2. Theodor W. Adorno, *Aesthetic Theory*, trans. Robert Hullot-Kentor (Minneapolis: University of Minnesota Press, 1997), 72; *Ästhetische Theorie*, vol. 7 of *Gesammelte Schriften*, ed. Rolf Tiedemann (Frankfurt am Main: Suhrkamp, 1997), 113. Hereafter abbreviated as "AT," with the English page number first, the German second.

3. Friedrich Nietzsche, "From: On Truth and Lie in an Extra-Moral Sense," in *The Portable Nietzsche*, ed. and trans. Walter Kaufmann (New York: Penguin, 1982), 42–47, here 46–47; "Über Wahrheit und Lüge im aussermoralischen Sinne," in *Kritische Studienausgabe*, ed. Giorgio Colli and Mazzino Montinari, vol. 1 (Munich: Deutscher Taschenbuch Verlag, and Berlin: de Gruyter, 1999), 873–97, here 881.

4. Martin Jay, *The Dialectical Imagination: A History of the Frankfurt School and the Institute of Social Research, 1923–1950* (Boston: Little, Brown), and Rolf Wiggershaus, *Die Frankfurter Schule: Geschichte—Theoretische Entwicklung—Politische Bedeutung* (Munich: Deutscher Taschenbuch Verlag, 1991).

5. Among these other affiliates of the Frankfurt School, it was first and foremost Max Horkheimer who also tried his hand at a collection of Denkbilder. Under the pseudonym "Heinrich Regius" he published *Dämmerung: Notizen in Deutschland* with a Swiss publisher in 1934. The collection, less polished and poetically stylized than those of his friends and colleagues treated here, turns on sociological topics that were to become core political concerns of the Frankfurt School's Critical Theory, including a critique of capitalism and its forms of bourgeois consciousness. Max Horkheimer, *Dämmerung: Notizen in Deutschland*, vol. 2 of *Gesammelte Schriften*, ed. Gunzelin Schmid Noerr (Frankfurt am Main: Suhrkamp, 1987), 309–452.

6. Although this planned volume on materialism never was realized, Bloch

expanded his own contribution to the project into his study *Das Materalismusproblem: Seine Geschichte und Substanz*, first published in 1972. Today it is volume 7 of Bloch's *Werkausgabe* (Frankfurt am Main: Suhrkamp, 1985).

7. Wiggershaus, *Die Frankfurter Schule*, 11.

8. Rolf Wiggershaus, "Ein abgrundtiefer Realist: Siegfried Kracauer, die Aktualisierung des Marxismus und das Institut für Sozialforschung," in *Siegfried Kracauer: Neue Interpretationen*, ed. Michael Kessler and Thomas Y. Levin (Tübingen: Stauffenburg, 1990), 284–95, here 284.

9. Jack Zipes, "Traces of Hope: The Non-Synchronicity of Ernst Bloch," in *Not Yet: Reconsidering Ernst Bloch*, ed. Jamie Owen Daniel and Tom Moylan (London: Verso, 1997), 1–12, here 3. For an account of the background against which the messianic concerns of the early Bloch and the early Benjamin gradually merged into the critical theory of the Frankfurt School, see Anson Rabinbach, "Between Apocalypse and Enlightenment: Benjamin, Bloch, and Modern German-Jewish Messianism," in *In the Shadow of Catastrophe: German Intellectuals between Apocalypse and Enlightenment* (Berkeley: University of California Press, 1997), 27–65.

10. See Mendieta's introduction to the volume "Religion as Critique: Theology as Social Critique and Enlightened Reason," in *The Frankfurt School on Religion: Key Writings by the Major Thinkers*, ed. Eduardo Mendieta (New York: Routledge, 2005), 1–17, here 12.

11. Walter Benjamin, *The Correspondence of Walter Benjamin, 1910–1940*, trans. Manfred R. Jacobson and Evelyn M. Jacobson (Chicago: University of Chicago Press, 1994), 148; *Gesammelte Briefe: Band II, 1919–1924*, ed. Christoph Gödde and Henri Lonitz (Frankfurt am Main: Suhrkamp, 1996), 46.

12. Theodor W. Adorno, "The Handle, the Pot, and Early Experience," in *Notes to Literature*, trans. Shierry Weber Nicholson, vol. 2 (New York: Columbia University Press, 1992), 211–19, here 212; "Henkel, Krug und frühe Erfahrung," in *Noten zur Literatur*, vol. 11 of *Gesammelte Schriften* (Frankfurt am Main: Suhrkamp, 1997), 556–66, here 557.

13. Theodor W. Adorno, "Brief an Ernst Bloch, 2. 10. 1937," in *Theodor W. Adorno und Max Horkheimer: Briefwechsel, 1927–1969; vol. 1, 1927–1937*, ed. Christoph Gödde and Henri Lonitz (Frankfurt am Main: Suhrkamp, 2003), 536–38, here 537.

14. Ernst Bloch, "Something's Missing: A Discussion between Ernst Bloch and Theodor W. Adorno on the Contradictions of Utopian Longing," in *The Utopian Function of Art and Literature: Selected Essays*, trans. Jack Zipes and Frank Mecklenburg (Cambridge, MA: MIT Press, 1988), 1–17; "Etwas fehlt . . . : Über die Widersprüche der utopischen Sehnsucht; Ein Rundfunkgespräch mit Theodor W. Adorno," in *Tendenz-Latenz-Utopie*, supplementary vol. to *Werkausgabe* (Frankfurt am Main: Suhrkamp, 1985), 350–68.

15. Kracauer in particular devoted a number of essays and books to the thought of Simmel. The most important among them is a monograph that appeared one

year after Simmel's death, *Georg Simmel: Ein Beitrag zur Deutung des geistigen Lebens unserer Zeit* (1919), as well as *Soziologie als Wissenschaft* (1922), a book that pivots on a dual analysis of Simmel and Max Weber.

16. Walter Benjamin, "On the Concept of History," trans. Harry Zohn, in *Selected Writings*, vol. 4, ed. Michael W. Jennings and Howard Eiland (Cambridge, MA: Harvard University Press, 2003), 389–400, here 392; "Über den Begriff der Geschichte," vol. 1 of *Gesammelte Schriften*, ed. Rolf Tiedemann and Hermann Schweppenhäuser (Frankfurt am Main: Suhrkamp, 1991), 691–704, here 697–98.

17. Ibid., 390 and 397; 694 and 704.

18. Ibid., 390; 695.

19. Walter Benjamin, "Berlin Childhood around 1900," trans. Howard Eiland, *Selected Writings*, vol. 3, ed. Howard Eiland and Michael Jennings (Cambridge, MA: Harvard University Press, 2002), 344–413, here 374; "Berliner Kindheit um neunzehnhundert (Fassung letzter Hand)," in *Gesammelte Schriften*, vol. 7, ed. Rolf Tiedemann and Hermann Schweppenhäuser (Frankfurt am Main: Suhrkamp, 1991), 385–433, here 416–17.

20. In the context of the early modern development, Benjamin cites, for instance, Ludwig Volkmann, *Bilderschriften der Renaissance: Hieroglyphik und Emblematik in ihren Beziehungen und Fortwirkungen* (Leipzig: Hiersemann, 1923).

21. Karoline Kirst, "Walter Benjamin's Denkbild: Emblematic Historiography of the Recent Past," *Monatshefte* 86, no. 4 (1994): 514–24, here 516.

22. Sabine Mödersheim, "Emblem, Emblematik," in *Historisches Wörterbuch der Rhetorik*, vol. 2, ed. Gert Ueding (Tübingen: Niemeyer, 1994), 1098–1108.

23. Here and in the rest of this paragraph, I follow the historical genealogy of the Denkbild as chronicled by Eberhard Wilhelm Schulz, "Zum Wort Denkbild," in *Wort und Zeit: Aufsätze und Vorträge zur Literaturgeschichte* (Neumünster: Wachholtz, 1968), 218–52, as well as Harro Müller-Michaels, "Herder: Denkbilder der Kulturen; Herders poetisches und didaktisches Konzept der Denkbilder," in *Nationen und Kulturen: Zum 250. Geburtstag Johann Gottfried Herders* (Würzburg: Königshausen & Neumann, 1996), 65–76, here 66–69.

24. Theodor W. Adorno, "Benjamin's *One-Way Street*," in *Notes to Literature*, vol. 2, trans. Shierry Weber Nicholsen (New York: Columbia University Press, 1992), 322–27, here 322f.; "Benjamins *Einbahnstraße*," in *Noten zur Literatur*, vol. 11 of *Gesammelte Schriften*, ed. Rolf Tiedemann (Frankfurt am Main: Suhrkamp, 1997), 680–85, here 680f.

25. Another basic issue worth exploring with regard to Adorno concerns the difference between Denkbilder and *Klangfiguren* ("sound figures"), the preferred term in his musicological reflections. One might interrogate the significance of the difference between a largely nonconceptual philosophical work that still will not fully abandon the conceptual along the visual-verbal mode of the Denkbild and the auditory mode of the *Klangfigur*. Adorno's *Klangfiguren* then would have be reread not only in relation to the Denkbild but also in relation to what Benjamin,

for whom musical *Klangfiguren* did not figure prominently, calls the "dialectical image."

26. Heinz Schlaffer, "Denkbilder: Eine kleine Prosaform zwischen Dichtung und Gesellschaftstheorie," in *Poesie und Politik: Zur Situation der Literatur in Deutschland*, ed. Wolfgang Kuttenkeuler (Stuttgart: Kohlhammer, 1973), 137–54, here 146. In addition to the seminal essays by Schlaffer and Schulz, more recent philological explorations of the Denkbild, together with extensive bibliographies, can be found in Ralph Köhnen, ed., *Denkbilder: Wandlungen literarischen und ästhetischen Sprechens in der Moderne* (Frankfurt am Main: Lang, 1996); Britta Leifeld, *Das Denkbild bei Walter Benjamin: Die unsagbare Moderne als denkbares Bild* (Frankfurt am Main: Lang, 2000); and Susanne Knoche, Lennart Koch, and Ralph Köhnen, eds., *Lust am Kanon: Denkbilder in Literatur und Unterricht* (Frankfurt am Main: Lang, 2003).

27. Theodor W. Adorno, *Minima Moralia: Reflections from Damaged Life*, trans. E. F. N. Jephcott (London: Verso, 1974), 16; *Minima Moralia: Reflexionen aus dem beschädigten Leben*, vol. 4 of *Gesammelte Schriften*, ed. Rolf Tiedemann (Frankfurt am Main: Suhrkamp, 1997), 14f.

28. Georg Wilhelm Friedrich Hegel, "Stellung der Kunst im Verhältnis zur endlichen Wirklichkeit und zur Religion und Philosophie," in *Vorlesungen über die Ästhetik*, vol. 1, vol. 13 of *Werke* (Frankfurt am Main: Suhrkamp, 1986), 127–44, here 130.

29. A question that cannot be addressed here but that deserves to be investigated in another place and at another time concerns the relation between the artwork as the post-conceptual other to pure abstraction and the Hegelian engagements with the trope of the "death" of art. If one were to follow the Hegel who lingers with the death or end of art, it also would be possible to read Schelling not exclusively as extending Hegel, as my following lines suggest, but also as reversing him in the sense that Schelling's project could be seen as revivifying the corpse of art that Hegel thought he had buried. In the meantime, compare further on the question of the "end" of art Alexander García Düttmann, *Kunstende: Drei ästhetische Studien* (Frankfurt am Main: Suhrkamp, 2000) and *Eva Geulen: Das Ende der Kunst; Lesarten eines Gerüchts nach Hegel* (Frankfurt am Main: Suhrkamp, 2002).

30. F. W. J. Schelling, *Philosophie der Kunst*, vol. 3 of *Werke*, ed. Manfred Schröter (Munich: Beck and Oldenbourg, 1927), 375–507, here 389 and 392.

31. Ernst Bloch, "Recollections of Walter Benjamin," trans. Michael W. Jennings, in *On Walter Benjamin: Critical Essays and Recollections*, ed. Gary Smith (Cambridge, MA: MIT Press, 1991), 338–45, here 340–41; "Erinnerungen an Walter Benjamin," *Über Walter Benjamin* (no editor named), (Frankfurt am Main: Suhrkamp, 1968), 16–23, here 17–18.

32. In recent years, philosophers who have taken up this question of the read-

ability of the world as a textual phenomenon include, among others, Hans Blumenberg. See especially such works as *Die Lesbarkeit der Welt* (Frankfurt am Main: Suhrkamp, 1986) and *Begriffe in Geschichten* (Frankfurt am Main: Suhrkamp, 1998).

33. Gilles Deleuze and Félix Guattari, *What Is Philosophy?* trans. Hugh Tomlinson and Graham Burchell (New York: Columbia University Press, 1994), 5.

34. Theodor W. Adorno, *Negative Dialectics*, trans. E. B. Ashton (New York: Continuum, 2000), 18; *Negative Dialektik*, vol. 6 of *Gesammelte Schriften*, ed. Rolf Tiedemann (Frankfurt am Main: Suhrkamp, 1997), 29.

35. Ibid., 33, 44.

36. Jacques Derrida, "The Law of Genre," trans. Avital Ronell, in *Acts of Literature*, ed. Derek Attridge (London: Routledge, 1992), 221–52, here 230–31.

37. The variegated formulations of the critical differences between inscription and description is at the core of de Man's essays collected in *The Resistance to Theory* (Minneapolis: University of Minnesota Press, 1986). For instance, in the essay "Hypogram and Inscription," in which de Man thematizes the "materiality of inscription," he argues: "Description, it appears, was a device to conceal inscription. Inscription is neither a figure, nor a sign, nor a cognition, nor a desire, nor a hypogram, nor a matrix, yet no theory of reading or of poetry can achieve consistency if . . . it responds to its powers only by a figural evasion which, in this case, takes the subtly effective form of evading the figural" (51). Much follows from these reflections. For tentative attempts to unpack some of these consequences, see especially Tom Cohen, *Ideology and Inscription: "Cultural Studies" after Benjamin, de Man, and Bakhtin* (Cambridge: Cambridge University Press, 1998), and the collection *Material Events: Paul de Man and the Afterlife of Theory*, ed. Tom Cohen, Barbara Cohen, J. Hillis Miller, and Andrzej Warminski (Minneapolis: University of Minnesota Press, 2001).

38. The paragraphs that constitute this section of the introduction are adapted and reworked from a review essay of mine, "Adorno's Scars, Bloch's Anacoluthon," *German Politics and Society* 18, no. 4 (Winter 2000): 93–112.

39. Theodor W. Adorno, "Commitment," in *Notes to Literature*, vol. 2, trans. Shierry Weber Nicholsen (New York: Columbia University Press, 1992), 76–94, here 93–94; "Engagement," in *Noten zur Literatur*, vol. 11 of *Gesammelte Schriften*, ed. Rolf Tiedemann (Frankfurt am Main: Suhrkamp, 1997), 409–30, here 430.

40. Bill Readings, *The University in Ruins* (Cambridge, MA: Harvard University Press, 1996).

41. J. Hillis Miller, *Black Holes* (Stanford: Stanford University Press, 1999), 49.

42. Christopher Fynsk, *The Claim of Language: A Case for the Humanities* (Minneapolis: University of Minnesota Press, 2004).

43. Fredric Jameson, "The Theoretical Hesitation: Benjamin's Sociological Predecessor," *Critical Inquiry* 25, no. 2 (1999): 267–88, here 267.

44. Adorno, *Minima Moralia*, 101; 114.

45. The terms of this intolerance and hostility are perceptively scrutinized in the essays collected in *Just Being Difficult? Academic Writing in the Public Arena*, ed. Jonathan Culler and Kevin Lamb (Stanford: Stanford University Press, 2003).

46. Paul de Man, "The Resistance to Theory," in *The Resistance to Theory*, 3–20, here 19.

47. Niklas Luhmann, *Liebe als Passion: Zur Codierung von Intimität* (Frankfurt am Main: Suhrkamp, 1994).

48. Roland Barthes, "The Reality Effect," in *The Rustle of Language*, trans. Richard Howard (Berkeley: University of California Press, 1989), 141–48.

49. See esp. Paul de Man, *Aesthetic Ideology* (Minneapolis: University of Minnesota Press, 1996), and Terry Eagleton, *The Ideology of the Aesthetic* (Oxford: Blackwell, 1990).

50. See Stanley Corngold's lucid perception of this point in his *Complex Pleasure: Forms of Feeling in German Literature* (Stanford: Stanford University Press, 1998), 176n.21.

51. Some of the terms in which this Adornean transformation can be thought specifically in relation to modernist painting are rigorously scrutinized in the new account by J. M. Bernstein, *Against Voluptuous Bodies: Late Modernism and the Meaning of Painting* (Stanford: Stanford University Press, 2006).

52. Ernst Bloch, "On a Simile in Keller," in *Literary Essays*, trans. Andrew Joron et al. (Stanford: Stanford University Press, 1998), 515–17, here 515; "Über ein Gleichnis Kellers," in *Literarische Aufsätze*, vol. 9 of *Werkausgabe* (Frankfurt am Main: Suhrkamp, 1985), 579–81, here 579.

53. "Simile," 516; "Gleichnis," 580.

54. Ernst Bloch, "Spoken and Written Syntax: Anacoluthon," in *Literary Essays*, 497–504, here 504; "Gesprochene und geschriebene Syntax: Anacoluth," in *Literarische Essays*, 560–67, here 567.

55. Sigmund Freud, "Trauer und Melancholie," in *Psychologie des Unbewußten*, Studienausgabe 3, ed. Alexander Mitscherlich, Angela Richards, and James Strachey (Frankfurt am Main: Fischer, 2000), 193–212.

56. For a historical reconsideration of loss, commemoration, and melancholia with regard to Benjamin's specific experience of World War I, see Martin Jay, "Walter Benjamin, Remembrance, and the First World War," *Benjamin Studies/Studien* 1 (2002): 185–208.

57. Theodor W. Adorno, "On Lyric Poetry and Society," in *Notes to Literature*, vol. 1, trans. Shierry Weber Nicholsen (New York: Columbia University Press, 1991), 37–54, here 43–44; "Rede über Lyrik und Gesellschaft," in *Noten zur Literatur, Gesammelte Schriften* 11:49–68, here 56–57.

For an insightful recent reading of Adorno's programmatic essay "On Lyric Poetry and Society" in light of related concerns, see Robert Kaufman, "Adorno's

Social Lyric, and Literary Criticism Today: Poetics, Aesthetics, Modernity," in *The Cambridge Companion to Adorno*, ed. Tom Huhn (Cambridge: Cambridge University Press, 2004), 354–75.

58. It would be necessary elsewhere to excavate how this Levinasian "wholly other" relates to Rudolf Otto's "das ganz Andere," which Horkheimer often evoked.

59. Paul de Man, "Anthropomorphism and Trope in the Lyric," in *The Rhetoric of Romanticism* (New York: Columbia University Press, 1984), 239–62, here 262.

60. Theodor W. Adorno and Walter Benjamin, *The Complete Correspondence, 1928–1940*, trans. Nicholas Walker (Cambridge, MA: Harvard University Press, 1999), 129; *Briefwechsel, 1928–1940*, ed. Henri Lonitz (Frankfurt am Main: Suhrkamp, 1994), 170.

61. Gayatri Chakravorty Spivak, *A Critique of Postcolonial Reason: Toward a History of the Vanishing Present* (Cambridge, MA: Harvard University Press, 1999), 145n49.

CHAPTER I

1. Walter Benjamin, "Goethe's Elective Affinities," trans. Stanley Corngold, in *Selected Writings*, Vol. 1: 1913–1926, ed. Marcus Bullock and Michael W. Jennings (Cambridge, MA: Harvard University Press, 1996), 297–360, here 333; "Goethes Wahlverwandtschaften," in *Gesammelte Schriften*, vol. 1, ed. Rolf Tiedemann and Hermann Schweppenhäuser (Frankfurt am Main: Suhrkamp, 1972–89), 123–201, here 172.

It is as though these published concerns had their siblings in unpublished ones, for instance in Benjamin's 1925 curriculum vitae, in which he writes that "I majored in philosophy and minored in modern German literary history and psychology. Since the center of gravity of my scholarly interests lies in aesthetics, my philosophical and literary studies have increasingly converged." Walter Benjamin, "Curriculum Vitae (I)," in *Selected Writings*, 1:422–23, here 422; "Lebenslauf (I)," in *Gesammelte Schriften*, 6:215–16, here 215.

2. I am thinking of Schlegel's poetological remark, made in the context of the literary and philosophical ambitions of his *Athenaeum* fragments, that "it is equally fatal for the mind both to have a system and to have none—hence, it will have to decide to combine both." Benjamin cites Schlegel's sentence in his dissertation on the German romantics. Walter Benjamin, "The Concept of Criticism in German Romanticism," trans. David Lachterman, Howard Eiland, and Ian Balfour, in *Selected Writings*, 1:116–200, here 140; "Der Begriff der Kunstkritik in der deutschen Romantik," in *Gesammelte Schriften*, 1:7–122, here 48. An extended reading of Benjamin's relationship to the concepts of the System and of Systematicity in both the early romantics and Hegel can be found in Philippe Lacoue-Labarthe and Jean-Luc Nancy, *The Literary Absolute: The Theory of Literature in*

German Romanticism, trans. Philip Barnard and Cheryl Lester (Albany: State University of New York Press, 1988).

3. Hannah Arendt, *Walter Benjamin, Bertolt Brecht: Zwei Essays* (Munich: Piper, 1971), 22.

4. Walter Benjamin, *One-Way Street*, trans. Edmund Jephcott, in *Selected Writings*, 1:444–88, here 457 and 476; *Einbahnstraße*, in *Gesammelte Schriften*, 4:83–148, here 105 and 131.

5. Detlef Schöttker, *Konstruktiver Fragmentarismus: Form und Rezeption der Schriften Walter Benjamins* (Frankfurt am Main: Suhrkamp, 1999), 181–85.

6. See Daniel Libeskind, *Erweiterung des Berlin Museums mit Abteilung Jüdisches Museum*, ed. Kristin Feireiss (Berlin: Ernst und Sohn, 1992), and Bernhard Schneider, *Daniel Libeskind: Jüdisches Museum Berlin: Zwischen den Linien*, preface by Daniel Libeskind, photographs by Stefan Müller (Munich: Prestel, 2001).

7. Victor Burgin, "The City in Pieces," in *In/Different Spaces: Place and Memory in Visual Culture* (Berkeley: University of California Press, 1996), 139–58, here 139.

8. This designation of *One-Way Street* is offered in Rainer Rochlitz, *The Disenchantment of Art: The Philosophy of Walter Benjamin*, trans. Jane Marie Todd (New York: Guilford, 1996), 126.

9. See Bernd Witte, "Walter Benjamins *Einbahnstraße*: Zwischen *Passage de l'Opéra* und *Berlin Alexanderplatz*," in *Walter Benjamin. 1892–1940*, ed. Uwe Steiner (Bern: Lang, 1992), 249–72. For a reading that places *One-Way Street* in the literary tradition of surrealism, see Josef Fürnkäs, *Surrealismus als Erkenntnis: Walter Benjamin, Weimarer Einbahnstraße und Pariser Passagen* (Stuttgart: Metzler, 1988). More recently, Michael W. Jennings situates *One-Way Street* in relation to the political and aesthetic forms of the historical avant-garde: "Walter Benjamin and the European Avant-Garde," in *The Cambridge Companion to Walter Benjamin*, ed. David Ferris (Cambridge: Cambridge University Press, 2004), 18–34.

10. See the Kantian rereading of Benjamin's category of experience through the notion of "color" recently proposed in Howard Caygill, *Walter Benjamin: The Colour of Experience* (London: Routledge, 1998).

11. The dedication, encrypting love, desire, and violence, reads: "This street is named / Asja Lacis Street / after her who / as an engineer / cut it through the author ("Diese Straße heißt / ASJA-LACIS-STRASSE / nach der / die sie als Ingenieur / im Autor durchgebrochen hat." Benjamin's preference for *durchgebrochen* over *durchbrochen* leaves an unsettling undecidability intact. Lacis both enabled and disabled this textual street: she broke it through the author and she broke it apart within him (*durchgebrochen*). For an extended reading of the relationship between Benjamin and Lacis and its significance for some of Benjamin's theoretical concerns, see Gerhard Richter, "Benjamin's Body: The Alterity of the Corpus in the Moscow Diary," in *Walter Benjamin and the Corpus of Autobiography* (Detroit: Wayne State University Press, 2000), 125–62.

12. Miriam Hansen, "Benjamin and Cinema: Not a One-Way Street," in *Ben-

jamin's Ghosts: Interventions in Contemporary Literary and Cultural Theory, ed. Gerhard Richter (Stanford: Stanford University Press, 2002), 41–73, here 48.

13. See Michael W. Jennings, "Trugbild der Stabilität. Weimarer Politik und Montage-Theorie in Benjamins *Einbahnstraße*," trans. Gerhard Richter and Michael W. Jennings, in *Global Benjamin*, vol. 1, ed. Klaus Garber and Ludger Rehm (Munich: Fink, 1999), 517–28, here 527. A consideration of *One-Way Street* in the context of the avant-garde aesthetics of Berlin constructivism is offered in Eckhardt Köhn, "'Nichts gegen die Illustrierte!' Benjamin, der Berliner Konstruktivismus und das avantgardistische Objekt," in *Schrift Bilder Denken: Walter Benjamin und die Künste*, ed. Detlev Schöttker (Frankfurt am Main: Suhrkamp; Berlin: Haus am Waldsee, 2004), 48–69, especially 58–59.

14. Walter Benjamin, "Surrealism," trans. Edmund Jephcott, in *Selected Writings*, Vol. 2: 1927–1934, ed. Michael W. Jennings, Howard Eiland, and Gary Smith (Cambridge, MA: Harvard University Press, 1999), 207–21, here 209; "Der Sürrealismus," *Gesammelte Schriften*, 2:295–310, here 298.

15. A sustained reading of the general relations between Benjamin and Husserlian phenomenology remains to be performed. An excellent start has been made by Peter Fenves, "The Genesis of Judgment: Spatiality, Analogy, and Metaphor in Benjamin's 'On Language as Such and on Human Language,'" in *Walter Benjamin: Theoretical Questions*, ed. David Ferris (Stanford: Stanford University Press, 1996), 75–93.

16. Walter Benjamin, *The Arcades Project*, trans. Howard Eiland and Kevin McLaughlin (Cambridge, MA: Harvard University Press, 1999), 460; *Das Passagen-Werk*, in *Gesammelte Schriften*, 5:574.

17. Walter Benjamin, *The Correspondence of Walter Benjamin, 1910–1940*, ed. Gershom Scholem and Theodor W. Adorno, trans. Manfred and Evelyn Jacobson (Chicago: University of Chicago Press, 1994), 322–23; *Gesammelte Briefe*, vol. 3, ed. Christoph Gödde and Henri Lonitz (Frankfurt am Main: Suhrkamp, 1997), 322–23.

18. Benjamin, *One-Way Street*, 446; *Einbahnstaße*, 88.

19. Benjamin, *Gesammelte Briefe*, 3:342.

20. Benjamin, *Correspondence*, 325; *Gesammelte Briefe*, 3:331.

21. Benjamin, *Arcades Project*, 461; *Passagen-Werk*, 575.

22. Benjamin, "Surrealism," 218; "Der Sürrealismus," 310.

23. Benjamin, *Arcades Project*, 463; *Passagen-Werk*, 578.

24. Benjamin himself makes this observation in his essay on Proust: "If the Romans, in Latin, called a text 'the web' or 'the woven,' then no one's text is more of a web or more densely woven than that of Marcel Proust." Walter Benjamin, "On the Image of Proust," trans. Harry Zohn, in *Selected Writings*, 2:237–47, here 238; "Zum Bilde Prousts," in *Gesammelte Schriften*, 2:310–24, here 311. This passage is interwoven with another in *One-Way Street*, where we read in the thought-image "Caution: Steps": "Work on good prose has three steps: a musical stage when it is

composed, an architectonic one when it is built, and a textile one when it is woven." Benjamin, *One-Way Street*, 455; *Einbahnstraße*, 102.

25. Benjamin, *One-Way Street*, 462; *Einbahnstraße*, 111.

26. See also Benjamin's letter of gratitude to Kracauer, dated 20 April 1926. *Gesammelte Briefe*, 3:145.

27. Benjamin, *Gesammelte Briefe*, 3:334.

28. Benjamin, *Correspondence*, 284; *Gesammelte Briefe*, 3:16, 85 (the early German edition on which the English translation is based omits Benjamin's first reference to the planned title). Benjamin's early title was inspired, as Schöttker suggests, by Hofmannsthal's book of aphorisms *Buch der Freunde*, which is listed in Benjamin's list of books read and which he cites in the *Arcades Project*. Benjamin also makes implicit reference to Novalis's plan, in 1799, to write a book of aphorisms "dedicated to friends," which would inscribe *One-Way Street* in an extended tradition that links aphoristic writing to friendship. Schöttker, *Konstruktiver Fragmentarismus*, 186–87.

29. Ernst Bloch, "Revueform in der Philosophie," in *Erbschaft dieser Zeit*, expanded ed. (Frankfurt am Main: Suhrkamp, 1985), 368–71, here 368.

30. Siegfried Kracauer, "On the Writings of Walter Benjamin," in *The Mass Ornament: Weimar Essays*, trans. Thomas Y. Levin (Cambridge, MA: Harvard University Press, 1995), 259–64, here 264; "Zu den Schriften Walter Benjamins," in *Schriften*, vol. 5, pt. 2, ed. Inka Mülder-Bach (Frankfurt am Main: Suhrkamp, 1990), 119–24, here 124.

31. Benjamin, *Correspondence*, 302; *Gesammelte Briefe*, 3:161.

32. Theodor W. Adorno, "Benjamin's *Einbahnstraße*," in *Notes to Literature*, vol. 2, trans. Shierry Weber Nicholson (New York: Columbia University Press, 1992), 322–27, here 322; "Benjamins *Einbahnstraße*," in *Noten zur Literatur*, vol. 11 of *Gesammelte Schriften*, ed. Rolf Tiedemann (Frankfurt am Main: Suhrkamp, 1997), 680–85, here 680.

33. Ibid., 323; 681–82.

34. Benjamin, *One-Way Street*, 481; *Einbahnstraße*, 138.

35. Ibid., 459; 107.

36. Walter Benjamin, *Origin of German Tragic Drama*, trans. John Osborne (London: New Left Books, 1977), 36; *Ursprung des deutschen Trauerspiels*, *Gesammelte Schriften*, 1:216.

37. Benjamin, *One-Way Street*, 476; *Einbahnstraße*, 131.

38. From a different perspective, a general discussion of the culture of distance in Weimar Germany can be found in Helmut Lethen, *Cool Conduct: The Culture of Distance in Weimar Germany*, trans. Don Reneau (Berkeley: University of California Press, 2001).

39. Walter Benjamin, "Gedanken zu einer Analysis des Zustands von Mitteleuropa," in *Gesammelte Schriften*, 4:916–35, here 923. I discuss this fragment at greater length in the context of Benjamin's, Derrida's, and Žižek's concepts of Europe and

the problems of Eurocentrism in "Sites of Indeterminacy and the Specters of Eurocentrism," *Culture, Theory and Critique* 43, no. 1 (2002): 51–65.

40. Benjamin, "Mitteleuropa," 924.

41. Walter Benjamin, "The Storyteller," trans. Harry Zohn, in *Selected Writings*, Vol. 3: 1935–1938, ed. Howard Eiland and Michael W. Jennings (Cambridge, MA: Harvard University Press, 2002), 143–66, here 143; "Der Erzähler," in *Gesammelte Schriften*, 2:438–65, here 438–39.

42. On the back cover of the hardbound first edition of the *Arcades Project*'s English translation.

43. Benjamin, *Arcades Project*, 833; *Passagen-Werk*, 1001.

44. For a discussion of the genesis of the dialectical image in Benjamin's thought, as well as a useful summary of previous attempts by Benjamin scholarship at reading this semi-concept, see Ansgar Hillach, "Dialektisches Bild," in *Benjamins Begriffe*, ed. Michael Opitz and Erdmut Wizisla (Frankfurt am Main: Suhrkamp, 2000), 186–229. In this context, compare further Rainer Nägele, "Thinking Images," in *Benjamin's Ghosts: Interventions in Contemporary Literary and Cultural Theory*, ed. Gerhard Richter (Stanford: Stanford University Press, 2002), 23–40.

45. Benjamin, *Arcades Project*, 462; *Passagen-Werk*, 576–77.

46. Theodor W. Adorno, "Erinnerungen," in *Gesammelte Schriften*, 20:173–78, here 177.

47. Theodor W. Adorno, "A Portrait of Walter Benjamin," in *Prisms*, trans. Samuel and Shierry Weber (Cambridge, MA: MIT Press, 1981), 227–41, here 240; "Charakteristik Walter Benjamins," in *Gesammelte Schriften*, 10:238–53, here 252.

48. See Walter Benjamin, *Denkbilder* (Frankfurt am Main: Suhrkamp, 1994), 125–27; in the standard editions as "Short Shadows (II)," trans. Rodney Livingstone, in *Selected Writings*, 2:699–702, here 699; "Kurze Schatten (II)," in *Gesammelte Schriften*, 4:425–28, here 425.

49. Walter Benjamin, "Literary History and the Study of Literature," trans. Rodney Livingstone, in *Selected Writings*, 2:459–65, here 464; "Literaturgeschichte und Literaturwissenschaft," in *Gesammelte Schriften*, 3:283–90, here 290.

50. In this movement, one should also hear the echoes of Benjamin's theory of translation. Benjamin suggests that "translation finds itself not in the center of the language forest but on the outside facing the wooded ridge; it calls into it without entering, aiming at that single spot where the echo is able to give, in its own language, the reverberation of the work in the alien one." Benjamin, "The Task of the Translator," trans. Harry Zohn, in *Selected Writings*, 1:253–63, here 258–59; "Die Aufgabe des Übersetzers," in *Gesammelte Schriften*, 4:9–21, here 16.

51. Benjamin, *Arcades Project*, 462–63; *Passagen-Werk*, 577–78.

52. Martin Heidegger, *Being and Time*, trans. John Macquarrie and Edward Robinson (New York: Harper Collins, 1962), 38; *Sein und Zeit* (Tübingen: Niemeyer, 1986), 17. For a discussion of the question of the historical index in

Benjamin and Heidegger, see Christopher Fynsk, "The Claim of History," *Diacritics* 22, no. 3–4 (Fall–Winter 1992): 115–26. The complex general relationship between the thought of Heidegger and that of Benjamin, beyond the tone of the merely polemical, is only now slowly coming into view. Useful recent examples are Martin Seel, "Sprache bei Benjamin und Heidegger," *Merkur* 46 (1992), 333–40; Howard Caygill, "Benjamin, Heidegger and the Destruction of Tradition," in *Walter Benjamin's Philosophy: Destruction and Experience*, ed. Andrew Benjamin and Peter Osborne (London: Routledge, 1994), 1–31; Samuel Weber, *Mass Mediauras: Form, Technics, Media* (Stanford: Stanford University Press, 1996); Stefan Knoche, *Benjamin-Heidegger: Über Gewalt; Die Politisierung der Kunst* (Vienna: Turia and Kant, 2000); and Beatrice Hanssen, "Benjamin or Heidegger: Aesthetics and Politics in an Age of Technology," in *Walter Benjamin and Art*, ed. Andrew Benjamin (New York: Continuum, 2005), 73–92.

53. Heidegger, *Being and Time*, 374; *Sein und Zeit*, 326.
54. Ibid.
55. Benjamin, *Arcades Project*, 456; *Passagen-Werk*, 570.
56. Paul de Man, "Semiology and Rhetoric," in *Allegories of Reading: Figural Language in Rousseau, Nietzsche, Rilke, and Proust* (New Haven: Yale University Press, 1979), 3–19, here 10.
57. For a general discussion of the categories of error and mistake in de Man, see Stanley Corngold, "Error in Paul de Man," in *The Yale Critics: Deconstruction in America*, ed. Jonathan Arac, Wlad Godzich, and Wallace Martin (Minneapolis: University of Minnesota Press, 1983), 90–108.
58. Benjamin, *One-Way Street*, 480; *Einbahnstraße*, 138.
59. Benjamin, *Arcades Project*, 463; *Passagen-Werk*, 579.
60. Adorno, "Portrait of Walter Benjamin," 241; "Charakteristik Walter Benjamins," 252–53.
61. Benjamin, "On the Image of Proust," 237; "Zum Bilde Prousts," 311.
62. Walter Benjamin and Gershom Scholem, *The Correspondence of Walter Benjamin and Gershom Scholem, 1932–1940*, ed. Gershom Scholem, trans. Gary Smith and Andre Lefevere (New York: Schocken, 1989), 135; Benjamin, *Gesammelte Briefe*, 4:478.

CHAPTER 2

1. Ernst Bloch, *The Spirit of Utopia*, trans. Anthony A. Nassar (Stanford: Stanford University Press, 2000), 115; *Der Geist der Utopie: Zweite Fassung*, vol. 3 of *Werkausgabe* (Frankfurt am Main: Suhrkamp, 1985), 149. Subsequent references are given in the text, using the abbreviations "S" for the English and "G" for the German edition.
2. Emmanuel Levinas, "On Death in the Thought of Ernst Bloch," in *Of God*

Who Comes to Mind, trans. Bettina Bergo (Stanford: Stanford University Press, 1998), 33–42, here 34.

3. Edward Said, "On the Transgressive Element in Music," in *Musical Elaborations* (New York: Columbia University Press, 1991), 35–72, here 40. Among the many general assessments of the relationship between music and language and considerations of music as a possible form of language, see the essays collected in *Sprache und Musik: Perspektiven einer Beziehung*, ed. Albrecht Riethmüller (Laaben: Laaber Verlag, 1999), as well as *Music and Text: Critical Inquiries*, ed. Steven Paul Scher (Cambridge: Cambridge University Press, 1992), and *Dichtung und Musik: Kaleidoskop ihrer Beziehungen*, ed. Günter Schnitzler (Stuttgart: Klett-Cotta, 1979), in the latter especially the contribution by Carl Dahlhaus, "Musik als Text," 11–28. Compare further Peter Faltin, "Ist Musik eine Sprache?" in *Die Zeichen*, vol. 2 of *Neue Aspekte der musikalischen Ästhetik*, ed. Hans Werner Henze (Frankfurt am Main: Suhrkamp, 1981), 32–50.

4. From this perspective, more traditional questions of music history and theory too could be expanded and recast as questions of textuality and of discourse in the broadest sense. Among the gestures toward that possible future direction, see for instance the historiographic and tropological concerns in Hayden White, "Form, Reference, and Ideology in Musical Discourse," in *Figural Realism: Studies in the Mimesis Effect* (Baltimore, MD: Johns Hopkins University Press, 1999), 147–76.

5. Ernst Bloch, *Spuren*, vol. 1 of *Werkausgabe* (Frankfurt am Main: Suhrkamp, 1985), 167.

6. Jacques Derrida, *Of Grammatology*, trans. Gayatri Chakravorty Spivak (Baltimore, MD: Johns Hopkins University Press, 1976), 158.

7. Jacques Derrida, "Afterword: Toward an Ethic of Discussion," trans. Samuel Weber, in *Limited Inc.* (Evanston, IL: Northwestern University Press, 1988), 111–54, here 136.

8. Ernst Bloch, *Experimentum Mundi*, vol. 15 of *Werkausgabe* (Frankfurt am Main: Suhrkamp, 1985), 248.

9. Jürgen Habermas, "Ein marxistischer Schelling," in *Über Ernst Bloch*, ed. Martin Walser et al. (Frankfurt am Main: Suhrkamp, 1968), 61–81.

10. Ernst Bloch, *Tübinger Einleitung in die Philosophie*, vol. 13 of *Werkausgabe* (Frankfurt am Main; Suhrkamp, 1985), 224.

11. A useful overview of the range of Bloch's aesthetic concerns can be found in his essay collection, selected from the vast *Werkausgabe* of his collected works, entitled *Ästhetik des Vorscheins*, ed. Gerd Ueding (Frankfurt am Main: Suhrkamp, 1974). Many of the most significant essays in this collection are available in English translation as *The Utopian Function of Art and Literature: Selected Essays*, trans. Jack Zipes and Frank Mecklenburg (Cambridge, MA: MIT Press, 1988).

12. For studies relevant to the multifaceted relationship between Bloch's philosophy of music and his politico-utopian concerns, cf. especially Anna Czajka-

Cunico, "'Wann lebt man eigentlich?' Die Suche nach der 'zweiten' Wahrheit und die ästhetische Erfahrung (Musik und Poesie) in Ernst Blochs *Geist der Utopie*," *Bloch-Almanach* 19 (2000): 103–57; Roger Behrens, "Hören im Dunkel des gelebten Augenblicks: Zur Musikphilosophie Ernst Blochs," *Bloch-Almanach* 17 (1998): 101–17; Albrecht Riethmüller, "Der Fortschritt in der Musik, gesehen von Bloch, Lukács und Adorno," *Bayrische Akademie der Schönen Künste Jahrbuch* 4 (1990): 75–95; Wolfgang Matz, *Musica Humana: Versuch über Ernst Blochs Philosophie der Musik* (Frankfurt am Main: Lang, 1988); Christopher Norris, "Utopian Deconstruction: Ernst Bloch, Paul de Man and the Politics of Music," *Paragraph* 11 (1988): 24–57; Robert Lilienfeld, "Music and Society in the 20th Century: Georg Lukács, Ernst Bloch, and Theodor W. Adorno," *International Journal of Politics, Culture, and Society* 1 (1987): 120–46; Frieder Reininghaus, "Musik wird Morgenrot: Ernst Bloch und die Musik," *Sozialistische Zeitschrift für Kunst und Gesellschaft* 3–4 (1977): 78–90; Heinz Paetzold, "Utopische Musiklehre," in *Neomarxistische Ästhetik I: Bloch und Benjamin* (Düsseldorf: Schwann, 1974), 113–24; and Gianni Vattimo, "Sprache, Utopie, Musik," *Philosophische Perspektiven* 4 (1972): 151–70.

13. A substantial selection of Bloch's writings on the philosophy of music was edited by his wife and appeared as *Zur Philosophie der Musik*, selected and ed. Karola Bloch (Frankfurt am Main: Suhrkamp, 1974). A partial English translation was published as *Essays on the Philosophy of Music*, trans. Peter Palmer (Cambridge: Cambridge University Press, 1985).

14. Bloch, *Experimentum Mundi*, 205.

15. Theodor W. Adorno, "Ernst Bloch's *Spuren*," in *Notes to Literature*, trans. Shierry Weber Nicholson, vol. 1 (New York: Columbia, 1991), 200–15, here 207; "Blochs Spuren," in *Noten zur Literatur*, vol. 11 of *Gesammelte Schriften* (Frankfurt am Main: 1997), 233–50, here 240.

16. Philippe Lacoue-Labarthe, *Musica Ficta (Figures of Wagner)*, trans. Felicia McCarren (Stanford: Stanford University Press, 1994), xvi.

17. I borrow the term "other-directedness" from Samuel Weber's discussion of textuality as "a figure that designates the *other-directedness of structures of signification*," which "entails an approach to the other as articulation and to articulation as other." "Catching Up with the Past," in *Mass Mediauras: Form, Technics, Media* (Stanford: Stanford University Press, 1996), 168–208, here 201.

18. Paul de Man, "The Resistance to Theory," in *The Resistance to Theory* (Minneapolis: University of Minnesota Press, 1986), 3–20, here 11. These concerns are enlarged and deepened in the essays collected in his *Aesthetic Ideology*, ed. Andrzej Warminski (Minneapolis: University of Minnesota Press, 1996).

19. For a general discussion of the status of music as a special kind of "text" and of resulting questions of composition and experimentation in post-traditional musical practices, see Claus-Steffen Mahnkopf, "Der Strukturbegriff der musikalischen Dekonstruktion," *Musik und Ästhetik* 21 (2002): 49–68.

20. Paul de Man, "The Rhetoric of Blindness: Jacques Derrida's Reading of Rousseau," in *Blindness and Insight: Essays in the Rhetoric of Contemporary Criticism*, 2nd ed. (Minneapolis: University of Minnesota Press, 1983), 102–41, here 130.

21. De Man, "Rhetoric of Blindness," 128–29.

22. Christopher Norris makes this point in his remarkable reading of Bloch and de Man, "Utopian Deconstruction," 52.

23. Ernst Bloch, *The Principle of Hope*, vol. 3, trans. Neville Plaice, Stephen Plaice, and Paul Knight (Cambridge, MA: MIT Press, 1986), 1062; *Das Prinzip Hoffnung*, vol. 3, in vol. 5 of *Werkausgabe* (Frankfurt am Main: Suhrkamp, 1985), 1248.

24. Jean-Luc Nancy, "Music," in *The Sense of the World*, trans. Jeffrey S. Librett (Minneapolis: University of Minnesota Press, 1997), 84–87, here 86.

25. Robert Bernasconi, "A Love That Is Stronger than Death: Sacrifice in the Thought of Levinas, Heidegger, and Bloch," *Angelaki: Journal of the Theoretical Humanities* 7, no. 2 (August 2002): 9–16, here 15.

26. Walter Benjamin, *Correspondence, 1910–1940*, trans. Manfred Jacobson and Evelyn M. Jacobson (Chicago: University of Chicago Press, 1994), 148; *Gesammelte Briefe*, vol. 2 (Frankfurt am Main: Suhrkamp, 1996), 46.

27. Theodor W. Adorno, "The Handle, the Pot, and Early Experience," in *Notes to Literature*, trans. Shierry Weber Nicholson, vol. 2 (New York: Columbia University Press, 1992), 211–19, here 212; "Henkel, Krug und frühe Erfahrung," in *Noten zur Literatur*, vol. 11 of *Gesammelte Schriften* (Frankfurt am Main: Suhrkamp, 1997), 556–66, here 557.

28. Ernst Bloch, "Grundsätzliche Unterscheidung der Tagträume von den Nachtträumen," in *Das Prinzip Hoffnung*, 86–128; "Traum von einer Sache," in *Philosophische Aufsätze zur objektiven Phantasie* (Frankfurt am Main: Suhrkamp, 1985), 163–69; and *Tagträume vom aufrechten Gang: Sechs Interviews mit Ernst Bloch*, ed. Arno Münster (Frankfurt am Main: Suhrkamp, 1977).

29. Bloch, *Principle*, 1069; *Prinzip*, 1257.

30. Immanuel Kant, *Critique of the Power of Judgment*, trans. Paul Guyer and Eric Matthews (Cambridge: Cambridge University Press, 2000), 205; *Kritik der Urteilskraft*, ed. Wilhelm Weischeded, vol. 10 of *Theorie-Werkausgabe* (Frankfurt am Main: Suhrkamp, 1991), 267.

31. Kant, *Judgment*, 206; *Urteilskraft*, 269.

32. Ibid., 207; 270.

33. "Ocularcentrism" and "anti-ocularcentrism" are the terms that Martin Jay suggests for the debate concerning the hegemony of "the noblest of the senses" in his philosophical history of vision, *Downcast Eyes: The Denigration of Vision in Twentieth-Century French Thought* (Berkeley: University of California Press, 1993).

34. Martin Heidegger, "Die Zeit des Weltbildes," in *Holzwege* (Frankfurt am

Main: Klostermann, 1980), 73–110. For a discussion of the role that music plays in the philosophies of German early (or Jena) Romantics such as Friedrich Schegel and Novalis, see Barbara Naumann, *Musikalisches Ideen-Instrument: Das Musikalische in Poetik und Sprachtheorie der Frühromantik* (Stuttgart: Metzler, 1990).

35. Derrida, *Of Grammatology*, 157.

36. Norris, "Utopian Deconstruction," 27.

37. Ernst Bloch, "Something's Missing: A Discussion between Ernst Bloch and Theodor W. Adorno on the Contradictions of Utopian Longing," in *The Utopian Function of Art and Literature: Selected Essays*, trans. Jack Zipes and Frank Mecklenburg (Cambridge, MA: MIT Press, 1988), 1–17, here 15; "Etwas fehlt . . . : Über die Widersprüche der utopischen Sehnsucht; Ein Rundfunkgespräch mit Theodor W. Adorno," in *Tendenz-Latenz-Utopie*, Werkausgabe, suppl. vol. (Frankfurt am Main: Suhrkamp, 1985), 350–68, here 366.

38. Ernst Bloch, *Heritage of Our Times*, trans. Neville and Stephen Plaice (Berkeley: University of California Press, 1990), 232; *Erbschaft dieser Zeit*, vol. 4 of *Werkausgabe* (Frankfurt am Main: Suhrkamp, 1985), 254.

39. Bertolt Brecht, *Aufstieg und Fall der Stadt Mahagonny: Stücke in einem Band* (Frankfurt am Main: Suhrkamp, 1987), 203–26, here 210–11 (scene 8).

40. I owe this image of wanting to experience music as slipping into a hot bathtub to my conversations about music with Jost Hermand, who reiterates it with eloquent ambivalence. Compare further his *Nach der Postmoderne: Ästhetik heute* (Cologne: Böhlau, 2004), 27. As an antidote to such hedonistic aberrations, see his *Konkretes Hören: Zum Inhalt der Instrumentalmusik* (Berlin: Argument, 1981), 142–50.

41. Friedrich Schlegel, "Kritische Fragmente," in *Schriften zur Literatur*, ed. Wolfdietrich Rasch (Munich: Deutscher Taschenbuch Verlag, 1985), 7–24, here 8.

42. Lacoue-Labarthe, *Musica Ficta*, 144–45.

43. Bloch, *Spuren*, 142.

44. Ernst Bloch, *Thomas Münzer als Theologe der Revolution*, vol. 2 of *Werkausgabe* (Frankfurt am Main: Suhrkamp, 1985), 198.

45. Bloch, *Tübinger Einleitung*, 100.

46. This according to his wife and posthumous editor, Karola Bloch, in the introduction to the edition of her husband's letters. "Zu dieser Ausgabe," in *Ernst Bloch: Briefe, 1903–1975*, vol. 1 (Frankfurt am Main: Suhrkamp, 1985), 7–12, here 11.

47. Roland Barthes, "Listening," in *The Responsibility of Forms: Critical Essays on Music, Art, and Representation* (Berkeley: University of California Press, 1991), 245–60, here 257.

48. Incisive commentaries on Bloch's *Spuren* can be found in the essays by his friends and fellow writers of the Denkbild, Kracauer and Adorno. See Kracauer's 1931 essay "Spuren," in *Ernst Blochs Wirkung: Ein Arbeitsbuch zum 90. Geburtstag* (Frankfurt am Main: Suhrkamp, 1975), 44–45, and the essay by Adorno, "Große Blochmusik," reprinted as "Blochs Spuren," in *Noten zur Literatur*.

For more recent suggestive studies of a variety of issues arising from Bloch's Denkbilder collected in *Spuren*, cf. Anna Czajka, "Poetik des Augenblicks. Zu Ernst Blochs *Spuren*," *Bloch-Jahrbuch* (1994): 36–49; Ekkehard Roeppert, "Erzählformen in Blochs *Spuren*," *Bloch-Almanach* 11 (1991): 137–48; Klaus L. Berghahn, "A View through the Red Window: Ernst Bloch's Spuren," in *Modernity and the Text: Revisions of German Modernism*, ed. Andreas Huyssen and David Bathrick (New York: Columbia University Press, 1989), 200–215; Martin Zerlang, "Ernst Bloch als Erzähler: Über Allegorie, Melancholie und Utopie in den *Spuren*," *Text und Kritik*, special issue on Ernst Bloch (1985): 61–75; and Rainer Hoffmann, *Montage im Hohlraum: Zu Ernst Blochs* Spuren (Bonn: Bouvier, 1977).

Finally, for a consideration of Bloch's narrative strategies, see Liliane Weissberg, "Philosophy and the Fairy Tale: Ernst Bloch as Narrator," *New German Critique* 55 (1992): 21–44, on *Spuren* especially 34–38.

49. Ernst Bloch, "From *Spuren* by Ernst Bloch," trans. Jamie Owen Daniel, in *Not Yet: Reconsidering Ernst Bloch*, ed. Jamie Owen Daniel and Tom Moylan (London: Verso, 1997), 215–23, here 215; *Spuren*, 11.

50. Bloch, *Spuren*, 130–31.

51. Bloch, *Principle*, 930; *Prinzip*, 1093.

52. Edgar Allan Poe, "The Facts in the Case of M. Valdemar," in *The Complete Works*, vol. 5 (New York: AMS, 1965), 154–66, here 163.

53. Bloch, *Tübinger Einleitung*, 98.

54. Bloch, *Principle*, 1062; *Prinzip*, 1248.

55. Bloch, *Principle*, 1088; *Prinzip*, 1279.

56. Bloch, *Principle*, 1375; *Prinzip*, 1627.

57. For extended discussions of the trumpet signal in *Fidelio* and its relation to the messianic tradition that links trumpet signals to expressions of hope, such as the biblical scenes of trumpet-playing angels and the playing of trumpets that opens graves and that causes the walls of Jericho to fall, cf. Francesca Vidal, "Bloch," in *Musik in der deutschen Philosophie: Eine Einführung*, ed. Stefan Lorenz Sorgner and Oliver Fürbeth (Stuttgart: Metzler, 2003), 135–54, here 144–48, as well as the discussion by Bloch's friend, Hans Mayer, "Der geschichtliche Augenblick des *Fidelio*," in *Abend der Vernunft: Reden und Vorträge, 1985–1990* (Frankfurt am Main: Suhrkamp, 1990), 33–45.

58. Ernesto Laclau and Chantal Mouffe, *Hegemony and Socialist Strategy: Toward a Radical Democratic Politics* (London: Verso, 1985), 193.

59. Ernst Bloch, *Atheism in Christianity: The Religion of the Exodus and the Kingdom*, trans. J. T. Swann (New York: Herder and Herder, 1972), motto, n.p.; *Atheismus im Christentum: Zur Religion des Exodus und des Reichs*, vol. 14 of *Werkausgabe* (Frankfurt am Main: Suhrkamp, 1985), motto, n.p.

60. Bloch, *Principle*, 1094; *Prinzip*, 1286.

CHAPTER 3

1. See Martin Heidegger's reading of the existential nature of building, dwelling, and thinking in his essay "Bauen Wohnen Denken" and in his discussion of Hölderlin's poetic mode of dwelling, "'... dichterisch wohnet der Mensch ...,'" both in *Vorträge und Aufsätze* (Stuttgart: Neske, 1954), 139–56 and 181–98, respectively.

2. Georg Lukács, *Die Theorie des Romans: Ein geschichtsphilosophischer Versuch über die Formen der großen Epik* (Darmstadt: Luchterhand, 1971), 21, 32.

3. I am grateful to Dirk Oschmann for reminding me of this point.

4. When in 1963 Kracauer selected thirty-three of his Weimar thought-images, which had originally appeared in the 1920s and 1930s in the *Frankfurter Zeitung*, for a collection with the title *Straßen in Berlin und anderswo* (Streets in Berlin and Elsewhere), he divided them into four sections: "Straßen" (Streets), "Lokale" (Sites), "Dinge" (Things), and "Leute" (People). The thought-image "Farewell to the Linden Arcade" appears in the first section and also was chosen by Kracauer to be included in a 1963 collection of longer essays of his Weimar period (1920–31), *Das Ornament der Masse* (*The Mass Ornament*). I cite Kracauer's texts from his collected works, whose three-book volume 5 contains many of his essays, albeit in strictly chronological order, an order that disrupts Kracauer's own constellation of texts and thought-images. I quote the English translation of Kracauer's thought-image from the English version of *Das Ornament der Masse*. Siegfried Kracauer, "Farewell to the Linden Arcade," in *The Mass Ornament: Weimar Essays*, ed. and trans. Thomas Y. Levin (Cambridge, MA: Harvard University Press, 1995), 337–42, here 340–41; "Abschied von der Lindenpassage," in *Schriften*, vol. 5, book 2, ed. Inka Mülder-Bach (Frankfurt am Main: Suhrkamp, 1990), 260–65, here 263.

5. For a general discussion of Kracauer's reception of Lukács, see Dirk Oschmann, *Auszug aus der Innerlichkeit: Das literarische Werk Siegfried Kracauers* (Heidelberg: Winter, 1999), 81–89

6. A title that Adorno takes verbatim from Kracauer's thought-images for his own in *Minima Moralia*.

7. That the trope of homelessness, in its Lukácsian inflection and beyond, was privileged among Kracauer and his friends is confirmed in the reflections of another Frankfurt School colleague, Leo Löwenthal. As he recalls, Kracauer "called himself homeless in a way. In October 1923 . . . on the occasion of my wedding to my first wife, I received a letter of congratulations in an envelope decorated by Kracauer and with the return address: 'General Headquarters of the Welfare Bureau for the Transcendentally Homeless'; and below, again in Teddie's [Wiesengrund Adorno's] handwriting: 'Kracauer and Wiesengrund. Agents of the Transcendentally Homeless. General Management in Frankfurt Oberrat.' That, of

course, was an allusion to Lukács's *Theory of the Novel*. But 'transcendentally homeless' is the true category for Siegfried Kracauer." Leo Löwenthal, "As I Remember Friedel," *New German Critique* 54 (Fall 1991): 5–17, here 12–13.

8. Martin Jay, "The Extraterritorial Life of Siegfried Kracauer," in *Permanent Exiles: Essays on the Intellectual Migration from Germany to America* (New York: Columbia University Press, 1986), 152–97, here 153.

9. These remarks by Roth and Kessler, respectively made in letters and diaries, are cited in Momme Brodersen, *Siegfried Kracauer* (Reinbek bei Hamburg: Rowohlt, 2001), 150. Further reflections on Kracauer's status as cultural outsider and his meditations on the dislocations of identity can be found in Ingrid Belke, "Identitätsprobleme Siegfried Kracauers (1889–1966)," in *Deutsch-Jüdisches Exil: Das Ende der Assimilation? Identitätsprobleme deutscher Juden in der Emigration*, ed. Wolfgang Benz and Marion Neiss (Berlin: Metropol, 1994), 45–65. Finally, for an analysis of how Kracauer's status as an outsider inflected his practice of philosophical journalism of the Weimar period, see Helmut Stalder, *Siegfried Kracauer: Das journalistische Werk in der "Frankfurter Zeitung," 1921–1933* (Würzburg: Königshausen und Neumann, 2003).

10. The overall sense that Kracauer's prose snapshots and philosophical miniatures from his Weimar years are best understood as belonging to the genre of the Denkbild, the form of the philosophically charged literary thought-image that also plays such a central role in the writings of his friends and colleagues Adorno, Benjamin, Bloch, Horkheimer, and others, is generally shared by Kracauer's readers. Several commentators suggest the term Denkbild for Kracauer's Weimar texts: Heinz Schlaffer, "Denkbilder: Eine kleine Prosaform zwischen Dichtung und Gesellschaftstheorie," in *Poesie und Politik. Zur Situation der Literatur in Deutschland*, ed. Wolfgang Kuttenkeuler (Stuttgart: Kohlhammer, 1973), 137–54; Inka Mülder, *Siegfried Kracauer: Grenzgänger zwischen Theorie und Literatur; Seine frühen Schriften, 1913–1933* (Stuttgart: Metzler, 1985), 103–6; Gerwin Zohlen, "Notizen zur Ausgabe und zum Autor," in Siegfried Kracauer, *Straßen in Berlin und anderswo*, with an essay by Gerwin Zohlen (Berlin: Das Arsenal, 1987), 120–28; Helmut Stalder, "Hieroglyphen-Entzifferung und Traumdeutung der Großstadt: Zur Darstellungsmethode in den 'Städtebildern' Siegfried Kracauers," in *Siegfried Kracauer: Zum Werk des Romanciers; Feuilletonisten, Architekten, Filmwissenschaftlers und Soziologen*, ed. Andreas Volk (Zürich: Seismo, 1996), 131–55; and Tom Levin, introduction to Kracauer's *The Mass Ornament*, 1–30.

11. Lili Kracauer's unpublished letter to Leo Löwenthal, in which she speaks of Kracauer's "extraterritoriality of chronological time," is cited in Dagmar Barnouw, *Critical Realism: History, Photography, and the Work of Siegfried Kracauer* (Baltimore, MD: Johns Hopkins University Press, 1994), 323n45.

12. Kracauer's letter to Löwenthal dated 27 October 1958 is now available in *In*

steter Freundschaft: Leo Löwenthal–Siegfried Kracauer, Briefwechsel, 1921–1966, ed. Peter-Erwin Jansen and Christian Schmidt (Springe: zu Klampen, 2003), 211–13, here 212.

13. Gilles Deleuze, "A Theory of the Other," in *The Deleuze Reader*, ed. Constantin V. Boundas (New York: Columbia University Press, 1993), 59–68, here 60.

14. Kracauer, "Farewell," 342; "Abschied," 263.

15. Ibid., 342; 264–65.

16. Walter Benjamin, "An Outsider Makes His Mark," trans. Rodney Livingstone, *Selected Writings: Volume 2, 1927–1934*, ed. Michael W. Jennings, Howard Eiland, and Gary Smith (Cambridge, MA: Harvard University Press, 1999), 305–10, here 310; "Ein Außenseiter macht sich bemerkbar: Zu S. Kracauer, 'Die Angestellten,'" in *Gesammelte Schriften*, vol. 3, ed. Hella Tiedemann-Bartes (Frankfurt am Main: Suhrkamp, 1972), 219–25, here 225.

17. Kracauer's two "Briefe zur Extraterritorialität" to Adorno, dated 25 October and 8 November 1963, are located among his papers at the Deutsches Literaturarchiv in Marbach. They are quoted in Mülder-Bach, "History as Autobiography: The Last Things before the Last," trans. Gail Finney, *New German Critique* 54 (Fall 1991): 139–57, here 154–55.

18. Jay, "Kracauer," 152–53. It is doubtful, however, that Kracauer's extraterritorial investment can be reduced to a "heightened expression for escape," as Mülder-Bach suggests. "History as Autobiography," 155.

19. As Gertrud Koch puts it, emphasizing the figural character of all of Kracauer's texts: "His philosophical treatises, just as much as his essays and short feuilletons, are connected by a literary style that turns them into an infinite simultaneous texture," even into a "rhetoric of metaphors." *Kracauer zur Einführung* (Hamburg: Junius, 1996), 8.

20. Siegfried Kracauer, *History: The Last Things before the Last*, ed. Paul Kristeller (Princeton: Wiener, 1995), 68–69. For a discussion of this passage in the context of Kracauer's effort to transform the self into an other by "disappearing" into his own texts, see Mülder-Bach, "History as Autobiography," 155–56. Given the subterranean affinity between Kracauer's project and Derrida's, it is perhaps no accident that Geoffrey Bennington makes a similar point regarding Derrida when he writes that "we have absorbed Derrida, his singularity and his signature, the event we were so keen to tell you about, into a textuality in which he may well have quite simply disappeared." Geoffrey Bennington, "Derridabase," in *Jacques Derrida*, trans. Geoffrey Bennington (Chicago: University of Chicago Press, 1993), 316.

21. Walter Benjamin, "*Trauerspiel* and Tragedy," trans. Rodney Livingstone, in *Selected Writings: Volume 1, 1913–1926*, ed. Marcus Bullock and Michael W. Jennings (Cambridge, MA: Harvard University Press, 1996), 55–58, here 55; in German: "Trauerspiel und Tragödie," in *Gesammelte Schriften*, vol. 2, ed. Rolf

Tiedemann and Hermann Schweppenhäuser (Frankfurt am Main: Suhrkamp, 1974), 134.

22. Jacques Derrida, "There Is No One Narcissism (Autobiophotographies)," in *Points... Interviews, 1974–1994*, ed. Elisabeth Weber, trans. Peggy Kamuf et al. (Stanford: Stanford University Press, 1995), 196–215, here 206.

23. Jacques Derrida, *Monolingualism of the Other, or, The Prosthesis of Origin*, trans. Patrick Mensah (Stanford: Stanford University Press, 1998), 73.

24. Paul de Man, "The Resistance to Theory," in *The Resistance to Theory* (Minneapolis: University of Minnesota Press, 1986), 3–20, here 19–20.

25. Jacques Derrida, *Memoirs: For Paul de Man*, revised ed., trans. Cecil Lindsay, Jonathan Culler, Eduardo Cadava, and Peggy Kamuf (New York: Columbia University Press, 1989), 73. For a general discussion of the relation between deconstruction and the very question of "foundations," see Rodolphe Gasché, "Deconstructive Methodology," in *The Tain of the Mirror: Derrida and the Philosophy of Reflection* (Cambridge, MA: Harvard University Press, 1986), 121–76, and Nicholas Royle, "Philosophy and the Ruins of Deconstruction," in *After Derrida* (Manchester: Manchester University Press, 1995), 124–42.

26. It is no accident that the German writer Reinhard Lettau reminds us, in his allegorical tale "Schwierigkeiten beim Häuserbauen," a story that, like E. T. A. Hoffmann's romantic tale "Rat Krespl," revolves around the very concept of building a house, that "the difficulties in building a house are enormous [*die Schwierigkeiten beim Häuserbauen sind gewaltig*]." "Schwierigkeiten beim Häuserbauen," in *Schwierigkeiten beim Häuserbauen* (Munich: Hanser, 1962), 89–95, here 94. By the same token, Kafka's tale "The Burrow" ("Der Bau") stages a self that obsessively constructs a home in the face of an imaginary other who never appears. Franz Kafka, *Das Ehepaar und andere Schriften aus dem Nachlaß, Gesammelte Werke*, vol. 8, ed. Hans-Gerd Koch (Frankfurt am Main: Fischer, 1994), 165–208.

27. For an autobiographically inflected meditation on his aporetic Jewish heritage, a Jewish heritage without a Jewish heritage, see Derrida's "Circumfession," a rhetorico-conceptual conflation of "confession" and "circumcision" that in turn unfolds in the margins, or circumference, of Geoffrey Bennington's attempt at presenting some major trajectories of Derrida's life and work. In the bottom margin of this "circumfession" Derrida comments on, modifies, challenges, and elaborates what is said "up" on the "official" page. "Circumfession," trans. Geoffrey Bennington, in Geoffrey Bennington and Jacques Derrida, *Jacques Derrida* (Chicago: University of Chicago Press, 1993).

28. The complex "Jewishness" of Derrida's thought and experience is insightfully discussed in John D. Caputo, *The Prayers and Tears of Jacques Derrida: Religion without Religion* (Bloomington: Indiana University Press, 1997). Compare further Joseph G. Kronick, "Edmond Jabès and the Question of the Jewish Unhappy Consciousness: Reflections on Deconstruction," in *Derrida and the*

Future of Literature (Albany: State University of New York Press, 1999), 69–99. From the perspective of a lifelong friend who shares Derrida's experience of being a French Jew in Algeria, Hélène Cixous investigates their mutual belonging and non-belonging in *Portrait of Jacques Derrida as a Young Jewish Saint*, trans. Beverly Bie Brahic (New York: Columbia University Press, 2004). Some of the multiple relays between Derrida's philosophy and the tradition and politics of "Frenchness" are explored by the essays collected in *The French Connections of Jacques Derrida*, ed. Julian Wolfreys, John Brannigan, and Ruth Robbins (Albany: State University of New York Press, 1999). The ways in which deconstruction transforms the very concepts of tradition, legacy, and inheritance are subtly analyzed in Michael Naas, *Taking on the Tradition: Jacques Derrida and the Legacies of Deconstruction* (Stanford: Stanford University Press, 2003). Finally, it would be necessary to supplement the current discussion with Derrida's recent meditations on traveling and "traveling with" as they are inflected by concepts of identity, topographical location, and spacing; see Catherine Malabou and Jacques Derrida, *Counterpath: Traveling with Jacques Derrida*, trans. David Wills (Stanford: Stanford University Press, 2004), especially chapter 5, "Of Algeria," 75–92.

29. Jacques Derrida, *The Other Heading: Reflections on Today's Europe*, trans. Pascale-Anne Brault and Michael E. Naas (Bloomington: Indiana University Press, 1992), 82–83.

30. Theodor W. Adorno, "Cultural Criticism and Society," in *Prisms*, trans. Samuel and Shierry Weber (Cambridge, MA: MIT Press, 1981), 17–34, here 23; "Kulturkritik und Gesellschaft," in *Gesammelte Schriften*, vol. 10, book 1, ed. Rolf Tiedemann (Frankfurt am Main: Suhrkamp, 1997), 11–30, here 16.

31. Jacques Derrida, "A 'Madness' Must Watch Over Thinking," in *Points . . . Interviews, 1974–1994*, ed. Elisabeth Weber, trans. Peggy Kamuf et al. (Stanford: Stanford University Press, 1995), 339–64, here 340.

32. Jacques Derrida, "Unsealing ('The Old New Language')," in *Points . . . Interviews, 1974–1994*, ed. Elisabeth Weber, trans. Peggy Kamuf et al. (Stanford: Stanford University Press, 1995), 115–31, here 120–21.

33. For a discussion of the friendship between Benjamin and Kracauer, especially as it centers on their common experiences as exiles in Marseilles, see Klaus Michael, "Vor dem Café: Walter Benjamin und Siegfried Kracauer in Marseille," in *"Aber ein Sturm weht vom Paradise her": Texte zu Walter Benjamin*, ed. Michael Opitz and Erdmut Wizisla (Leipzig: Reclam, 1992), 203–21. Elements of their complex personal and philosophical friendship become readable in what survives of their correspondence: Walter Benjamin, *Briefe an Siegfried Kracauer: Mit vier Briefen von Siegfried Kracauer an Walter Benjamin* (Marbach: Deutsches Literaturarchiv and Theodor W. Adorno-Archiv, 1987). For a reflection on Kracauer's general theory of friendship, see Gerhard Richter, "Siegfried Kracauer and the Folds of Friendship," *German Quarterly* 70, no. 3 (Summer 1997): 233–46.

34. Theodor W. Adorno, "Nach Kracauers Tod," in *Gesammelte Schriften*, vol. 20, book 1, 195.

35. I borrow the paragraphs on Derrida in this section from an earlier essay of mine in which I address the concepts of universalism and Eurocentrism in the work of Slavoj Žižek, Benjamin, and Derrida: "Sites of Indeterminacy and the Specters of Eurocentrism," *Culture, Theory and Critique* 43, no. 1 (2002): 51–65. These sentences appear here in revised form.

36. The politics of the *arrivant* should also be put into conversation with other names for the political in Derrida. For attempts to elaborate some of these other names, see, among others, Richard Beardsworth, *Derrida and the Political* (London: Routledge, 1996), and Geoffrey Bennington, "Derrida and Politics," in *Jacques Derrida and the Humanities: A Critical Reader*, ed. Tom Cohen (Cambridge: Cambridge University Press, 2001), 193–212. Derrida's engagement with Marxian politics in particular, as it emerges in his *Specters of Marx*, has occasioned a collection of responses, collected in *Ghostly Demarcations: A Symposium on Jacques Derrida's Specters of Marx*, ed. Michael Sprinker (London: Verso, 1999). This volume also includes an illuminating response by Derrida to his political respondents, "Marx & Sons," trans. G. M. Goshgarian, 213–69.

37. Derrida, *The Other Heading*, 12–13.

38. Ibid., 13.

39. This notion of the *tout autre*, inspired in part by Levinas, traverses much of Derrida's work of the last two decades. For a recent discussion of the *tout autre*, see further J. Hillis Miller, *Black Holes* (Stanford: Stanford University Press, 1999), 157–69.

40. Jacques Derrida, *Aporias: Dying—Awaiting (One Another at) the "Limits of Truth,"* trans. Thomas Dutoit (Stanford: Stanford University Press, 1993), 34.

41. Ibid., 33–36.

42. Jacques Derrida and Bernard Stiegler, *Échographies de la télévision: Entretiens filmés* (Paris: Éditions Galilée, 1996). Compare further, among other texts on the problem of the image, Derrida's reflections on Barthes's study of photography in "The Deaths of Roland Barthes," trans. Pascale-Anne Brault and Michael Naas, *Philosophy and Non-Philosophy since Merleau-Ponty*, ed. Hugh Silverman (New York: Routledge, 1989), 259–96; his conversation on the photographic image in "Die Photographie als Kopie, Archiv und Signatur: Im Gespräch mit Hubertus v. Amelunxen und Michael Wetzel," *Theorie der Fotografie*, vol. 4, 1980–1995, ed. Hubertus v. Amelunxen (Munich: Schirmer/Mosel, 2000), 280–96; his extended reading of the images by Belgian photographer Marie-Françoise Plissart in *Right of Inspection*, trans. David Willis (New York: Monacelli, 1998); his meditations on painted self-portraits in *Memoirs of the Blind*, trans. Pascale-Anne Brault and Michael Naas (Chicago: University of Chicago Press, 1993); and his investigations of drawings and paintings, including Valerio Adami's drawing "Ritratto di Walter

Benjamin," in *The Truth in Painting*, trans. Geoffrey Bennington and Ian McLeod (Chicago: University of Chicago Press, 1987). Finally, a general meditation on the relation, in Derrida's texts, between the image of the artwork and questions of mourning can be found in David Farrell Krell, *The Purest of Bastards: Works of Mourning, Art, and Affirmation in the Thought of Jacques Derrida* (University Park: Pennsylvania State University Press, 2000).

43. Kracauer, *History*, 4.

44. Siegfried Kracauer, "On Photography," in *The Mass Ornament*, 47–63, here 56; "Die Photographie," in *Schriften*, vol. 5, book 2, 83–98, here 91.

45. Marcel Proust, *Remembrance of Things Past*, vol. 1, trans. C. K. Scott Moncrieff (New York: Boni, 1930), 814–15. Kracauer quotes this passage in *Theory of Film: The Redemption of Physical Reality*, introd. Miriam Hansen (Princeton, NJ: Princeton University Press, 1997), 14.

46. It will be necessary to read Kracauer's theory of photography more rigorously in the comparative contexts of the history of such theories, and specifically in relation to Roland Barthes, whose theory of photography exhibits many similarities with Kracauer's. Writing several decades later, he does not seem to have been aware of Kracauer's reflections. For a useful beginning of an investigation of the relation between Kracauer and Barthes, see Heide Schlüpmann, "Stellung zur Massenkultur: Barthes' 'Bemerkung zur Fotografie' mit Kracauer gelesen," in *Ein Detektiv des Kinos: Studien zu Siegfried Kracauers Filmtheorie* (Basel: Stromfeld, 1998), 55–65.

47. Kracauer, *History*, 83–84.

48. For a discussion of Kracauer's image in the context of Benjamin's theory of photography, see Hubertus von Amelunxen, "Ein Eindruck der Vergängnis. Vorläufige Bemerkungen zu Walter Benjamin," *Fotogeschichte* 9 (1989): 3–10.

49. Walter Benjamin, *The Arcades Project*, trans. Howard Eiland and Kevin McLaughlin (Cambridge, MA: Harvard University Press, 1999), 476; *Das Passagen-Werk*, vol. 5 of *Gesammelte Schriften*, ed. Rolf Tiedemann (Fankfurt am Main: Suhrkamp, 1982), 596; Kracauer, *History*, 149.

50. By focusing on the "surface-level" quality of the photograph, we enact with respect to Kracauer's texts the stance that he wishes to apply to the reading of entire historical paradigms. As he writes in "The Mass Ornament," three years before this picture was taken: "The position that an epoch occupies in the historical process can be determined more strikingly from an analysis of its inconspicuous surface-level expressions than from that epoch's judgments about itself . . . The surface-level expressions . . . by virtue of their unconscious nature, provide unmediated access to the fundamental substance of the state of things. Conversely, knowledge of this state of things depends on the interpretation of these surface-level expressions. The fundamental substance of an epoch and its unheeded impulses illuminate each other reciprocally." Kracauer, "The Mass Ornament," in *The Mass Ornament*, 75–86, here 75; in German: "Das Ornament der Masse," in *Schriften* 5.2, 57–67, here 57.

For discussions of Kracauer's engagement with the surface structure of modern culture, see Miriam Hansen, "Mass Culture as Hieroglyphic Writing: Adorno, Derrida, Kracauer," *New German Critique* 56 (Spring–Summer 1992): 43–73, as well as Inka Mülder-Bach, "Der Umschlag der Negativität: Zur Verschränkung von Phänomenologie, Geschichtsphilosophie und Filmästhetik in Siegfried Kracauers Metaphorik der Oberfläche," *Deutsche Vierteljahrsschrift* 61, no. 2 (1987): 359–73.

51. Kracauer, "On Photography," 56; "Die Photographie," 91–92.
52. Derrida, *Monolingualism of the Other*, 13.
53. The most extensive treatment of this general aspect of Derrida's work is Robert Smith, *Derrida and Autobiography* (Cambridge: Cambridge University Press, 1995).
54. Derrida, *Monolingualism of the Other*, 57.
55. Ibid., 69.
56. Ibid., 17.
57. Ibid., 28.
58. Ibid., 40.
59. Ibid., 22.
60. Ibid., 60–61.
61. Ibid., 61.
62. See Benedict Anderson, *Imagined Communities: Reflections on the Origin and Spread of Nationalism* (London: Verso, 1983), and Homi K. Bhabha, "DissemiNation: Time, Narrative, and the Margins of the Modern Nation," in *The Location of Culture* (London: Routledge, 1994), 139–70. For a book-length treatment of the question of "origin," compare further John Pizer, *Toward a Theory of Radical Origin: Essays on Modern German Thought* (Lincoln: University of Nebraska Press, 1995).
63. Derrida, *Monolingualism of the Other*, 25.
64. Theodor W. Adorno, "On the Question: 'What Is German?'," trans. Thomas Y. Levin, *New German Critique* 36 (Fall 1985): 131; "Auf die Frage: Was ist deutsch," in *Gesammelte Schriften*, vol. 10, book 2, 691–701.
65. This significance of the "between" in acts of cultural recognition is made vivid by Alexander García Düttmann, *Zwischen den Kulturen: Spannungen im Kampf um Anerkennung* (Frankfurt am Main: Suhrkamp, 1997).
66. Werner Hamacher, "One 2 Many Multiculturalisms," trans. Dana Hollander, in *Violence, Identity, and Self-Determination*, ed. Hent de Vries and Samuel Weber (Stanford: Stanford University Press, 1997), 284–325, here 298.
67. Ibid., 325.

CHAPTER 4

1. Theodor W. Adorno and Walter Benjamin, *The Complete Correspondence, 1928–1940*, trans. Nicholas Walker (Cambridge, MA: Harvard University Press, 1999), 212–12; *Briefwechsel, 1928–1940* (Frankfurt am Main: Suhrkamp, 1994), 276.

2. The term "annihilationist anti-Semitism" was suggested to me by Peter Fenves. For recent discussions of the status of anti-Semitism in the work of Adorno, see Anson Rabinbach, "'Why Were the Jews Sacrificed?' The Place of Anti-Semitism in Adorno and Horkheimer's *Dialectic of Enlightenment*," in *Adorno: A Critical Reader*, ed. Nigel Gibson and Andrew Rubin (Oxford: Blackwell, 2002), 132–49, as well as Jan Plug, "Idiosyncracies of Anti-Semitism," in *Rereading Adorno*, ed. Gerhard Richter, special issue of *Monatshefte* 94, no. 1 (Spring 2002): 43–66.

3. Philippe Lacoue-Labarthe and Jean-Luc Nancy, "The Nazi Myth," trans. Brian Holmes, *Critical Inquiry* 16, no. 2 (Winter 1990): 291–312, here 312.

4. It would be necessary to place Adorno's reflections on Hitler, performed in American exile, into dialogue with the rhetorical analyses of Hitler that were unfolding in the work of American thinkers at roughly the same time. I am thinking, for instance, of Kenneth Burke's 1939 essay, "The Rhetoric of Hitler's 'Battle.'" Burke's essay, which originally appeared in the *Southern Review*, is reprinted in *Language and Politics*, ed. Michael Shapiro (New York: New York University Press, 1984), 61–80.

5. Compare further Jost Hermand, "Ein wildgewordener Kleinbürger? Hitler-Parodien bei Chaplin und Brecht," in *"Das 'Ewig-Bürgerliche' widert mich an". Brecht-Aufsätze* (Berlin: Theater der Zeit, 2001), 351–63.

6. While *The Great Dictator* was not released until 1940, as early as August 1934, shortly after the death of former *Reichspräsident* Paul von Hindenburg, Benjamin devoted a reflection to Chaplin's analytical potential with regard to Hitler: "Hitler's Diminished Masculinity," in *Selected Writings: Volume 2, 1927–1934*, ed. Michael W. Jennings, Howard Eiland, and Gary Smith (Cambridge, MA: Harvard University Press, 1999), 792–93; "Hitlers herabgeminderte Männlichkeit," in *Gesammelte Schriften*, vol. 6, ed. Rolf Tiedemann and Hermann Schweppenhäuser (Frankfurt am Main: Suhrkamp, 1985), 103–4. For Adorno's analytical comments and his recollections of meeting Chaplin, see "Zweimal Chaplin," in *Ohne Leitbild: Parva Aesthetica*, vol. 10 of *Gesammelte Schriften*, ed. Rolf Tiedemann (Frankfurt am Main: Suhrkamp, 1997), 362–66. The first part of this essay, reading Chaplin through Kierkegaard, was originally published in 1930, the second part in 1964, on the occasion of Chaplin's seventy-fifth birthday.

7. The term "Hitlerism" can be defined, with Lacoue-Labarthe and Nancy, as "the exploitation—lucid but not necessarily cynical, for convinced of its own truth—of the modern masses' openness to myth." "The Nazi Myth," 312. For Art Spiegelman's comment, see his "Drawing Pens and Politics: Mightier than the Sorehead," *Nation*, 17 January 1994, 46. A discussion of Spiegelman's stance in the context of general issues of Holocaust presentation and the aporias of historiography can be found in my "Holocaust und Katzenjammer: Lektüreprotokolle zu Art Spiegelmans Comic *Maus*," *German Studies Review* 23, no. 1 (2000): 85–114.

8. Theodor W. Adorno, *Aesthetic Theory*, trans. Robert Hullot-Kentor (Minneapolis: University of Minnesota Press, 1997), 5; *Ästhetische Theorie*, vol. 7 of *Gesammelte Schriften*, 15.

9. Not to be confused with the Second Viennese School of music, which included Adorno's music teachers and colleagues such as Alban Berg, Arnold Schönberg, and Eduard Steuermann.

10. Ludwig Wittgenstein, *Culture and Value*, trans. Peter Winch, ed. G. H. von Wright, in collaboration with Heikki Nyman (Chicago: University of Chicago Press, 1980), 24; cited in Marjorie Perloff, *Wittgenstein's Ladder: Poetic Language and the Strangeness of the Ordinary* (Chicago: University of Chicago Press, 1996), xix.

11. This double stress on the aesthetic permeates in various modulations and intensities Adorno's entire oeuvre, culminating in his final text, *Aesthetic Theory*. For an examination of the conditions of possibility of such a double mobilization of the aesthetic in critical theory, see Rüdiger Bubner, "Kann Theorie ästhetisch werden? Zum Hauptmotiv der Philosophie Adornos," in *Materialien zur ästhetischen Theorie Theodor W. Adornos: Konstruktionen der Moderne*, ed. Burkhardt Lindner and W. Martin Lüdke (Frankfurt am Main: Suhrkamp, 1979), 108–37.

12. Representative of this standard reading of *Minima Moralia* in Adorno scholarship is Rolf Wiggershaus's evenhanded study *Theodor W. Adorno* (Munich: Beck, 1998), 11.

13. Theodor W. Adorno, "On Lyric Poetry and Society," in *Notes to Literature*, vol. 1, trans. Shierry Weber Nicholsen (New York: Columbia University Press, 1991), 37–54, here 43–44; "Rede über Lyrik und Gesellschaft," in *Noten zur Literatur*, vol. 11 of *Gesammelte Schriften*, 49–68, here 56–57.

14. Theodor W. Adorno, *Negative Dialectics*, trans. E. B. Ashton (New York: Continuum, 2000), 18; *Negative Dialektik*, vol. 6 of *Gesammelte Schriften*, ed. Rolf Tiedemann (Frankfurt am Main: Suhrkamp, 1997), 29.

15. Ibid., 33–34; 44.

16. Theodor W. Adorno, "Words from Abroad," in *Notes to Literature*, 1:185–99, here 197; "Wörter aus der Fremde," in *Noten zur Literatur*, vol. 11 of *Gesammelte Schriften*, 216–32, here 230.

17. Adorno, *Aesthetic Theory*, 87; *Ästhetische Theorie*, 135.

18. Adorno, "Words from Abroad," 189; "Wörter aus der Fremde," 221.

19. Adorno, *Negative Dialectics*, 55; *Negative Dialektik*, 65.

20. Theodor W. Adorno, "Einleitung zum 'Positivismusstreit in der deutschen Soziologie,'" in *Gesammelte Schriften*, vol. 8, 280–353, here 317–18.

21. Adorno, *Aesthetic Theory*, 124; *Ästhetische Theorie*, 135.

22. For a general discussion of Adorno's conception of the aesthetic in terms of their nonpropositional cognitive character, see Simon Jarvis, *Adorno: A Critical Introduction* (New York: Routledge, 1998), 90–91.

23. I borrow the hyphen from Fredric Jameson, *Late Marxism: Adorno, or, The Persistence of the Dialectic* (London: Verso, 1990), 86.

24. Helmut Schnädelbach, "Dialektik der Vernunftkritik. Zur Konstruktion des Rationalen bei Adorno," in *Adorno-Konferenz 1983*, ed. Ludwig von Friedeburg and Jürgen Habermas (Frankfurt am Main: Suhrkamp, 1983), 66–93, here 90.

25. Theodor W. Adorno, *Minima Moralia: Reflections from Damaged Life*, trans. E. F. N. Jephcott (London: Verso, 1974), 39; *Minima Moralia: Reflexionen aus dem beschädigten Leben*, in *Gesammelte Schriften*, 4:43. Henceforth, all references to this text will be given parenthetically, preceded by the abbreviation *MM*. The first number indicates the page number of the English-language edition, the second number that of the German edition.

26. See Hans Robert Jauss, "The Literary Process of Modernism from Rousseau to Adorno," trans. Lisa C. Roetzel, *Cultural Critique* 11 (Winter 1988–89): 27–61.

27. Jürgen Habermas, "Theodor W. Adorno: Ein philosophierender Intellektueller," in *Philosophisch-politische Profile*, expanded ed. (Frankfurt am Main: Suhrkamp, 1987), 160–66, here 162. For a discussion of *Minima Moralia*'s public reception in the context of postwar Germany, see Alex Demirovic, "Zwischen Nihilismus und Aufklärung. Publizistische Reaktionen auf die *Minima Moralia*," in *Kritische Theorie und Kultur*, ed. Rainer Erd et al. (Frankfurt am Main: Suhrkamp, 1989), 153–72.

28. For a theoretico-political discussion of Adorno's presence, through the composer Schönberg and Thomas Mann's figure Leverkühn, in the novel *Doctor Faustus*, see Jean-François Lyotard, "Adorno as the Devil," trans. Robert Hurley, *Telos* 19 (Spring 1974), 127–37.

29. Theodor W. Adorno and Thomas Mann, *Briefwechsel, 1943–1955*, ed. Christoph Gödde and Thomas Sprecher (Frankfurt am Main: Suhrkamp, 2002), 91.

30. Ibid., 97.

31. Ibid., 122.

32. Ibid., 128–29. Although Adorno's "carrying owls to Athens" translates idiomatically as "carrying coals to Newcastle," I render it literally from the German in order to preserve Adorno's pun on Hegel's owl that takes flight at dusk.

33. *Minima Moralia* as a whole implicitly announces itself in its first line—"The melancholy science from which I make this offering to my friend [*Die traurige Wissenschaft, aus der ich meinem Freunde einiges darbiete*]" [*MM* 15; 13]—as a chiasmic citation of Nietzsche's *Joyous Science* (*Fröhliche Wissenschaft*). The specific sentence, "Es gibt kein richtiges Leben im falschen," bookmarks Adorno's 1963 lecture course on moral philosophy: he mentions it in both his first and his last lecture. He begins his first lecture by cautioning that his lectures will not provide a practical guide to ethics or the good life but that, instead, "we will have to make do with the claim I made at the beginning of that book [*Minima Moralia*] that

'there can be no right life within the false one.' An assertion, incidentally, that—as I discovered later—comes very close to one made by Nietzsche." His last lecture takes up this reference when Adorno says that he "wanted to use this last hour to say something about the nature of moral philosophy today. This is to assume that it is possible to say anything at all on the subject in the light of the statement I tried to make sound persuasive to you in my discussion of the ethics of conviction and the ethics of responsibility, namely that in the false life, a right life is not possible. Incidentally, long after I formulated this sentence I discovered a similar statement in Nietzsche, although it is very differently phrased." Theodor W. Adorno, *Problems of Moral Philosophy*, trans. Rodney Livingstone, ed. Thomas Schröder (Stanford: Stanford University Press, 2001) 1, 167; *Probleme der Moralphilosohie*, ed. Thomas Schröder (Frankfurt am Main: Suhrkamp, 1996), 9, 248. While Adorno does not specify the passage in Nietzsche that he has in mind, his German editor suggests that he is referring to sections 33 and 34 in part 1 of *Human, All Too Human*. There, Nietzsche discusses the necessity of error and of erroneous assumptions about life as a vital necessity for life itself, that is, as both misleading and enabling categories. Friedrich Nietzsche, *Menschliches, Allzumenschliches*, vol. 2 of *Kritische Studienausgabe*, ed. Giorgio Colli and Mazzino Montinari (Berlin: de Gruyter, 1980), 52–54. We could say that *Minima Moralia* is also connected to *Human, All Too Human* because the latter is often considered by Nietzsche's readers as marking a rupture in his writing. In its fragmentary and aphoristic form, it inaugurates a new tone as well as new concerns in Nietzsche's corpus—just as *Minima Moralia*, with its constellation of Denkbilder, marked a formal rupture in Adorno's style. And in the same way that *Human, All Too Human* was in part precipitated by a deep personal rupture—Nietzsche's break with Richard Wagner—*Minima Moralia* was marked by the rupture of personal life that exile from Hitler imposed upon Adorno.

34. Adorno's gesture here convenes with Maurice Blanchot's observation: "'Optimists write badly.' (Valéry.) But pessimists do not write." *The Writing of the Disaster*, trans. Ann Smock (Lincoln: University of Nebraska Press, 1995), 113.

35. After I had completed this chapter, two incisive studies that consider Adorno's well-known sentence in the context of its broader moral-philosophical implication appeared: Jochen Hörisch, *Es gibt (k)ein richtiges Leben im falschen* (Frankfurt am Main: Suhrkamp, 2003), and Alexander García Düttmann, *So ist es: Ein philosophischer Kommentar zu Adornos* Minima Moralia (Frankfurt am Main: Suhrkamp, 2004).

36. For accounts of Adorno's intellectual life in the United States and the ways in which it interacts with his thinking, see his "Scientific Experiences of a European Scholar in America," in *Critical Models: Interventions and Catchwords*, trans. Henry Pickford (New York: Columbia University Press, 1998), 215–42; "Wissenschaftliche Erfahrungen in Amerika," in *Gesammelte Schriften*, vol. 10, book 2,

702–38. Critical readings of Adorno's production in American exile can be found in, among others, Martin Jay, "Adorno in America," in *Permanent Exiles: Essays on the Intellectual Migration from Germany to America* (New York: Columbia University Press, 1986), 120–37; Peter Uwe Hohendahl, "The Philosopher in Exile," in *Prismatic Thought: Theodor W. Adorno* (Lincoln: University of Nebraska Press, 1995), 21–44; and chapters 3 and 4 of Rolf Wiggershaus, *The Frankfurt School: Its History, Theories, and Political Significance*, trans. Michael Robertson (Cambridge, MA: MIT Press, 1994). A sustained reading of the relationship between Adorno's California exile and *Minima Moralia* specifically is offered in Nico Israel, "Damage Control: Adorno, Los Angeles, and the Dislocation of Culture," *Yale Journal of Criticism* 10, no. 1 (1997): 85–113. For a (rather uneven) general attempt to consider the Frankfurt School's sociological relation to German fascism and Hitler's anti-Semitism, see Erich Cramer, *Hitlers Antisemitismus und die "Frankfurter Schule": Kritische Faschismus-Theorie und geschichtliche Realität* (Düsseldorf: Droste, 1979). More recently, compare further Michael Wilson, *Das Institut für Sozialforschung und seine Faschismusanalyse* (Frankfurt am Main: Campus, 1983).

37. See Jacques Derrida's suggestive discussion of dreaming in *Minima Moralia* and in Benjamin in his acceptance speech of the 2001 Theodor W. Adorno Prize in Frankfurt: *Fichus* (Paris: Galilée, 2002).

38. An alternative possibility of reading the sentence "The splinter in your eye is the best magnifying glass [*Der Splitter in deinem Auge ist das beste Vergrößerungsglas*]" is suggested to me by Fritz Breithaupt. If one emphasized "your" to mean, literally, "in *your* eye" (rather than in mine), one would not primarily hear in Adorno's phrase the general or collective "your" that signals "one's," that is, yours *and* mine. From that perspective, the case could be made that Adorno is playing with the German proverb "ein Brett vor dem Kopf haben" (literally, to have a wooden board in front of one's head), which means being thick, slow to catch on, incapable of thinking straight. In that case, one would be eager to detect the tiny splinter in the eye of the other, while being oblivious to the huge board one carries before one's own head.

I would add that this incapability would indeed make one a *Holzkopf* (a "woodenhead" or numbskull) and that Adorno's allusion here is not only idiomatic but also biblical (Matthew 7:3–6 and Luke 6:41–42). In Matthew 7:3–6, we encounter (in the revised modern German translation, based on Luther's): "Was siehst du aber den Splitter im Auge deines Bruders und nimmst nicht den Balken in deinem Auge wahr? Oder wie kannst du zu deinem Bruder sagen: Halt, ich will dir den Splitter aus deinem Auge ziehen? Und siehe, ein Balken steckt in deinem Auge. Du Heuchler, zieh zuerst den Balken aus deinem Auge; danach sieh zu, wie du den Splitter aus dem Auge deines Bruders ziehst." The King James Version reads: "And why beholdest thou the mote that is in your brother's eye, but considerest not the beam that is in thine own eye? Or how wilt thou say to thy brother, Let me pull out the mote out of thine eye; and behold, a beam is in thine own eye? Thou hypocrite, first cast out the beam out of thine own eye; and then shalt thou see clearly to cast out the mote out of thy brother's eye."

39. Blanchot, *The Writing of the Disaster*, 145.

40. An exception is the illuminating discussion of Adorno's intricate reweavings of Hegel in the dedication of *Minima Moralia* in the context of a theory of love and of a displaced father-son constellation in Thomas Pepper, "Guilt by (Un)free Association: Adorno on Romance *et al.*, with Some References to the Schlock Experience," in *Singularities: Extremes of Theory in the Twentieth Century* (Cambridge: Cambridge University Press, 1997), 20–48.

41. Martin Heidegger, *Was ist Metaphysik?* (Frankfurt am Main: Vittorio Klostermann, 1992), 51.

42. See Martin Heidegger, *Elucidations of Hölderlin's Poetry*, trans. Keith Hoeller (Amherst, NY: Humanity, 2000); *Erläuterungen zu Hölderlins Dichtung*, 4th expanded ed. (Frankfurt am Main: Vittorio Klostermann, 1971).

43. Martin Heidegger, *What Is Called Thinking?*, trans. Fred Wieck and J. Glenn Gray (New York: Harper and Row, 1968), 138–39; *Was heißt Denken?* (Tübingen: Niemeyer, 1954), 91.

44. It would also be necessary to theorize the entire friendship between Adorno and Horkheimer in a way that takes into account the full range of their writings to and about each other, such as a variety of short essays and letters. Adorno's publications on Horkheimer—a biographical sketch, a transcript of a radio broadcast, an open letter, a congratulatory missive, and a preface—are collected in volume 20, book 1 of his *Gesammelte Schriften* (149–68).

45. Max Horkheimer, "Himmel, Ewigkeit und Schönheit: Spiegel—Interview mit Max Horkheimer zum Tode Theodor W. Adornos," *Der Spiegel*, 11 August 1969.

46. See Roland Barthes, *Camera Lucida: Reflections on Photography*, trans. Richard Howard (New York: Noonday, 1993), 96.

47. Georg Wilhelm Friedrich Hegel, *Lectures on the Philosophy of History: Introduction; Reason in History*, trans. H. B. Nisbet, introd. Duncan Forbes (Cambridge: Cambridge University Press, 1975), 85; *Vorlesungen über die Philosophie der Geschichte*, Theorie-Werkausgabe 12 (Frankfurt am Main: Suhrkamp, 1985), 47.

In mobilizing Hegel in order to inscribe him with and against himself, Adorno performs precisely that task of reading of which scholars such as Duncan Forbes are afraid. In his introduction to the British translation of Hegel, he complains: "After a survey of the literature one is left wondering why modern philosophers of history bother with Hegel at all. Mostly they only muddy the waters of interpretation without advancing the cause of the philosophy of history." Hegel, *Philosophy of History*, xxv. In his belief that philosophical questions are questions of reading and interpretation, and in his notion that such interpretive reading cannot unfold in isolation from the linguistic constitution of a text and its predicaments, Adorno would certainly qualify as one of those writers who "muddy the waters of interpretation" that Forbes so fears. But all of Adorno's thought, even when it is concerned with the philosophy of history, would seem to take issue with Forbes's "only" and the prohibition against *reading* that it implies. Here, Adorno is much closer to Paul de Man, who writes that his *Allegories of Reading* "started out as a historical study" but he found himself "unable to progress beyond local difficulties of interpretation," so that he was forced to "shift from historical definition to the problematics of reading." Paul de Man, *Allegories of Reading: Figural Language in Rousseau, Nietzsche, Rilke, and Proust* (New Haven, CT: Yale University Press, 1979), ix.

For a recent discussion of Adorno's concerns with problems of reading in the context of his studies of Hegel, see Samuel Weber, "'As Though the End of the World Had Come and Gone . . .': Critical Theory and the Task of Reading, or, *Allemal ist nicht immergleich*," *New German Critique* 81 (Fall 2000): 83–105.

48. Adorno, *Negative Dialectics*, 365; *Negative Dialektik*, 358.

49. In this context, compare further Adorno's discussion of metaphysics and the Kantian imperative after Auschwitz in his 1965 lecture course: "I could, if you like, give this a moral-philosophical twist and say that Hitler has placed a new imperative on us: that, quite simply, Auschwitz should not be repeated and that nothing like it should ever exist again. It is impossible to found this imperative on logic—it has that in common with the Kantian imperative. When Kant states that his own imperative is simply given, that assertion doubtless contains all kinds of grimly authoritarian and irrationalist elements, but also—as I tried to explain to you in my lectures last semester—an awareness that the sphere of right action does not coincide with mere rationality, that it has an 'addendum.'" Theodor W. Adorno, *Metaphysics: Concepts and Problems*, ed. Rolf Tiedemann, trans. Edmund Jephcott (Stanford: Stanford University Press, 2001), 116; *Metaphysik. Begriff und Probleme*, ed. Rolf Tiedemann (Frankfurt am Main: Suhrkamp, 1998), 181. For a discussion of the categorical imperative after Auschwitz in the context of issues of naming and the name, see Alexander García Düttmann, who suggests that to act and to think in such a way that Auschwitz does not happen again means to "act and think as if Auschwitz could happen again, as if it had *already* happened several times. (If Auschwitz happens only once, it is because this name points to an event which will never stop happening)." Alexander García Düttmann, *The Gift of Language: Memory and Promise in Adorno, Benjamin, Heidegger, and Rosenzweig*, trans. Arline Lyons (Syracuse, NY: Syracuse University Press, 2000), 94.

50. Here, Adorno's reading of Hegel could be said to exhibit certain affinities to that of Jean-Luc Nancy, who attempts to offer innovative and radical readings of Hegel's Absolute that are no longer confined by traditional interpretations of the Absolute as a synthesizing and totalizing closure of thought. For Nancy, the "absolute is between us. It is there in itself and for itself, and, one might say, the self itself is between us. But 'the self itself is unrest': between us, nothing can be at rest, nothing is assured of presence or of being—and we pass each after the others as

much as each into the others. Each with the others, each *near* the others: the *near* of the absolute is nothing other than our *near* each other." *Hegel: The Restlessness of the Negative*, trans. Jason Smith and Steven Miller (Minneapolis: University of Minnesota Press, 2002), 78–79. In this context, compare further Nancy, *The Speculative Remark (One of Hegel's Bons Mots)*, trans. Céline Surprenant (Stanford: Stanford University Press, 2001).

51. Adorno, *Negative Dialectics*, 364–65; *Negative Dialektik*, 357–58.

52. Walter Benjamin, *One-Way Street*, trans. Edmund Jephcott, in *Selected Writings: Volume 1, 1913–1926*, ed. Marcus Bullock and Michael W. Jennings (Cambridge, MA: Harvard University Press, 1996), 444–88, here 459; *Einbahnstraße*, vol. 4 of *Gesammelte Schriften*, ed. Tillman Rexroth (Frankfurt am Main: Suhrkamp, 1972), 83–148, here 107.

53. For a different reading of this sentence that attempts to link it to Nietzsche's philosophy of irony and his transvaluation of all values, see Gillian Rose, *The Melancholy Science: An Introduction to the Thought of Theodor W. Adorno* (New York: Columbia University Press, 1978), 18–24.

54. Giorgio Agamben, *Remnants of Auschwitz: The Witness and the Archive*, trans. Daniel Heller-Roazen (New York: Zone, 1999), 80.

55. Ibid., 81.

56. Ibid., 81–82.

57. Adorno, *Negative Dialectics*, 366; *Negative Dialektik*, 359.

58. Sigmund Freud, *Civilization and Its Discontents*, in *The Future of an Illusion, Civilization and Its Discontents, and Other Works*, vol. 21 of *The Standard Edition of the Complete Psychological Works of Sigmund Freud*, ed. and trans. James Strachey (London: Hogarth, 1961), 59–145; *Das Unbehagen in der Kultur*, in *Fragen der Gesellschaft/Ursprünge der Religion*, Studienausgabe 9, ed. Alexander Mitscherlich, Angela Richards, and James Strachey (Frankfurt am Main: Fischer, 2000).

59. Sigmund Freud, "Notes upon a Case of Obsessional Neurosis, in Two Case Histories ('Little Hans' and the 'Rat Man')," in *The Standard Edition of the Complete Pyschological Works of Sigmund Freud*, vol. 10, ed. and trans. James Strachey (London: Hogarth, 1955), 152–318, here 214–18; *Bemerkungen über einen Fall der Zwangsneurose*, in *Zwang, Paranoia und Perversion*, Studienausgabe 7, ed. Alexander Mitscherlich, Angela Richards, and James Strachey (Frankfurt am Main: Fischer, 2000), 31–103, here 78–79.

60. Indeed, as Düttmann has shown, for Adorno and Horkheimer there can hardly be a thought—a thought that wishes to take its own aporias seriously for its own effectiveness—that does not theorize its abiding dependence on an element of exaggeration. For "how would one establish with certainty that the exaggerating trait of thinking, the gesture without which the insight into the dialectic of enlightenment would have remained hidden, does not express itself in this exaggeration?" "Thinking as Gesture: A Note on *Dialectic of Enlightenment*," *New German Critique* 81 (Fall 2000): 143–52, here 152.

61. Freud, *Notes*, 215–16; *Bemerkungen*, 79.

62. Here, Adorno echoes Benjamin's multiple readings of the interlaced status of culture, violence, and barbarism that traverse, among other texts, his essay on the collector Fuchs as well as his theses on the concept of history. It would be necessary, too, to read the activities of the rat-clubbing innkeeper at length in the terms offered by Benjamin's distinction between mythical and divine violence in his 1921 essay "On the Critique of Violence." For now, Benjamin's reading of violence is the focus of the volumes *Deconstruction and the Possibility of Justice*, ed. Drucilla Cornell, Michael Rosenfeld, and David Gray Carlson (New York: Routledge, 1992), and *Gewalt und Gerechtigkeit: Derrida–Benjamin*, ed. Anselm Haverkamp (Frankfurt am Main: Suhrkamp, 1994). For a discussion that embeds Benjamin's concepts of violence in contemporary debates, see Beatrice Hanssen, *Critique of Violence: Between Poststructuralism and Critical Theory* (London: Routledge, 2000).

63. Adorno, *Negative Dialectics*, 366–67; *Negative Dialektik*, 359–60.

64. Theodor W. Adorno, "Cultural Criticism and Society," in *Prisms*, trans. Samuel and Shierry Weber (Cambridge, MA: MIT Press, 1981), 34; "Kulturkritik und Gesellschaft," in *Gesammelte Schriften*, vol. 10, ed. Rolf Tiedemann (Frankfurt am Main: Suhrkamp, 1997), 30. Adorno's various formulations of this statement regarding lyric poetry "after Auschwitz" have now been collected, along with responses by a variety of German-language poets and critics: *Lyrik nach Auschwitz? Adorno und die Dichter*, ed. Petra Kiedaisch (Stuttgart: Reclam, 1995).

65. Adorno shares with Horkheimer this general logic in which reason, in the very act of its articulation, is always already inscribed with what it may seek to overcome—irrationality, myth, superstition, slavery, dependency, exploitation. As Horkheimer writes: "If one were to speak of a disease affecting reason, this disease should be understood not as having stricken reason at some historical moment, but as being inseparable from the nature of reason in civilization as we have known it so far." He adds that "the 'recovery' depends on insight into the nature of the original disease, not on a cure of the latest symptoms." Max Horkheimer, "On the Concept of Philosophy," *German 20th Century Philosophy: The Frankfurt School*, ed. Wolfgang Schirmacher (New York: Continuum, 2000), 1–17, here 10.

66. Berel Lang, *Heidegger's Silence* (Ithaca, NY: Cornell University Press, 1996), 22.

67. "'Negative Dialectics,'" as Jarvis reminds us, "does not mean that dialectic is now positive and ought to become negative, but that genuinely dialectical thought already is negative. Adorno's idea of negative dialectic is not simply a reversal of Hegel, another attempt brusquely to 'stand dialectics on its feet.' Adorno prefers another of Marx's metaphors: he suggests that German Idealism can be made to 'dance to its own tune.' Adorno attempts to prevent a dialectical thinking of which he takes Hegel to be the outstanding exponent from freezing into a method or a world-view and thereby becoming, precisely, undialectical." *Adorno*, 168. For a discussion of the various meanings that "negative" can assume

in negative dialectics, see Michael Theunissen, "Negativität bei Adorno," in *Adorno-Konferenz 1983*, ed. Ludwig von Friedeburg and Jürgen Habermas (Frankfurt am Main: Suhrkamp, 1983), 41–65.

68. Hegel, *Philosophy of History*, 89; *Philosophie der Geschichte*, 49.

69. Jean-François Lyotard, quoted in Hubertus von Amelunxen, "Fotografie *nach* der Fotografie: Das Entsetzen des Körpers im digitalen Raum," in *Fotografie nach der Fotografie*, ed. Hubertus von Amelunxen, Stefan Iglhaut, and Florian Rötzer (Dresden: Verlag der Kunst, 1995), 116–23, here 116.

70. These essays are now available in English translation in a volume that comprises Adorno's essay collections *Eingriffe* and *Stichworte*: Theodor W. Adorno, *Critical Models*, trans. and with a preface by Henry Pickford (New York: Columbia University Press, 1998).

71. Adorno, *Negative Dialectics*, 408; *Negative Dialektik*, 399–400.

72. It would be necessary to expand our discussion to include the relation of Adorno's project to various other semantic levels of *Fall*: as a grammatical, psychoclinical, and even criminological case.

73. The extensive notes and fragments comprising the *Graeculus* project will eventually be made available by the archive. Selections, arranged thematically, are in the process of being published on an annual basis in the archive's yearbooks, the *Frankfurter Adorno Blätter*. A first selection, comprising Adorno's musicological notes, was included in *Frankfurter Adorno Blätter 7*, ed. Rolf Tiedemann (Munich: Edition Text + Kritik, 2001), 9–36. My remarks on Adorno's *Graeculus* project are based on the philological information provided by Adorno's German editor, Rolf Tiedemann, in his introductory pages (9–10).

CODA

1. Jacques Derrida, "The Taste of Tears," trans. Pascale-Anne Brault and Michael Naas, in *The Work of Mourning*, ed. Pascale-Anne Brault and Michael Naas (Chicago: University of Chicago Press, 2001), 107–10, here 107 and 110. I also am indebted to the editors' splendid introduction to that volume.

2. For a moving example of the imbrication of friendship and the project of a transformed Critical Theory, see Horkheimer's text written on the occasion of, and published two days after, Adorno's death: "Über seinen Gefährten: Zum Tode Theodor W. Adornos," in *Frankfurter Schule und Studentenbewegung: Von der Flaschenpost zum Molotowcocktail, 1946–1995*, vol. 2, ed. Wolfgang Kraushaar (Hamburg: Roger & Bernhard bei Zweitausendeins, 1998), 672.

A literary reflection—a Denkbild in its own right—of the scene of Adorno's funeral is offered by his former student Alexander Kluge, "Gefahrenmoment für die Letzten der Kritischen Theorie bei Adorno's Beerdigung," in *Die Lücke, die der Teufel läßt: Im Umfeld des neuen Jahrhunderts* (Frankfurt am Main: Suhrkamp, 2003), 640–41.

Index

Adami, Valerio, 215*n*42
Adorno, Theodor W., 1, 2, 4, 5, 6, 7, 8, 11–14, 17, 19, 22, 24, 26–28, 30–32, 33, 34, 35, 36, 37, 40, 47, 52, 53–55, 62, 71, 77, 82, 97, 110, 112, 127, 143–145, 147–190, 192, 193*n*2, 194*nn*12–13, 195*nn*24–25, 196*n*27, 197*n*34, 197*n*39, 197*n*44, 198*n*57, 199*n*60, 202*n*32, 203*nn*46–47, 204*n*60, 206*n*15, 207*n*27, 208*n*37, 208*n*48, 210*n*6, 211*n*10, 214*n*30, 215*n*34, 217*n*64, 217*n*1, 218*n*4, 218*n*6, 219*n*8, 219*nn*11–22, 220*n*25, 220*nn*28–33, 221*n*34–36, 222*n*38, 223*n*44, 223*n*47–50, 225*n*51, 225*n*57, 225*n*60, 226*nn*62–65, 226*n*67, 227*n*70–73
Agamben, Giorgio, 173–175, 225*n*54–56
Alexander the Great, 168
Althusser, Louis, 87
Amelunxen, Hubertus von, 216*n*48, 227*n*69
Anderson, Benedict, 142, 217*n*62
Aragon, Louis, 46
Arendt, Hannah, 44, 143, 173, 200*n*3
Arnheim, Rudolf, 111
Augustine, Saint, 119

Baader, Franz von, 11
Bach, Johann Sebastian, 85, 92, 94, 101, 102
Barnouw, Dagmar, 211*n*11
Barthes, Roland, 28, 96, 134, 198*n*48, 208*n*47, 215*n*42, 223*n*46
Baudelaire, Charles, 12, 48, 176

Baumgarten, Alexander, 29
Beardsworth, Richard, 215*n*36
Beethoven, Ludwig van, 32, 85, 94, 101, 102
Behrens, Roger, 206*n*13
Belke, Ingrid, 211*n*9
Benjamin, Walter, 1, 2, 4, 5, 6, 7, 8–13, 14, 16, 17, 18, 19, 20, 21, 22, 34, 37, 38, 43–71, 76, 82, 93–94, 97, 110, 112, 114–115, 116, 117, 119, 127, 138, 147, 148, 150, 153, 157, 170, 172, 192, 194*n*11, 195*n*16, 195*n*19, 199*n*60, 199*nn*1–2, 199*n*4, 200*n*11, 201*nn*14–24, 202*n*25–28, 202*n*31, 202*n*34, 202*nn*36–37, 202*n*39, 203*nn*40–41, 203*n*43, 203*n*45, 203*n*48–52, 204*n*55, 204*n*58–59, 204*n*61–62, 207*n*26, 211*n*10, 212*n*16, 212*n*21, 214*n*33, 215*n*35, 216*n*49, 218*n*6, 225*n*52, 226*n*62
Bennington, Geoffrey, 212*n*20, 213*n*27, 215*n*36
Berg, Alban, 219*n*9
Berghahn, Klaus, 209*n*48
Bernasconi, Robert, 81, 207*n*25
Bernstein, J. M., 198*n*51
Bhabha, Homi, 142, 217*n*62
Bismarck, Otto von, 167
Bizet, Georges, 85
Blanchot, Maurice, 159, 223*n*39
Bloch, Ernst, 1, 2, 4, 5, 6, 7, 11, 13, 14, 17–18, 22, 23, 33, 34, 37, 38–39, 47, 48, 52–53, 72–106, 153, 157, 192, 193*n*6, 194*n*14, 196*n*31, 198*n*52, 198*n*54, 202*n*29, 204*n*1,

Bloch, Ernst (*continued*)
  205*n*5, 205*n*8, 205*n*10, 206*n*14, 207*n*23, 207*n*28–29, 208*nn*37–38, 208*n*43–45, 209*n*49–51, 209*n*53–56, 209*n*59–60, 211*n*10
Bloch, Karola, 208*n*46
Blumenberg, Hans, 197*n*32
Boehme, Jacob, 11
Bolzani, Giovanni, 11
Borchardt, Rudolf, 12
Borgia, Cesare, 166–167
Bradley, F. H., 175
Brahms, Johannes, 77, 85
Brecht, Bertolt, 1, 8, 12, 40, 59, 90, 92, 148, 177, 181, 208*n*39
Breithaupt, Fritz, 222*n*38
Brodersen, Momme, 211*n*9
Bruckner, Anton, 76
Bubner, Rüdiger, 219*n*11
Burckhardt, Jacob, 117
Burgin, Victor, 200*n*7
Burke, Kenneth, 218*n*4

Caesar, Julius, 168
Caputo, John, 213*n*28
Caygill, Howard, 200*n*10, 204*n*52
Celan, Paul, 30, 119, 143
Chaplin, Charlie, 40, 148, 218*n*6
Cicero, Marcus Tullius, 189
Cixous, Hélène, 214*n*28
Cohen, Tom, 197*n*37
Corngold, Stanley, 198*n*50, 204*n*57
Cramer, Erich, 222*n*36
Czajka-Cunico, Anna, 205*n*12, 209*n*48

Dahlhaus, Carl, 205*n*3
Darwin, Charles, 167
Debord, Guy, 1
Deleuze, Gilles, 18, 110, 113, 197*n*33, 212*n*13
DeLillo, Don, 149
de Man, Paul, 1, 24, 29, 36, 67–69, 78–79, 122–123, 197*n*37, 198*n*46, 198*n*49, 199*n*59, 204*n*56, 206*n*18, 207*n*21, 213*n*24, 224*n*47

Demirovic, Alex, 220*n*27
Derrida, Jacques, 1, 19–20, 37, 39, 59, 74, 89, 97, 107–146, 158, 191, 193*n*1, 197*n*36, 202*n*39, 205*n*6–7, 208*n*35, 212*n*20, 213*n*22–23, 213*n*25, 213*n*27–28, 214*n*29, 214*n*31–32, 215*nn*35–42, 217*n*52–61, 217*n*63, 222*n*37, 227*n*1
Descartes, René, 87–88
Disney, Walt, 40, 148
Döblin, Alfred, 46
Düttmann, Alexander García, 196*n*29, 217*n*65, 221*n*35, 224*n*49, 225*n*60

Eagleton, Terry, 29, 198*n*49
Einstein, Albert, 189
Eisler, Hanns, 153
Engels, Friedrich, 156, 183

Faltin, Peter, 205*n*3
Fenves, Peter, 201*n*15, 218*n*2
Flaubert, Gustave, 25, 29
Foucault, Michel, 1
Forbes, Duncan, 223*n*47
Freud, Sigmund, 1, 3, 34, 96–97, 99, 178–180, 182, 183, 198*n*55, 225*n*58–59, 226*n*61
Fromm, Erich, 4
Fürnkäs, Josef, 200*n*9
Fynsk, Christopher, 23, 197*n*42, 204*n*52

Gadamer, Hans-Georg, 120
Gasché, Rodolphe, 213*n*25
George, Stefan, 12, 155
Geulen, Eva, 196*n*29
Giehlow, Karl, 11
Goebbels, Joseph, 157
Goethe, Johann Wolfgang, 11, 51, 180
Guattari, Félix, 18, 110, 197*n*33

Habermas, Jürgen, 75, 154, 205*n*9, 220*n*27
Hamacher, Werner, 59, 145, 217*n*66
Hamann, Johann Georg, 11
Hansen, Miriam, 46, 200*n*12, 217*n*50

Hanssen, Beatrice, 204*n*52, 226*n*62
Harsdörfer, Georg Phillip, 11
Heartfied, John, 40, 148
Hegel, Georg Wilhelm Friedrich, 1, 3, 14–17, 22, 25, 35, 43–44, 61, 87, 119, 123, 149, 156, 157, 162, 167, 168–169, 170, 171, 175, 185, 196*nn*28–29, 220*n*32, 223*n*40, 223*n*47, 224*n*50, 226*n*67, 227*n*68
Heidegger, Martin, 1, 65–66, 88, 108, 119, 123, 140, 162–163, 173, 203*n*52, 204*n*53, 207*n*34, 210*n*1, 223*n*41–43
Herder, Johann Gottfried, 7, 11
Hermand, Jost, 208*n*40, 218*n*5
Hillach, Ansgar, 203*n*44
Hindenburg, Paul von, 218*n*6
Hitler, Adolf, 40–41, 71, 147–190, 218*nn*6–7, 221*n*35, 224*n*49
Hoffmann, E. T. A., 213*n*26
Hoffmann, Rainer, 209*n*48
Hofmannsthal, Hugo von, 50, 202*n*28
Hohendahl, Peter Uwe, 222*n*36
Hölderlin, Friedrich, 17, 43–44, 93, 162
Hörisch, Jochen, 221*n*35
Horkheimer, Max, 4, 5, 6, 40, 47, 110, 127, 153, 160–161, 163–165, 192, 193*n*5, 199*n*58, 211*n*10, 223*n*44–45, 225*n*60, 226*n*65, 227*n*2
Husserl, Edmund, 91, 119

Israel, Nico, 222*n*36

Jameson, Fredric, 24, 197*n*43, 220*n*23
Jarvis, Simon, 219*n*22, 226*n*67
Jauss, Hans Robert, 154, 220*n*26
Jay, Martin, 3, 111, 116, 193*n*4, 198*n*56, 207*n*33, 211*n*8, 212*n*18, 222*n*36
Jennings, Michael W., 200*n*9, 201*n*13
Jephcott, E. F. N., 161
Joyce, James, 119
Jünger, Ernst, 8
Juvenal, 189

Kafka, Franz, 1, 25, 59, 119, 143, 170, 213*n*26

Kant, Immanuel, 3, 11, 15, 22, 25, 46, 56, 85, 86–87, 89, 119, 149, 169–170, 207*n*30–31, 224*n*49
Kaufman, Robert, 198*n*57
Khatibi, Abdelkebir, 143
Keller, Gottfried, 33, 70
Kessler, Harry Graf, 111, 211*n*9
Kierkegaard, Sören, 149, 218*n*6
Kirchheimer, Otto, 4
Kirst, Karoline, 195
Klee, Paul, 8–9
Kluge, Alexander, 227*n*2B
Knoche, Lennart, 196*n*26
Knoche, Stefan, 204*n*52
Koch, Gertrud, 212*n*19
Köhnen, Ralph, 196*n*26
Kracauer, Lili, 112, 211*n*11
Kracauer, Siegfried, 1, 2, 4, 5, 7, 11, 13, 14, 17, 22, 37, 39, 47, 50, 51, 52–53, 97, 107–146, 153, 192, 194*n*15, 202*n*26, 202*n*30, 208*n*48, 210*n*4, 210*n*7, 211*n*9, 211*n*12, 212*n*14–15, 212*n*17, 212*n*20, 214*n*33, 216*n*43–47, 216*n*50, 217*n*51
Kraus, Karl, 8, 12, 45
Krell, David Farrell, 216*n*42
Kronick, Joseph, 213*n*28
Kürnberger, Ferdinand, 173, 175

Lacan, Jacques, 1
Lacis, Asja, 46, 111, 200*n*11
Laclau, Ernesto, 103, 209*n*58
Lacoue-Labarthe, Philippe, 72, 77, 93, 148, 199*n*2, 206*n*16, 208*n*42, 218*n*3, 218*n*7
Lang, Berel, 184, 226*n*66
La Rochefoucauld, François de, 26
Leifeld, Britta, 196*n*26
Libeskind, Daniel, 46, 200*n*6
Lessing, Gotthold Ephraim, 11
Lethen, Helmut, 202*n*38
Lettau, Reinhard, 213*n*26
Levin, Thomas Y., 211*n*10
Levinas, Emmanuel, 1, 73, 81, 100, 129, 143, 199*n*58, 204*n*2
Lilienfeld, Robert, 206*n*12

Löwenthal, Leo, 4, 112, 210*n*7, 211*nn*11–12
Luhmann, Niklas, 26, 198*n*47
Lukács, Georg, 17, 76, 77, 108, 110, 210*n*2, 211*n*7
Lyotard, Jean-François, 186, 220*n*28, 227*n*69

Mahler, Gustav, 77
Mahnkopf, Claus-Steffen, 206*n*19
Malabou, Catherine, 214*n*28
Mallarmé, Stéphane, 12
Mann, Thomas, 154–155, 220*n*28–31
Marcuse, Herbert, 4
Marx, Karl, 1, 3, 21–22, 38, 46, 73, 75, 82, 103, 108, 111, 156, 157, 170, 183, 226*n*67
Matz, Wolfgang, 206*n*12
Mayer, Hans, 111, 209*n*57
Mendieta, Eduardo, 5, 6, 194*n*10
Merleau-Ponty, Maurice, 87
Michael, Klaus, 214*n*33
Miller, J. Hillis, 23, 197*n*41, 215*n*39
Möller van den Bruck, Arthur, 8
Mouffe, Chantal, 103, 209*n*58
Mozart, Wolfgang Amadeus, 77, 85, 92, 101, 102
Mülder-Bach, Inka, 116, 211*n*10, 212*nn*17–18, 212*n*20, 217*n*50
Müller-Michaels, Harro, 195*n*23
Musil, Robert, 8, 12

Naas, Michael, 214*n*28
Nägele, Rainer, 203*n*44
Nancy, Jean-Luc, 80, 148, 199*n*2, 207*n*24, 218*n*3, 218*n*7, 224*n*50
Napoleon, 168–169
Naumann, Barbara, 208*n*34
Neumann, Franz, 4
Nietzsche, Friedrich, 1, 2, 3, 11, 45, 77, 89, 151, 155, 156, 193*n*3, 220*n*33, 225*n*53
Norris, Christopher, 90, 206*n*12, 207*n*22, 208*n*36
Novalis (Friedrich Leopold, Baron Freiherr von Hardenberg), 14, 88, 108, 202*n*28, 208*n*34

Oschmann, Dirk, 210*n*3, 210*n*5
Otto, Rudolf, 199*n*58

Paetzold, Heinz, 206*n*12
Pepper, Thomas, 223*n*40
Perloff, Marjorie, 219*n*10
Pizer, John, 217*n*62
Plato, 12, 87, 119
Plissart, Marie-Françoise, 215*n*42
Plug, Jan, 218*n*2
Poe, Edgar Allan, 99, 209*n*52
Pollack, Friedrich, 4
Proust, Marcel, 12, 25, 59, 71, 133–134, 201*n*24, 216*n*45

Rabinbach, Anson, 194, 218*n*2
Readings, Bill, 21, 197*n*40
Reininghaus, Frieder, 206*n*12
Riethmüller, Albrecht, 206*n*12
Rilke, Rainer Maria, 173
Rochlitz, Rainer, 200*n*8
Roeppert, Ekkehard, 209*n*48
Rose, Gillian, 225*n*53
Rosenzweig, Franz, 143
Roth, Joseph, 111, 211*n*9
Rousseau, Jean-Jacques, 78, 89, 119
Royle, Nicholas, 213*n*25

Saavedra Fajardo, Diego de, 11
Said, Edward, 74, 205*n*3
Salomon, Ernst von, 8
Sartre, Jean-Paul, 87
Scheerbart, Paul, 48
Schelling, Friedrich Wilhelm Joseph, 14, 16–17, 43–44, 75, 196*n*30
Schlaffer, Heinz, 14, 196*n*26, 211*n*10
Schlegel, Friedrich, 1, 14, 16, 44, 45, 92, 199*n*2, 208*n*34, 208*n*41
Schlüppmann, Heide, 216*n*46
Schnädelbach, Helmut, 153, 220*n*24
Schneider, Bernhard, 200*n*6
Schoen, Ernst, 6, 82

Scholem, Gershom, 49, 71, 143, 204*n*62
Schönberg, Arnold, 32, 93, 219*n*9, 220*n*28
Schopenhauer, Arthur, 77, 78, 79, 89, 135
Schöttker, Detlef, 200*n*5, 202*n*28
Schuler, Alfred, 62
Schulz, Eberhard Wilhelm, 195
Schwitters, Kurt, 45
Seel, Martin, 204*n*52
Seuss, Dr. (Theodor Seuss Geisel), 40, 148
Shakespeare, William, 94
Simmel, Georg, 7, 98, 194*n*15
Smith, Robert, 217*n*53
Sohn-Rethel, Alfred, 181
Spengler, Oswald, 8
Spiegelman, Art, 148, 218*n*7
Spivak, Gayatri, 37, 199*n*61
Stalder, Helmut, 211*nn*9–10
Steuermann, Eduard, 219*n*9
Stiegler, Bernard, 215*n*42
Stone, Sascha, 45
Strauss, David Friedrich, 166–167

Theunissen, Michael, 227*n*67
Tieck, Ludwig, 14, 26

Tiedemann, Rolf, 227*n*73
Tschichold, Jan, 45

Valéry, Paul, 45
Vattimo, Gianni, 206*n*12
Vico, Giambattista, 117
Vidal, Francesca, 209*n*57
Volkmann, Ludwig, 195,

Wagner, Richard, 76, 85, 221*n*33
Weber, Max, 195*n*15
Weber, Samuel, 204*n*52, 206*n*17, 224*n*47
Weil, Felix, 3
Weissberg, Liliane, 209*n*48
White, Hayden, 205*n*4
Wiggershaus, Rolf, 3, 5, 193*n*4, 194*nn*7–8, 219*n*12, 222*n*36
Wilson, Michael, 222*n*36
Winkelmann, Johann Joachim, 11
Witte, Bernd, 200*n*9
Wittfogel, Karl August, 4
Wittgenstein, Ludwig, 150, 219*n*10

Zerlang, Martin, 209*n*48
Zincgref, Julius Wilhelm, 11
Zipes, Jack, 5, 6, 194*n*9
Žižek, Slavoj, 202*n*39, 215*n*35
Zohlen, Gerwin, 211*n*10

Cultural Memory in the Present

Ranjana Khanna, *Algeria Cuts: Women and Representation, 1830 to the Present*

Esther Peeren, *Bakhtin and Beyond: Intersubjectivities and Popular Culture*

Eyal Peretz, *Becoming Visionary: Brian De Palma's Cinematic Education of the Senses*

Diana Sorensen, *A Turbulent Decade Remembered: Scenes from the Latin American Sixties*

Hubert Damisch, *A Childhood Memory by Piero della Francesca*

Asja Szafraniec, *Beckett, Derrida, and the Event of Literature*

Sara Guyer, *Romanticism After Auschwitz*

Alison Ross, *The Aesthetic Paths of Philosophy: Presentation in Kant, Heidegger, Lacoue-Labarthe, and Nancy*

Bella Brodzki, *Can These Bones Live? Translation, Survival, and Cultural Memory*

Rodolphe Gasché, *The Honor of Thinking: Critique, Theory, Philosophy*

Brigitte Peucker, *The Material Image: Art and the Real in Film*

Natalie Melas, *All the Difference in the World*

Jonathan Culler, *The Literary in Theory*

Michael G. Levine, *The Belated Witness: Literature, Testimony, and the Question of Holocaust Survival*

Jennifer A. Jordan, *Structures of Memory*

Christoph Menke, *Reflections of Equality*

Marlène Zarader, *The Unthought Debt: Heidegger and the Hebraic Heritage*

Jan Assmann, *Religion and Cultural Memory: Ten Studies*

David Scott and Charles Hirschkind, *Powers of the Secular Modern: Talal Asad and His Interlocutors*

Gyanendra Pandey, *Routine Violence: Nations, Fragments, Histories*

James Siegel, *Naming the Witch*

J. M. Bernstein, *Against Voluptuous Bodies: Late Modernism and the Meaning of Painting*

Theodore W. Jennings, Jr., *Reading Derrida / Thinking Paul: On Justice*

Richard Rorty and Eduardo Mendieta, *Take Care of Freedom and Truth Will Take Care of Itself: Interviews with Richard Rorty*

Jacques Derrida, *Paper Machine*

Renaud Barbaras, *Desire and Distance: Introduction to a Phenomenology of Perception*

Jill Bennett, *Empathic Vision: Affect, Trauma, and Contemporary Art*

Ban Wang, *Illuminations from the Past: Trauma, Memory, and History in Modern China*

James Phillips, *Heidegger's* Volk: *Between National Socialism and Poetry*

Frank Ankersmit, *Sublime Historical Experience*

István Rév, *Retroactive Justice: Prehistory of Post-Communism*

Paola Marrati, *Genesis and Trace: Derrida Reading Husserl and Heidegger*

Krzysztof Ziarek, *The Force of Art*

Marie-José Mondzain, *Image, Icon, Economy: The Byzantine Origins of the Contemporary Imaginary*

Cecilia Sjöholm, *The Antigone Complex: Ethics and the Invention of Feminine Desire*

Jacques Derrida and Elisabeth Roudinesco, *For What Tomorrow . . . : A Dialogue*

Elisabeth Weber, *Questioning Judaism: Interviews by Elisabeth Weber*

Jacques Derrida and Catherine Malabou, *Counterpath: Traveling with Jacques Derrida*

Martin Seel, *Aesthetics of Appearing*

Nanette Salomon, *Shifting Priorities: Gender and Genre in Seventeenth-Century Dutch Painting*

Jacob Taubes, *The Political Theology of Paul*

Jean-Luc Marion, *The Crossing of the Visible*

Eric Michaud, *The Cult of Art in Nazi Germany*

Anne Freadman, *The Machinery of Talk: Charles Peirce and the Sign Hypothesis*

Stanley Cavell, *Emerson's Transcendental Etudes*

Stuart McLean, *The Event and Its Terrors: Ireland, Famine, Modernity*

Beate Rössler, ed., *Privacies: Philosophical Evaluations*

Bernard Faure, *Double Exposure: Cutting Across Buddhist and Western Discourses*

Alessia Ricciardi, *The Ends of Mourning: Psychoanalysis, Literature, Film*

Alain Badiou, *Saint Paul: The Foundation of Universalism*

Gil Anidjar, *The Jew, the Arab: A History of the Enemy*

Jonathan Culler and Kevin Lamb, eds., *Just Being Difficult? Academic Writing in the Public Arena*

Jean-Luc Nancy, *A Finite Thinking*, edited by Simon Sparks

Theodor W. Adorno, *Can One Live after Auschwitz? A Philosophical Reader*, edited by Rolf Tiedemann

Patricia Pisters, *The Matrix of Visual Culture: Working with Deleuze in Film Theory*

Andreas Huyssen, *Present Pasts: Urban Palimpsests and the Politics of Memory*

Talal Asad, *Formations of the Secular: Christianity, Islam, Modernity*

Dorothea von Mücke, *The Rise of the Fantastic Tale*

Marc Redfield, *The Politics of Aesthetics: Nationalism, Gender, Romanticism*

Emmanuel Levinas, *On Escape*

Dan Zahavi, *Husserl's Phenomenology*

Rodolphe Gasché, *The Idea of Form: Rethinking Kant's Aesthetics*

Michael Naas, *Taking on the Tradition: Jacques Derrida and the Legacies of Deconstruction*

Herlinde Pauer-Studer, ed., *Constructions of Practical Reason: Interviews on Moral and Political Philosophy*

Jean-Luc Marion, *Being Given That: Toward a Phenomenology of Givenness*

Theodor W. Adorno and Max Horkheimer, *Dialectic of Enlightenment*

Ian Balfour, *The Rhetoric of Romantic Prophecy*

Martin Stokhof, *World and Life as One: Ethics and Ontology in Wittgenstein's Early Thought*

Gianni Vattimo, *Nietzsche: An Introduction*

Jacques Derrida, *Negotiations: Interventions and Interviews, 1971–1998*, ed. Elizabeth Rottenberg

Brett Levinson, *The Ends of Literature: The Latin American "Boom" in the Neoliberal Marketplace*

Timothy J. Reiss, *Against Autonomy: Cultural Instruments, Mutualities, and the Fictive Imagination*

Hent de Vries and Samuel Weber, eds., *Religion and Media*

Niklas Luhmann, *Theories of Distinction: Re-Describing the Descriptions of Modernity*, ed. and introd. William Rasch

Johannes Fabian, *Anthropology with an Attitude: Critical Essays*

Michel Henry, *I Am the Truth: Toward a Philosophy of Christianity*

Gil Anidjar, *"Our Place in Al-Andalus": Kabbalah, Philosophy, Literature in Arab-Jewish Letters*

Hélène Cixous and Jacques Derrida, *Veils*

F. R. Ankersmit, *Historical Representation*

F. R. Ankersmit, *Political Representation*

Elissa Marder, *Dead Time: Temporal Disorders in the Wake of Modernity (Baudelaire and Flaubert)*

Reinhart Koselleck, *The Practice of Conceptual History: Timing History, Spacing Concepts*

Niklas Luhmann, *The Reality of the Mass Media*

Hubert Damisch, *A Childhood Memory by Piero della Francesca*

Hubert Damisch, *A Theory of /Cloud/: Toward a History of Painting*

Jean-Luc Nancy, *The Speculative Remark: (One of Hegel's bon mots)*

Jean-François Lyotard, *Soundproof Room: Malraux's Anti-Aesthetics*

Jan Patočka, *Plato and Europe*

Hubert Damisch, *Skyline: The Narcissistic City*

Isabel Hoving, *In Praise of New Travelers: Reading Caribbean Migrant Women Writers*

Richard Rand, ed., *Futures: Of Jacques Derrida*

William Rasch, *Niklas Luhmann's Modernity: The Paradoxes of Differentiation*

Jacques Derrida and Anne Dufourmantelle, *Of Hospitality*

Jean-François Lyotard, *The Confession of Augustine*

Kaja Silverman, *World Spectators*

Samuel Weber, *Institution and Interpretation: Expanded Edition*

Jeffrey S. Librett, *The Rhetoric of Cultural Dialogue: Jews and Germans in the Epoch of Emancipation*

Ulrich Baer, *Remnants of Song: Trauma and the Experience of Modernity in Charles Baudelaire and Paul Celan*

Samuel C. Wheeler III, *Deconstruction as Analytic Philosophy*

David S. Ferris, *Silent Urns: Romanticism, Hellenism, Modernity*

Rodolphe Gasché, *Of Minimal Things: Studies on the Notion of Relation*

Sarah Winter, *Freud and the Institution of Psychoanalytic Knowledge*

Samuel Weber, *The Legend of Freud: Expanded Edition*

Aris Fioretos, ed., *The Solid Letter: Readings of Friedrich Hölderlin*

J. Hillis Miller / Manuel Asensi, *Black Holes / J. Hillis Miller; or, Boustrophedonic Reading*

Miryam Sas, *Fault Lines: Cultural Memory and Japanese Surrealism*

Peter Schwenger, *Fantasm and Fiction: On Textual Envisioning*

Didier Maleuvre, *Museum Memories: History, Technology, Art*

Jacques Derrida, *Monolingualism of the Other; or, The Prosthesis of Origin*

Andrew Baruch Wachtel, *Making a Nation, Breaking a Nation: Literature and Cultural Politics in Yugoslavia*

Niklas Luhmann, *Love as Passion: The Codification of Intimacy*

Mieke Bal, ed., *The Practice of Cultural Analysis: Exposing Interdisciplinary Interpretation*

Jacques Derrida and Gianni Vattimo, eds., *Religion*

The authorized representative in the EU for product safety and compliance is:
Mare Nostrum Group
B.V Doelen 72
4831 GR Breda
The Netherlands

www.ingramcontent.com/pod-product-compliance
Lightning Source LLC
Chambersburg PA
CBHW030538230426
43665CB00010B/939